ALSO BY MYRA KORNFELD

The Voluptuous Vegan:

More Than 200 Sinfully Delicious Recipes for

Meatless, Eggless, and Dairy-Free Meals

The Healthy Hedonist

More Than 200 Delectable Flexitarian Recipes
for Relaxed Daily Feasts

MYRA KORNFELD

Illustrations by Sheila Hamanaka

SIMON & SCHUSTER PAPERBACKS
New York • London • Toronto • Sydney

To all those I love

who have shared meals at my table

SIMON & SCHUSTER PAPERBACKS
Rockefeller Center
1230 Avenue of the Americas
New York, NY 10020

Copyright © 2005 by Myra Kornfeld
Illustrations copyright © 2005 by Sheila Hamanaka

First Simon & Schuster paperback edition 2005

SIMON & SCHUSTER PAPERBACKS and colophon are registered trademarks of Simon & Schuster, Inc.

For information about special discounts for bulk purchases, please contact
Simon & Schuster Special Sales: 1-800-456-6798 or business@simonandschuster.com.

Designed by Dana Sloan

Manufactured in the United States of America
1   3   5   7   9   10   8   6   4   2

Library of Congress Cataloging-in-Publication Data

Kornfeld, Myra.
The healthy hedonist : more than 200 delectable flexitarian recipes for relaxed daily feasts /
Myra Kornfeld ; illustrations by Sheila Hamanaka.
p. cm.
1. Cookery. 2. Vegetarian cookery. I. Title.
TX714.K657   2005
641.5—dc22   2005044147

ISBN-13: 978-0-7432-5570-7
ISBN-10:   0-7432-5570-4

Acknowledgments

I am so grateful for the love, generosity, and support of so many people, without whom this book would not have been possible.

A heartfelt thanks to everyone at Simon and Schuster—especially to my editor, Sydny Miner, who undertook the project with enthusiasm, edited the manuscript with grace and meticulousness, and is a pleasure to work with, as is Sarah Hochman, whom I would also like to thank. My warmest thanks to Dana Sloan for such a beautiful interior design and layout.

Thanks to all the people who graciously tested the recipes and offered excellent suggestions: Roberta Barabash, Charlotte Kornfeld, Glynnis Osher, David Anderson, Sally Nash, and Sara Parks. Thank you to Laura Pagano Gouy, Donna Daniels, Janet Rosenthal, Colombe Jacobson, and Tolga Klein for hours spent in my kitchen testing. Special thank-yous go to the following people: my dear angel friend Alison Dearborn Rieder, who generously went out of her way to test more than half of the recipes while "effortlessly" maintaining an intensely full personal schedule; my dear friend Lynne Forte, who shared many hilarious days helping me in my kitchen; and to solid-gold, supportive, and able Russell Lehrer, for untold hours spent cooking with me.

So much love goes to my fabulous friends Linda Erman and Glynnis Osher, for supporting me on the project day in and day out. I am eternally grateful to Linda for going above and beyond the call of duty in spending hours in editing marathons with me, hammering out just the right words, and to Glynnis for going to great lengths to design the perfect voluptuous cover. My gratitude goes to Sheila Hamanaka for her beautiful, clear illustrations.

The Natural Gourmet Cookery School in New York City deserves special acknowledgment for being such a vital center devoted to delicious and healthy cooking; special thanks to founder Annemarie Colbin for being the "grand dame" of natural foods cooking and for being a vital source of inspiration to me. Thanks so much to director Jenny Matheau for the opportunity to teach and learn so much from my students.

A special word of gratitude goes to the following people:

Agent Melanie Jackson, for her intelligence, hard work, and enthusiastic support from the very beginning.

Clara Rosamarda for clear, intuitive, and sage advice at just the right moments.

Diane Carlson, whose Conscious Gourmet retreats have added so much to my life.

Frances Gozland, for expanding my cultural horizens.

My sweet husband, Stephen, whose love, support, editorial feedback, and encouragement enable me to shine.

Thanks to other supportive friends at my table: Margaret Peot, Ruth Teitel, Elaine Ryan, Ruth Simon, Marla Meritzer, and Diana Miller. My heartfelt gratitude goes to Sally Nash, Ron Singer, Sara Parks, and John Purdy, my Washington "family," for their hospitality and spiritual support.

I am grateful to my parents, Irving and Charlotte Kornfeld, for their unwavering devotion.

Thanks to Sur La Table, Classic Thyme, the Institute of Culinary Education, and the Upper West Side Jewish Community Center in New York for wonderful teaching venues. Thanks to Kathy Kingsley of *Vegetarian Times* for supporting my writing work.

Thanks so much to Be Yoga in New York for helping me to maintain balance in the midst of a crazy schedule.

Most of all, thanks so much to all my students everywhere, who have shared with me their interests and concerns, and who have given me such valuable information and feedback. You make the effort worthwhile.

Contents

Introduction

The Healthy Hedonist is a book of vibrant, healthful, great-tasting recipes designed to satisfy a wide variety of palates. Many of us have had the experience of finishing a meal only to feel heavy, stuffed, and guilty shortly thereafter. A true hedonist, "a person who pursues pleasure," is passionate about food. A real hedonist also wants to feel good. The *healthy* hedonist anticipates a good meal, savors it, *and* feels energetic and nourished afterward. ◎ Different people have different ideas about what constitutes healthy eating habits. Many are bewildered by the myriad choices available. Some thrive on a vegetarian diet; others do not. Some eschew dairy, while others don't respond well to soy. Some don't eat certain foods or combinations of foods because of their religious or spiritual convictions. Some eat a variety of foods but are not sure what is going to make them feel their best. Many are struggling with weight issues. ◎ I came to natural foods years ago when I was a fashion designer. Cooking was a way to relax after an exhausting day on New York's Fashion Avenue. I had a wonderful time playing with newly discovered ingredients like quinoa and lentils and umeboshi vinegar. For the first time, I realized that there was a direct connection between what I put into my body and how I felt. Soon after, I discovered Annemarie Colbin's Natural Gourmet Cookery School, and "for the fun of it" I enrolled in its first part-time chef training program. Annemarie was my first natural foods mentor. To this day, I often repeat her maxim "If it's not real, don't eat it." ◎ My love affair with cooking had begun, and my training in fashion design influenced my cooking. I still pay attention to how dishes complement each other—how they "hang together"—and I envision garnishes as accessories to a dish. ◎ Nowadays I spend my work life teaching and writing about food. This book reflects much of what I have learned over my past five years of teaching, in large part as a response to the questions, concerns, and requests of my students. I teach many kinds of cooking classes to all kinds of people, from those who are conversant with natural foods to those who are more in the mainstream. The recipes in this book are those that my students have loved. ◎ Many of us are what could now be called "flexitarians." A flexitarian may be primarily a vegetarian but may eat some animal products on occasion.

Or a flexitarian may be an omnivore who often chooses to eat vegetarian. Some people call themselves vegetarian; then they add that they eat some fish, or perhaps fish and chicken. They too are flexitarians. In addition, some people often have to cook for others who do not have the same eating habits as they do. For example, one of my students was a mother who found herself at a loss when it came to cooking for her vegan teenage daughter. One of my students was a vegan whose wife was not a vegetarian, and he did all the household cooking. Some of my students reported that they had been eating only raw foods for years, then realized that they needed to add animal products as well as cooked food back into their diets.

Many of the recipes presented here are vegetarian, although there are a good number of fish and chicken dishes. Many of these dishes can be made several ways. The flounder with an orange glaze is also delicious when made with tofu. The chicken with mushroom ragout is equally tasty when made with tempeh. The Moroccan stew is succulent whether it is made with braised chicken or with chickpeas for the vegetarian. A spinach and roasted shiitake mushroom salad with a rosemary lemon balsamic vinaigrette makes an excellent starter to a wholesome meal; the addition of crispy tempeh croutons transforms the salad into a light vegetarian entrée.

Most of the dairy in the book is optional. A baby greens salad with roasted red pepper vinaigrette has warm walnut-crusted goat cheese medallions for a tasty flourish—but the salad is still delicious without the cheese. Some of the soups include a yogurt garnish, but tofu cream can be substituted. It's up to you to decide which version suits your needs or preference.

Many of us have only a limited time to spend in the kitchen, but we still want to make fresh and delicious food. Shortcut methods are offered whenever they can be applied without compromising the taste and healthfulness of the dish. For instance, the roasted red pepper soup is best made with homemade stock and home-roasted peppers. However, if you substitute jarred peppers and store-bought stock, the results are still impressive and the total prep time is under thirty minutes. The whole-grain dough for the pizza crusts takes only forty-five seconds to mix and knead in the food processor. The whole-grain risottos are baked, and the easy polenta is made in a double boiler, so there is no need to spend time glued to the pot, stirring.

These recipes are for the unfussy food that I make on a day-to-day basis in my home kitchen. They are also perfect for entertaining. Many can be made in advance. Best of all, they are inspired by ethnic flavors from all over the world, including India, Morocco, Turkey, Mexico, Thailand, Colombia, El Salvador, Lebanon, Greece,

Italy, France, Iran, China, Vietnam, and the United States. The recipes will pique the interest of even the most seasoned cook.

I have included low-key but satisfying recipes for a variety of needs. When you want to give your body a break, try the spring tonic garlic soup and the dhal; when you are feeling indulgent, make a batch of the brownies. Since the focus here is on real food, there is no emphasis on low-fat high-carb, or high-protein low-carb, cooking. The recipes call for sufficient salt to draw all the flavors together and sufficient fat for each particular dish; however, most of the dishes in the book are naturally on the lighter side.

Try to cook with ingredients that are as natural as possible. The less refined a food is, the more it nurtures the body. Whole grains, which have their nutrients intact, are more satisfying and filling than refined ones, so the recipes in this book include whole-grain pizza dough, crêpes, pilafs, and pastries. Of course some dishes call for refined grains, such as basmati and jasmine rice, which are more appropriate for some meals.

"Whole food" often means food with fewer ingredients. Real nut butters contain nuts, and nuts only, and perhaps some salt. Shoyu, or natural soy sauce, contains only soy, wheat, water, and salt. Some of the common commercial ingredients to stay away from are hydrogenated fats, high-fructose corn syrup, sugar substitutes such as aspartame, and chemical preservatives. Read the labels. Chances are that if the list of ingredients includes long polysyllabic terms that you can barely pronounce, it's not a healthy product.

Eat organic as much as possible. Organic food tastes better, and it is healthier. You just have to taste a can of conventional beans after testing an organic variety to understand the difference. Educate yourself on what's out there so that you can make intelligent choices.

Real food also means fresh food—food that is not canned, processed, or frozen. This does not mean that I have not made a few notable exceptions in putting these recipes together. I use canned organic tomatoes, canned coconut milk, canned hearts of palm, and bottled roasted peppers. From time to time I'll use frozen organic corn and frozen peas, two vegetables that have little water content and do not suffer too badly from being frozen. Frozen peas are often better than their fresh counterparts, since they are frozen while young. When you have to pick your battles, shelling peas is just one step too many! Although I prefer to start with dry beans and soak and cook them, for the sake of efficiency I frequently turn to canned.

If you have a greenmarket near you, get acquainted with your local farmers. You'll be able to purchase vegetables that were picked the day before, vegetables that are vibrant and full of life. In these markets, there is often a more interesting and unusual selection than you can find in a supermarket. After many years of visiting the Union Square Greenmarket in New York City, I am still inspired when I see the vast array of luscious vegetables and fruits, fresh cheeses, and breads offered there.

Something wonderful happens when you bring fresh, vibrant food into your home. Whether you're an accomplished cook or a novice, with a variety of great food at your fingertips, you're likely to become a healthy hedonist.

A hedonist ought to have a good time when cooking for friends. Don't be afraid to alter something to your preference, or to mix and match recipes to create a meal. It is your energy that goes into what you cook, so splash blessings on your food as you sauté and stir and simmer. Load your pantry and your refrigerator with tasty, delicious, good-quality ingredients. Celebrate the pleasures of coconut oil and ghee, whole eggs and chocolate. Fill your belly with luscious food. Dare to be a healthy hedonist.

Salt

You don't need to give up salt to be a healthy hedonist. Salt draws out essential flavors that would otherwise remain neutral or latent. For this reason, some food gurus believe the art of salting is what distinguishes a mediocre cook from a very good one.

Many people today are afraid to season their food properly because of the misconception that salt is bad for you; true, there is generally too much sodium in many processed and packaged foods. But salt, especially sea salt, is your friend, not your enemy. The proper amount of salt added during cooking releases the flavors of the food without making it taste salty. Salt added at the table, on the other hand, does not permeate the food properly. When you cook your own food, learn to salt to taste, and before long you'll recognize when a dish is seasoned perfectly. Well-seasoned food leaves a rounded flavor on the tongue. In addition, pleasantly spicy foods sometimes feel as if they are overly spicy. Once the correct amount of salt is added—and that might mean only a pinch—the constituent flavors are drawn together harmoniously and the food comes alive.

In the recipes here, I indicate an amount of salt that is *close* to the amount I think the dish needs. The recipe will usually need one or two pinches more to draw out the flavors; it is impossible to include that tiny amount in the recipe, and it may vary depending on the ingredients. I call this extra amount a "grandma pinch," which means a good fat pinch, not a speck. (If you tend to be heavy-handed, however, make your pinch a baby pinch.)

The best sea salts available, Celtic Sea Salt and *Fleur de sel*, are harvested by professional salt farmers in northern France, along the coast of Brittany. These are wind- and sun-dried only, with nothing added or taken out. The minerals remain in ionized form, in the same balance they have in the ocean, which is the same balance of minerals that we need in our body. The eighty or so trace minerals are responsible for the light gray color, and the grains are a bit moist. Fine-ground Celtic salt is my choice all-purpose salt, for both savory and sweet recipes.

Fats

Fats make up a part of a healthy diet. To be physically and mentally healthy, to insulate and to keep the body warm, you need a certain amount of fats. The fat-soluble vitamins A, D, E, and K need dietary fat in order to be used by the body.

All fats are made up of a combination of monounsaturated, polyunsaturated, and saturated fats. We cannot say one oil is good because it is monounsaturated or polyunsaturated. The length of the fatty acid chain—whether it is a short, medium, or long chain—is more telling about the nature of the fat.

Avoid refined oils whenever possible. The use of high temperature and chemical solvents, as well as exposure to light and oxygen, in the processing of nearly all refined oils destroys much of the essential omega-3 and omega-6 fatty acids, and also creates rancidity and oxidation. Refined fats suppress the immune system. Polyunsaturated oils, which are highly unstable, are not suitable as cooking oils for the most part. Consuming large quantities of polyunsaturated oil increases serum cholesterol.

It's actually difficult *not* to get enough omega-6 oils in a normal diet; they are readily available in nuts and seeds. In nuts they include natural antioxidants to protect them from going rancid. Polyunsaturated oils become toxic when they are exposed to heat, light, and air. Oxidation causes the formation of harmful free radicals. Most important, refrain from consuming any products containing "partially hydrogenated" oils, which are molecularly altered and produce trans-fatty acids, fats known to be disease-causing.

Omega-3 fatty acids are best obtained from eating flax seeds or consuming some flax oil daily, and by eating fatty fish such as salmon, mackerel, anchovies, sardines, and herring.

The oils that I advocate for cooking are stable oils that can take heat without becoming rancid or oxidized. These include extra-virgin olive oil, coconut oil, and organic butter and ghee. I use small amounts of unrefined sesame oil and toasted sesame oil; and I use unrefined nut oils, such as hazelnut oil and walnut oil, in salad dressings. Extra-virgin olive oil is a stable liquid with a high percentage of oleic acid, which makes it ideal for cooking and for salads. It is also rich in antioxidants, which prevent it from becoming rancid. It is over 70 percent monounsaturated and 16 percent saturated fat.

Organic butter is a stable fat made from cream with a wide range of short, medium, and odd-chain fatty acids as well as typical saturated, monounsaturated, and some polyunsaturated fatty acids. Butter contains fat-soluble vitamins, including vitamins A, D, and E. Butter has short- and medium-chain fatty acids (15 percent) and conjugated linoleic acid (CLA), which has strong anticancer properties. It is rich in selenium, a vital antioxidant. All of these properties are only in the fat part of the milk. Butter and cream contain little lactose or casein and are usually well tolerated even by those who are sensitive to dairy. All the recipes use unsalted butter.

Ghee is especially well tolerated by most people, because the milk solids are removed. In traditional Indian medicine, ghee is considered the most *satvic*, or health-promoting, fat available. You can purchase organic or hormone-free ghee, but it is easy

Ghee

MAKES 1½ CUPS

1 pound unsalted butter, preferably organic

Warm the butter in a small saucepan over medium-low heat until it has melted completely, about 5 minutes. The butter will start to gurgle as the water evaporates, and the top will be covered with foam. Simmer uncovered over low heat until the milk solids start to brown on the bottom of the pot, 10 to 15 minutes. (Check after 10 minutes and then frequently after that, by pushing aside the foam and tilting the pan to see if the solids have browned.) As soon as the solids turn brown, remove the pan from the heat and let the residue settle to the bottom. Then carefully pour the clear liquid through a strainer lined with a double layer of cheesecloth into a heat-resistant container. Discard the solids.

Ghee will stay fresh on the kitchen counter 4 to 6 weeks; in the refrigerator for 4 months; and indefinitely in the freezer.

to make at home. As the ghee forms, the milk solids sink to the bottom of the pot, leaving only the pure stable fat, which is suitable for high-heat sautéing.

Sesame oil contains a high percentage of omega-6 fatty acids. It also contains sesamin, a natural antioxidant that enhances its stability, making it suitable for stir-fries. I also use it for Asian dressings. Toasted sesame oil, which burns easily and should not be used to cook with, is wonderful as a condiment.

Canola oil is almost always refined, so I use it only once in a great while, when I need a flavorless liquid fat.

Coconut oil is a completely stable oil and does not need to be refrigerated. The smoking point is fairly high, 350°F. Coconut oil does not get absorbed by the food as much as other oils do, so food cooked in coconut oil does not taste greasy. It is the per-

Health Properties of Coconut Oil

Long vilified, coconut oil is finally getting the attention it deserves for being the incredibly healthy fat that it is. Coconut oil is a traditional food in many areas of the world, from India, to the Pacific Islands, to Southeast Asia. Coconut oil is a highly saturated fat, made up mostly of medium-chain fatty acids. The length of the chain is a key factor in determining the way dietary fat is digested and metabolized and how it affects the body: Medium-chain fatty acids are broken down and used predominantly for energy production, and thus seldom end up as body fat or as deposits in arteries or anywhere else. They produce energy, not fat, and have a neutral effect on blood cholesterol. Coconut oil does not increase platelet stickiness.

Coconut oil is composed mostly of lauric acid, which is a highly protective fatty acid found in mother's milk. Coconut oil, or some derivative of it, is used in hospital formulas to feed the very young, the critically ill, and those with digestive problems. Coconut oil does not oxidize, even when heated to high temperatures, and it does not create free radicals in the body; rather, it helps fight them. It is so resistant to free radicals that it acts as an antioxidant, helping to prevent the oxidation of other oils. Coconut milk, which contains about 24 percent coconut oil, is also a good source of medium-chain fatty acids. For sources for coconut oil, check the Resources section in the back of this book.

fect oil for high-heat sautéing or pan-frying. It is semisolid at room temperature and melts at 76°F.

There are two types of coconut oil: extra-virgin and deodorized. Extra-virgin tastes and smells like coconut, so use it when you want a subtle coconut flavor. The deodorized oil is excellent for all cooking purposes. I have included my favorite brands of both types of coconut oil in the Resources section.

Dairy Products

The less processed they are, the healthier and more delicious dairy products are. The Weston Price Foundation and its affiliated physicians (see Resources) offer compelling data on the superiority of raw milk, which is non-pasteurized and non-homogenized.

The cream in milk normally rises to the surface. Homogenization is a process in which the fat particles are distributed throughout the milk so that they cannot rise. However, homogenization makes fat and cholesterol more susceptible to rancidity and oxidation.

Pasteurization is a process in which a liquid is heated to a certain point in order to destroy bacteria. However, when milk comes from contained herds that are pasture fed, it is not tainted in the first place. Raw milk and raw-milk cheeses contain a full complement of enzymes, and they are more easily digested than their pasteurized counterparts. Raw milk contains lactic-acid-producing bacteria, which protect against pathogens. Pasteurization destroys the enzymes that help the body to absorb calcium in milk. It also alters milk's mineral components, such as calcium, chlorin, magnesium, phosphorus, potassium, sodium, and sulfur. The present-day level of sanitation in modern milking methods, such as the use of stainless steel tanks and efficient packaging and distribution, have rendered the need for pasteurization virtually obsolete.

Although it is difficult to find raw milk in the United States, there is a growing movement of people who are buying milk directly from farmers who feed their livestock only grass (see Resources). If you have an opportunity to purchase this type of milk do so for the sheer pleasure of tasting such delicious dairy. Many stores now carry non-homogenized milk from cows raised on natural feed. That milk is used to make good cultured products, such as yogurt, cultured buttermilk, and cultured cream. Look for yogurt labeled "with the cream on top." I have noticed a huge increase in the quantities and varieties of raw-milk cheeses that have become available in recent years. A lot of it is imported and of good quality. Many of my students who are sensitive to milk and cheese find themselves reacting well to raw-milk cheeses.

The next best choice is organic milk, which comes from a cow that has been raised on organic feed and, most importantly, has not been injected with bovine growth hormones. This milk is widely available.

The Well-Stocked Kitchen

No matter how big a kitchen, there may be no need to crowd it with superfluous gadgets. Here's a rundown on the most essential pieces of equipment:

A good set of saucepans: The basics are a small pan (1½ to 2 quarts), a medium saucepan (about 4 quarts), and a soup pot (about 6 quarts).

Two 10-inch skillets—one of them nonstick—are also essential, as is a 3-quart skillet with straight sides and a lid, which I call a large skillet.

The best pots and skillets consist of three layers: the layer that touches the food should be stainless steel; the middle layer, which conducts heat, should be aluminum; and the outside layer can be any material you prefer, such as stainless steel, aluminum, or copper. Nonstick cookware should also be of high quality so it does not scratch easily.

Good knives are indispensable. A chef's knife, a paring knife, and a serrated knife are all you need to do just about anything. A boning knife may or may not be useful to you. When you are purchasing a knife, hold a variety of them in your hand and choose the one that is most comfortable. Most people are comfortable with an 8-inch blade. I like heavier-style knives for when I want to cut into something hard, like a winter squash.

An 8- or 9-inch cast-iron skillet is great for toasting chiles and spices and for searing food over high heat.

A food processor and a standing blender are both important kitchen machines. An immersion, or stick, blender is useful for creating smooth soups or vegetable purées, but it's not necessary. It does not replace a standing blender, which can handle fibrous hard-to-blend vegetables. Other tools that make a difference in the kitchen:

Oven thermometer: I have found that most ovens vary 25 to 75 degrees from the reading on the dial. That makes a huge difference, especially when you're baking. If your baked goods get crusty on top but stay soft in the middle, chances are your oven is running hot. With a thermometer inside, you'll have an accurate read.

Microplane zester: A tool modeled after a carpenter's rasp, this grates citrus zest in seconds. It can also be used to grate hard cheese, chocolate, and fresh nutmeg. Microplanes come in various degrees of fineness.

Spice grinder: For the best flavor, always start with whole spices and grind them fresh. An inexpensive electric coffee mill makes a great spice grinder. Freshly ground pepper from a peppermill puts the stale jar variety to shame. A mortar and pestle is useful for crushing garlic and salt together. It's also good for grinding or "bruising" toasted spices.

A pressure cooker: Makes cooking beans from scratch convenient. Pressure cookers are easy to use and reduce the cooking time of foods by more than 75 percent.

A citrus squeezer or reamer: My current favorites are the squeezers that are shaped like a citrus fruit. The two handles are squeezed together and the juice comes out already strained.

A salad spinner: A must-have for washing greens. Get the kind with the basket that lifts out; you can use the basket like a strainer when you wash the greens before spinning them.

I also love Y-shaped vegetable peelers. They make it easy to peel thick skins, such as those on winter squash.

A mandoline (a plastic one works fine) is wonderful for making paper-thin slices of vegetables for salads and gravies. Fennel tastes especially delicious when sliced this way.

Other equipment includes a selection of bowls (I recommend stainless steel of various sizes), measuring spoons, dry and wet measuring cups, wooden spoons, plastic spatulas, metal spatulas (including an offset spatula for spreading icing and other toppings), a pie spatula, and a nonstick spatula. A slotted spoon, a soup ladle, and a whisk are also essential.

Don't forget tongs. Mine are stationed on the oven door so that I can grab them easily.

A strainer—get a fairly large one—will multi-task as a flour sifter, stock and soup strainer, and mini colander.

A grill pan is a fun piece of equipment if you don't have or want to use an outdoor grill.

Some other useful tools include a box grater, a potato masher (for potatoes and refried beans), a steamer rack, a colander, and a can opener. A skimmer is good for lifting things out of a liquid, such as gnocchi or ravioli. A melon baller is great for getting the hairy choke out of an artichoke as well as for making melon balls for fruit salads.

For poultry, you should have an instant-read thermometer to take the internal temperature of the bird. Kitchen shears are handy for cutting through the backbone to butterfly a chicken. A roasting rack elevates the bird off the bottom of the baking pan.

If you like to bake, you'll need a couple of baking sheets, cake pans, and bread pans.

Make sure to have cheesecloth around to make herbal bouquets. A pastry brush is important if you're going to make anything with phyllo.

Some tools that are fun to have for specialty cooking include a baking stone for bread and pizzas, and a pizza peel as well as a pizza cutter.

My new favorite tool is a chile roaster, a metal grate that you set over a burner. It makes charring chiles or bell peppers or eggplants really easy. See Sweet Snacks and Desserts (page 274) for other essential equipment.

The Pantry

With these items in your pantry, you'll just need to pick up the fresh ingredients for any recipe in this book.

ON THE SHELVES

Oils: extra-virgin olive oil, coconut oil, ghee, small bottle of organic canola oil.

Vinegars: balsamic, red wine, brown rice, apple cider, and umeboshi. White wine and sherry vinegars are also nice to have on hand.

Jars, bottles, and packages: shoyu, Thai fish sauce, kalamata olives, capers, mustard, dried porcini mushrooms, dried shiitake mushrooms, sun-dried tomatoes, tomato paste, dried chestnuts, roasted red peppers, chipotle chiles in adobo sauce, peanut butter, almond butter, tahini, liquid smoke (a small bottle). Cans of coconut milk, fire-roasted tomatoes, chickpeas, cannellini beans, black beans, and kidney beans. Small bottles of liquor such as rum, brandy, and Grand Marnier for flavoring desserts. Sake, mirin, and sherry. A bottle of dry white wine and a bottle of red wine, such as Merlot.

Dried fruit: raisins, apricots, dates, coconut, currants.

Sea vegetables: arame, hijiki, wakame, kombu, nori, dulse.

Grains: brown basmati, white basmati, and wild rice. Quinoa, millet, corn grits, steel-cut oats, rolled oats, barley, farro, spelt berries, seven-grain cereal, polenta, soba noodles, whole-grain pasta, and rice sticks.

Dry beans and lentils: brown lentils, French lentils, red lentils, chickpeas, black turtle beans, moong dhal, adzuki beans, Great Northern beans, split peas, cannellini beans, red kidney beans, pinto beans.

Spices: whole dried chiles (chipotle, ancho, New Mexican, pasilla), whole and ground cumin seed, whole and ground coriander seed, caraway seed, fennel seed, black peppercorns, turmeric, ground cinnamon, cinnamon sticks, paprika, chile powder, cardamom (pod and ground), ground ginger, ground mustard, fenugreek, allspice, thyme, oregano, basil, asafetida, whole and ground cloves, star anise.

PANTRY SHELVES, REFRIGERATOR, OR FREEZER

Nuts and seeds, such as sesame seeds, pumpkin seeds, sunflower seeds, pecans, walnuts, almonds, pistachios, peanuts, pine nuts, and hazelnuts, are best kept in cold storage in the refrigerator or freezer to prevent them from going rancid. If you don't have the space, keep only small quantities on your pantry shelf and replenish them frequently.

Flours, such as whole-wheat flour, spelt flour, whole-wheat pastry flour, unbleached white flour, cornmeal, oat flour, rye flour, and semolina flour, are also best kept refrigerated or in the freezer to keep them fresher longer.

IN THE REFRIGERATOR

Sesame oil, toasted sesame oil, walnut oil, hazelnut oil, and organic butter.

Miso: one dark, such as barley, rice, or hatcho; one light, such as sweet white; and one mellow barley miso for a tasty all-purpose variety.

Additional pantry supplies are listed in Sweet Snacks and Desserts.

Basic Techniques

Proper cutting techniques make the difference between having a good experience in the kitchen and struggling.

A *round* is a circular slice. To make rounds, cut across a cylindrical vegetable—a carrot, daikon, cucumber, or jalapeño—at even intervals. The basic round cut can be varied by cutting the vegetable on an angle to create elongated or oval disks. This is a diagonal cut. This cut exposes a larger surface area, so the vegetable will need a shorter cooking time.

Half-moons are used for elongated vegetables like carrots and parsnips. Cut the vegetable in half lengthwise; then cut each half crosswise into half rounds. Quarter moons are made the same way, except that you cut the halves lengthwise into quarters, then cut them into pieces.

To make *matchsticks*, first cut the vegetable or fruit into thin diagonal slices of the same length. Then stack the slices and cut them into long thin pieces.

To *dice* is to cut a vegetable into uniform pieces. First cut off a slice to make a flat base so the vegetable sits solidly on the cutting surface. Then cut the vegetable into slabs—¼-inch, ⅓-inch, ½-inch, or 1-inch, depending on the size dice you want. Stack a few slabs on top of each other and cut them into julienne of the same width. Now cut the matchsticks into cubes. Be sure to cut the same width at each stage: For example, ¼-inch slabs are cut into ¼-inch julienne, which in turn become ¼-inch dice. When a recipe calls for small dice, cut into ¼-inch; ⅓-inch is a medium dice, and ¾-inch is a large dice. Tiny ⅛-inch dice is also called *brunoise*.

Onions are singular vegetables. *Peel* an onion by cutting off the stem and the root ends, leaving enough of the root to hold the onion together. Halve the onion and peel off the skin and the underlying layer.

Thinly slice an onion by cutting the halved onion lengthwise, from the root end to the tip.

Slice an onion crosswise for *half rings*, which are attractive in a salad.

To *dice,* lay one half cut side down, root end away from you. Make even slices the width that you want the dice to be, without cutting through the root end. Then turn the onion and cut into dice.

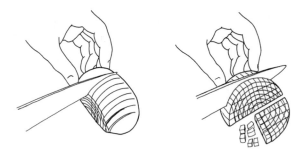

A medium onion weighs about 6 ounces and yields 1 cup chopped. All the recipes in this book call for medium onions. A medium clove of garlic yields 1 teaspoon minced. Large cloves can be considered 2 or even 3 cloves, and a small clove might be considered a half clove. Adjust accordingly.

A *rough cut* is made by cutting the vegetable without regard to shape. This cut is used for stocks, and for soups and sauces that are going to be pureéd. Though the shape doesn't matter, the size of these cuts should be more or less uniform. For a vegetable stock a rough cut is fine, but do not cut the pieces more than an inch thick so they can fully impart their flavor during the cooking time.

To *mince* is to chop into very fine pieces. Garlic, shallots, and fresh herbs are often minced. This is easiest to do with a chef's knife, which has a slightly curved blade. First slice or chop the vegetables or herbs into small pieces. Then position the blade above the pile of chopped pieces, with the tip of the knife resting on the cutting board. Using the palm or fingers of your other hand to press on the back edge of the blade, chop the pieces rapidly by rocking the blade back and forth, keeping the tip on the board. Continue chopping, inching left and right, until the pieces are uniformly very small.

To *shred* means to slice leaves very thin. This cut is often used on cabbages and leafy greens. To shred cabbage, first quarter the cabbage and cut out the tough centers. Then lay each quarter on a cut side and thinly slice across, working the knife from one end of the quarter to the other, until it's all shredded. For Napa or Chinese cabbage, pull off and discard the outer leaves, then thinly slice across.

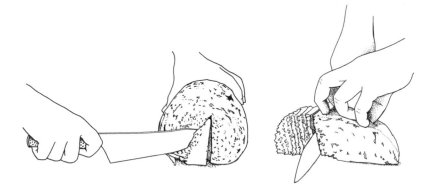

A *chiffonade* is made by very finely shredding leaves, most often leaves that have been stacked and rolled. Stack same-size leaves together, roll them up tightly, and then slice across the rolled leaves until the roll has been transformed into wispy little shreds. This technique is used on basil and on large leafy greens such as spinach and chard.

A *roll cut* is a basic cut for long thin root vegetables, such as carrots, parsnips, and daikon. Place the peeled root on a cutting board, and make a diagonal cut to remove the stem end. Roll the root over and slice through on the same diagonal, keeping the knife where it was for the first cut, creating a wedge shape. Repeat until the entire root has been cut.

If the vegetable is thicker at one end, roll it only a quarter of the way around and then make the diagonal cut. The result will be an irregular piece with angled edges facing different ways. Continue to roll partway and slice on the diagonal. The cut and size varies depending on the angle at which the vegetable rests in relation to the knife.

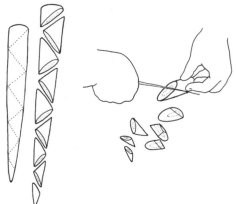

CUTTING PARSLEY AND CILANTRO: Wash these herbs and dry them well, keeping the bunch intact. Hold the herbs by the stem on an angle, leafy part on the board. Angle the knife downward to shave off the leaves, avoiding cutting the stems as much as possible. Pull out any big stems that you may find in the pile. Chop the pile of herbs to the desired size. Refrain from turning your herbs into "grass stains," which is what happens when herbs that have not been dried properly are minced until they are unrecognizable.

PEELING AND CUTTING GINGER: The easiest way to peel ginger is with a knife. Anchor the ginger on a cutting board and cut the skin off. (A few tiny protruding knobs may be sacrificed.) Slice the ginger lengthwise into thin slabs. Cut the slabs into matchsticks and cut the matchsticks into tiny dice. If necessary, you can mince the diced pieces even more.

PEELING A TOMATO: Bring a pot of water to a boil. Cut out the core of the tomato by inserting the tip of a paring knife about one inch into the tomato just outside of the core. Rotate the tomato as you cut with a sawing motion until the core is cut free. Discard the core and drop the tomato into the boiling water. Let it cook for 15 to 30 seconds, depending on its ripeness. Remove the tomato with a slotted spoon and let it cool for a minute. The skin should peel right off. To seed, cut the tomato in half and squeeze out the seeds. Scoop out the remaining seeds with your fingers or a spoon.

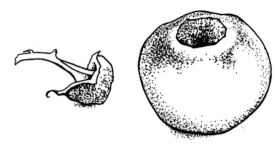

ABOUT LEEKS: Use only the white and light green parts of the leek. Save the dark green part for making stock. It's easiest to remove the dirt from leeks after you cut them. To cut leeks, slice them lengthwise down the middle of the white part and cut into the desired size pieces. Then wash by placing the cut pieces in a bowl of water and swishing them around. Lift out the pieces, leaving the dirt behind. Repeat this process one more time if necessary, until no dirt remains.

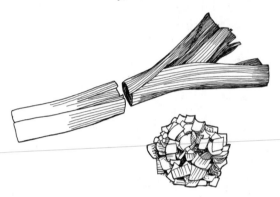

TRIMMING FENNEL: Cut off any protruding tops from the bulb. Shave off any discolored or bruised parts. Cut the bulb in half lengthwise, and remove the hard core with a paring knife. Lay the fennel cut side down and thinly slice with a knife, or use a mandoline.

CUBING BUTTERNUT SQUASH: Cut the squash at the point where the neck (the straight part) meets the rounded bottom. Peel the neck with a Y-shaped peeler or a knife. Cut it into ½-inch-thick slabs, and cut the slabs into batons. Cut each baton into ½-inch cubes. Peel, seed, and halve the rounded part. Cut each half into wedges. Cut each wedge into ½-inch pieces.

TO THICKEN YOGURT: Place 2 cups (preferably whole-milk) yogurt over a cheesecloth-lined strainer set in a bowl. Place the bowl in the refrigerator and let the yogurt drain for at least 2 hours and up to overnight. Two cups of yogurt will become 1 cup thickened yogurt ("yogurt cheese").

TO PREVENT MINCED GARLIC FROM BURNING WHILE SAUTÉING: Place the oil and garlic in the cold skillet and heat them together. The garlic will slowly become golden, and you will be able to control the cooking.

CLEANING OUT YOUR SPICE GRINDER: To get rid of the potent odor of whatever spice you have ground, place a handful of white rice or a piece of bread in the grinder, grind it, and then discard.

MAKING BREAD CRUMBS: Remove the crusts and cut a loaf of bread, preferably sourdough or whole-grain, into cubes. If the bread is a couple of days old and a little firm, process the cubes in a food processor until crumbs form. If it is fresh and spongy, slice the bread and put it in a 200°F oven for a few minutes to dry out a bit before processing. Make a large batch and freeze any leftover bread crumbs in a resealable bag. Bread crumbs defrost almost immediately.

TOASTING NUTS AND SEEDS: Spread nuts or seeds on a baking sheet and toast in a preheated 350°F oven until lightly golden and fragrant, 8 to 10 minutes. Pine nuts take only about 6 minutes. Alternatively, dry-toast the nuts or seeds in a heavy-bottomed skillet, stirring frequently, until brown spots begin to appear, about 3 minutes.

SKINNING WALNUTS: Walnuts have a loose skin that often dislodges when they are chopped. After toasting them, rub the walnuts against a strainer for a minute or two (place the strainer over the sink or a wastebasket) to loosen the skins. Remove the walnuts from the strainer, leaving the skins behind.

SKINNING HAZELNUTS: To remove the skins from hazelnuts, toast the hazelnuts in a preheated 350°F oven for 8 to 10 minutes, until the papery skins start to loosen. Wrap a few of the warm hazelnuts in a kitchen towel and rub them against one another to loosen the skins. Transfer the cleaned hazelnuts to a bowl. Repeat several times with the remaining nuts until most of the skins are removed.

STORING GREENS: Keep fragile herbs and lettuce, such as basil and arugula, fresh by storing them in the refrigerator with the stem ends in containers of water. Cover the leaves with a plastic bag.

Roasted Peppers

Bell peppers, any color

Place the pepper directly on the grate over a gas burner. Turn the heat to high and cook until the skin is blistered and charred. Use tongs to turn the pepper over, and cook each side until the whole surface is blackened. This should take only a few minutes. Place the pepper in a plastic or paper bag, or under an inverted bowl, for about 15 minutes to steam the skin loose. When the pepper is cool enough to handle, remove the charred skin, using a paring knife if necessary. Don't run the pepper under water to remove the skin, as that washes away a lot of flavor. (I like to have a small bowl of water nearby to dip my fingers in; this makes slipping off the skin much easier.) Discard the seeds and stem, and cut the pepper into thin slices.

Another method is to halve the pepper and remove the stem, seeds, and white membranes. Place the pepper, cut side down, on an oiled or parchment-covered baking sheet and place it in a very hot oven (450°F) or under a broiler. Roast or broil until it is evenly charred, turning it as necessary. Remove from the oven or broiler and cover immediately; steam and then remove the skin as described above.

Roasted Garlic

1 head garlic
1 teaspoon extra-virgin olive oil
Pinch of salt

Preheat the oven to 350°F. Peel the excess papery skin from the head of garlic. Slice the top fifth off the head and place the garlic on a piece of foil. Drizzle the oil and salt over the exposed area. Wrap in foil and cook until softened, about 45 minutes. Let cool a few minutes. Squeeze the garlic out of the cloves into a bowl, and mash it.

Nibbles and Spreads

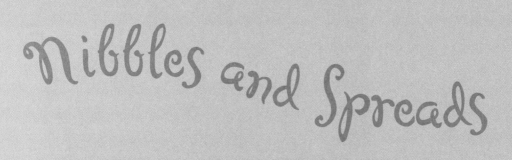

Sweet Potato–Red Pepper Spread

Roasted Asparagus and Garlic Tapenade

Portobello Mushroom Tapenade

Onion-Rosemary Fig Jam

A Festival of Sour Cream and Onion Dips

   The Classic

   Yogurt and Onion Dip

   Tofu "Sour Cream" and Onion Dip

Vegan Dill Sour Cream

Roasted New Potato Cups

Spanakopita Party Triangles

Vegetable Quesadillas with Basil Pesto

Crispy Thai Wontons with Shoyu Dipping Sauce

Yuca Cakes with Mango Mojo

Roasted Eggplant and Pepper Salad

Spreads and dips

are wonderful for entertaining. They are easy to make, convenient, and can be prepared in advance. Set out a variety of crackers and dips while your guests gather; they'll appreciate having something to nibble on right away and you'll be free to attend to other last-minute preparations. For large parties, offer a variety of spreads surrounded by Cornmeal-Dusted Broiled Vegetable Chips (page 113) as well as crackers, breads, and crudités. I've included a recipe for roasted potato cups, which make excellent bite-size containers for dips. They look adorable and taste delectable. Keep some cut vegetables and a dip or two in the refrigerator for those moments when you feel the urge to snack. The Portobello Mushroom Tapenade and Sweet Potato–Red Pepper Spread both make lovely tea party sandwiches, bag lunches, or picnic fare when spread on whole-grain bread. Onion-Rosemary Fig Jam is an unusual breakfast spread. Crisp wontons, quesadillas, yuca cakes, and mini spanakopita triangles are a great combination for passed hors d'oeuvres. Even though they require a little more effort than the spreads, they can all be made in advance, and they freeze and reheat beautifully. When simmered like pasta and served in a porcini broth, the wontons make a meal. Add some sautéed tempeh and asparagus, and the yuca cakes are substantial enough for lunch or a light dinner. The quesadilla, with its pile of vegetables and layers of cheese and pesto, also makes a delicious lunch. There are additional spreads scattered throughout the book, along with many dishes that make wonderful first courses. The Vietnamese Spring Roll Salad (page 216) is an elegant example. I serve Zucchini Latkes (page 118) most often as an appetizer. Any of the burgers, made a bit smaller, can be a delicious first course, as is the Easy Polenta (page 192), cut into small squares and topped with pesto or tapenade. The Roasted Eggplant and Pepper Salad makes a good pre-dinner spread as well as a wonderful side dish. Whether a particular dish is called an appetizer, main course, or side dish often depends on the portion size and when it is served. Enjoy mixing and matching and tailoring the recipes according to your own preference.

Sweet Potato–Red Pepper Spread

This light pink purée is festive with flecks of red and green. Tahini is the secret in-gredient: It provides the fat necessary for a smooth texture, but the flavor is unobtru-sive. Try this delectable spread on a chicken or vegetable sandwich.

MAKES 2 CUPS

3/4 pound sweet potatoes, peeled and cut into 1/2-inch-thick rounds (2 cups)
1/4 cup tahini, preferably roasted
3/4 teaspoon salt
1 garlic clove, minced
1 tablespoon fresh lemon juice
Freshly ground black pepper to taste
1/2 cup bottled roasted red bell peppers *or* 1 fresh red bell pepper,
   roasted; cut into small dice
1/4 cup minced fresh chives

Place a vegetable steamer over simmering water in a saucepan, and steam the sweet potatoes until tender, about 10 minutes.

Combine the sweet potatoes, tahini, salt, garlic, lemon juice, and a sprinkling of black pepper in a food processor, and process until smooth. Add the red pepper and chives, and pulse until combined. Taste, and add salt if necessary.

This can be stored, covered, in the refrigerator for up to 4 days.

Roasted Asparagus and Garlic Tapenade

This chunky relish combines some of my all-time favorite foods. Spread it on toasted baguette slices or take it over the top with a garnish of shaved Parmesan.

MAKES 1 CUP

1 pound asparagus, hard ends removed, chopped into 1/2-inch pieces
2 tablespoons extra-virgin olive oil
Salt
1/4 cup sun-dried tomatoes
1/4 cup pine nuts
1 head garlic, roasted (see page 19)
1 tablespoon fresh lemon juice
1/2 teaspoon grated lemon zest
Freshly ground black pepper
1/4 cup chopped fresh parsley

Preheat the oven to 375°F.

Combine the asparagus with the oil in a medium bowl, and toss to lightly coat the asparagus with oil. Sprinkle with salt. Spread the asparagus on a parchment-covered baking sheet, and roast until tender and beginning to brown, about 20 minutes, depending on size.

Soak the sun-dried tomatoes in hot water to cover until softened, about 10 minutes. Drain, discarding the soaking liquid. Slice the tomatoes into thin pieces and set them aside.

Dry-toast the pine nuts in a heavy-bottomed skillet over medium heat until lightly golden, about 3 minutes.

Squeeze the garlic out of its skin into the bowl of a food processor. Add half of the asparagus along with the pine nuts, 1/2 teaspoon salt, the lemon juice and zest, and a sprinkling of black pepper. Process until smooth.

Spoon the mixture into a medium bowl and add the remaining asparagus, the parsley, and the sun-dried tomatoes. Taste, and add a sprinkling of salt if necessary. This will keep, covered and refrigerated, for up to 4 days.

Portobello Mushroom Tapenade

This spread is incredibly light, yet rich enough to take the edge off a voracious appetite. Spread the tapenade on crackers, or stuff it into mushrooms and bake them. For heartier fare, try it on a sandwich layered with hummus.

MAKES 1½ CUPS

2 tablespoons extra-virgin olive oil
1 onion, diced (1 cup)
½ pound portobello mushrooms, stems removed,
    caps chopped (about 3 cups)
3 garlic cloves, minced
1 teaspoon ground cumin
½ teaspoon dried thyme leaves
2 tablespoons tomato paste
Salt
2 tablespoons shoyu
¾ cup walnuts, toasted
Freshly ground black pepper
¼ cup chopped fresh parsley

Warm the olive oil in a large skillet over medium heat. Add the onions and mushrooms, and sauté for 5 minutes. Then add the garlic, cumin, thyme, tomato paste, ½ teaspoon salt, and shoyu. Scrape the bottom of the pan to deglaze it, and sauté until dry, a few minutes more.

Transfer the mixture to a food processor, and add the walnuts. Process until finely chopped. Add a sprinkling of black pepper and stir in the parsley. Taste and add a sprinkling of salt if necessary. Serve at room temperature.

This will keep, covered and refrigerated, for up to 4 days.

Onion-Rosemary Fig Jam

Slather this spread on bread with hedonistic abandon. Slow-cooked onions, figs, and pecans make a delicious combination that is at once savory and sweet. The flavor improves as it sits, so this is a good choice to keep on hand for unexpected company.

MAKES 2 CUPS

1 tablespoon extra-virgin olive oil
4 cups thinly sliced onions (sliced lengthwise)
Salt
1/2 pound (about 18) dried black Mission figs, hard stems removed
1/2 cup pecans, toasted
2 teaspoons finely minced fresh rosemary

In a medium skillet, combine the oil, onions, and a large pinch of salt. Cook slowly over low heat until the onions have released their juices and reduced to about 1 cup, about 20 minutes.

In a small pot, cover the figs with water and bring to a boil. Remove the pot from the heat and let the figs soak for a few minutes until tender. Drain, reserving the soaking liquid.

Combine the figs, onions, pecans, and rosemary in a food processor and process until smooth, adding a little of the reserved fig liquid as needed. (You'll probably need between 1/4 and 1/2 cup.) Stir in a sprinkling of salt. Let the mixture rest for at least 30 minutes to allow the flavors to marry. Then taste, and add more salt if necessary.

Store, covered, in the refrigerator for up to 2 weeks.

A Festival of Sour Cream and Onion Dips

As a kid, I was crazy about sour cream and onion dip. As an adult, I read the label on a popular packaged dip: hydrogenated oil, corn syrup, caramel coloring . . . Here are several healthful ways to make this party favorite: with sour cream, with yogurt, and with dairy-free tofu. All are fabulous. Dried onions, sold as "instant minced onion" in the spice department, are browned and crisped to give this dip its authentic flavor. Serve the dip with chips or crudités, or stuff it into a baked potato. These will all keep, covered and refrigerated, for up to 5 days.

The Classic (MAKES 1 CUP)

1 cup sour cream, preferably organic
1 teaspoon natural sugar, such as Sucanat, maple sugar,
    or evaporated cane sugar
1/2 teaspoon salt
1 tablespoon minced shallots
2 tablespoons canola oil
1 tablespoon dried onion flakes

Place the sour cream in a bowl, and stir in the sugar, salt, and shallots.

Warm the oil in a small skillet over medium heat. Add the onion flakes and sauté until golden, about 1 minute. Immediately pour the onions into the bowl and stir to combine with the other ingredients. Refrigerate for 20 minutes to allow the flavors to marry.

Yogurt and Onion Dip (MAKES 1 CUP)

Although I like all the onion dip variations, this is my favorite of the three.

2 cups plain full-fat yogurt, preferably organic
1 teaspoon natural sugar, such as Sucanat, maple sugar,
    or evaporated cane sugar
1/2 teaspoon salt
1 tablespoon minced shallots
2 tablespoons canola oil
1 tablespoon dried onion flakes

Place a cheesecloth-lined strainer over a bowl, and pour the yogurt into the strainer. Place the bowl in the refrigerator. Let the yogurt drain for at least 2 hours and up to overnight.

Measure out 1 cup of the thickened yogurt. (If you use a thin variety of yogurt, you'll have 1 cup. If you start with a thicker type, you may have a bit extra.) Place the yogurt in a bowl, and stir in the sugar, salt, and shallots.

Warm the oil in a small skillet over medium heat. Add the onion flakes and sauté until golden, about 1 minute. Immediately pour the onions into the bowl and stir to combine with the other ingredients. Refrigerate for 20 minutes to marry the flavors.

Tofu "Sour Cream" and Onion Dip (MAKES 1 CUP)

Your guests will never know that this dairy-free version is made with tofu!

6 ounces ($\frac{1}{2}$ box) firm silken tofu
1 teaspoon brown rice vinegar
1 teaspoon natural sugar, such as maple sugar, Sucanat,
    or evaporated cane sugar
$\frac{1}{2}$ teaspoon salt
2 tablespoons canola oil
1 tablespoon dried onion flakes
1 tablespoon minced shallots

Combine the tofu, vinegar, sugar, and salt in a food processor and process to combine.

Warm the oil in a small skillet over medium heat. Add the onion flakes and sauté until golden, about 1 minute. Immediately transfer the onions to the processor. Add the shallots and process to combine. Transfer to a small bowl and refrigerate for 20 minutes to marry the flavors.

Homemade tortilla chips are delicious with this dip. Cut a corn tortilla into 6 pieces. Place the pieces in a single layer on an oiled-parchment-covered baking sheet. Brush the tops of the chips lightly with extra-virgin olive oil, sprinkle with salt, and bake in a 375°F oven until crisp, about 10 minutes.

Vegan Dill Sour Cream

This is a delicious cream to swirl into lentil soup or borscht. Boxed tofu has very little flavor, providing a neutral background for the dill. Use the remaining tofu to make another batch, and serve it with baked potatoes.

MAKES ½ CUP

6 ounces (½ box) firm silken tofu
1 tablespoon extra-virgin olive oil
1 tablespoon fresh lemon juice
¼ teaspoon salt
Freshly ground white pepper to taste
½ cup chopped fresh dill

Combine all the ingredients in a food processor and process until smooth. Store in the refrigerator, covered, for up to 5 days.

Roasted New Potato Cups

These cups make great little containers for a variety of tasty toppings, such as the Herbed Olive Tapenade (page 170), Vegan Dill Sour Cream (page 28), or Basil Pesto (page 171). Filled with sour cream and topped with caviar, they become quite elegant. For best results, use potatoes that are equal in size.

You can make these up to a day in advance and reheat them for 10 minutes in a 350°F oven.

MAKES ABOUT 24 PIECES

1 pound (about 12 walnut-size) small thin-skinned potatoes
1 tablespoon extra-virgin olive oil
Salt

Preheat the oven to 400°F.

Cut each potato in half, and cut a thin slice off the bottom of each half so it can sit upright. Using a melon baller or a teaspoon-size measuring spoon, scoop out a small half-round of potato to make a little cup-shaped holder.

Place the potato cups in a medium bowl and toss them gently with the oil and a sprinkling of salt. Arrange the potatoes, hollow side up, on a parchment-covered baking sheet and roast until they are golden and tender, 20 to 30 minutes. Remove them from the oven and fill with a dollop of filling. Serve warm.

Spanakopita Party Triangles

Spanakopita triangles are one of my favorite hors d'oeuvres, no matter how large the gathering. Convenient to make in advance, they can go straight from the freezer to the oven with only a few extra minutes cooking time. The olives in this version add a distinctive and wonderful flavor, but they're delicious without them, too.

MAKES 22 APPETIZER-SIZE OR ABOUT 65 COCKTAIL-SIZE TRIANGLES

Filling

1 1/2 pounds fresh spinach, stemmed, washed, and chopped, *or* 20 ounces baby spinach, rinsed and chopped, *or* one 10-ounce package frozen spinach, defrosted

2 tablespoons extra-virgin olive oil

1 onion, finely chopped (1 cup)

1 1/2 cups (1/2 pound) crumbled feta cheese, preferably Greek sheep's-milk feta

1/4 cup finely chopped fresh dill

1/2 cup chopped fresh parsley

1 egg, lightly beaten

1/4 teaspoon ground nutmeg

1/2 teaspoon salt

Freshly ground black pepper

1/2 cup pitted olives, preferably kalamata, chopped into small pieces, optional

Pastry

3/4 pound frozen phyllo dough, defrosted

Extra-virgin olive oil or melted clarified butter

Preheat the oven to 375°F.

Prepare the filling: Place the chopped fresh spinach in a large pot or skillet. Cover and place over medium-low heat. Cook, stirring or tossing with tongs frequently to push the uncooked leaves to the bottom of the pot, for a few minutes, just long enough to wilt the spinach so the juices can run out freely. (You don't have to add water to the pot; the water clinging to the wet leaves is enough to cook them.)

Drain the spinach well in a colander, pressing it with a spoon to remove as much liquid as possible. If you are using defrosted frozen spinach, drain it well and chop it. Place the drained spinach in a mixing bowl.

Warm the oil in a medium skillet over medium-low heat, and sauté the onions until softened, about 8 minutes.

Add the onions to the spinach along with the cheese, herbs, egg, nutmeg, and salt. Mix well to combine; then add a generous sprinkling of black pepper. Stir in the olives if using.

Prepare tha pastry: Cut the sheets of phyllo in half lengthwise. Stack the pieces into a single pile. Cover the stack of phyllo with a kitchen towel, and then place a damp towel over the dry one; this will prevent the phyllo from drying out while you work. Be sure to cover the phyllo each time after pulling off a layer.

Make the triangles: Lay one sheet of phyllo on your work surface. Brush it with oil, and fold it in half lengthwise. Oil the exposed side. Place 1½ tablespoons of filling at the bottom end of the strip. Fold the pastry up from the corner, forming a triangle, and then continue folding as illustrated in the drawing. Fold down the last edge and brush the entire triangle with oil. Transfer the triangle to a parchment-covered baking sheet. Repeat with the remaining phyllo and filling. (If you are making cocktail-size triangles, cut each sheet of phyllo into 4 widthwise strips, and use just ½ tablespoon of the filling for each phyllo triangle.) Bake for 25 to 35 minutes, or until the triangles are golden brown. Serve hot.

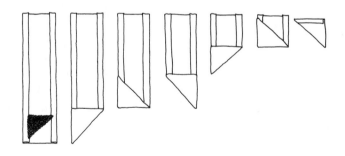

NOTES: *If you own a ricer, use it to squeeze the water out of the spinach. It's the best way—even when the spinach is boiling hot!*

Feta cheese comes in a variety of types. Bulgarian feta is the saltiest, followed by Greek, and then French, which is the mildest. For this recipe I prefer the Greek style.

Vegetable Quesadillas with Basil Pesto

This is a winning combination that always gets rave reviews at parties; it also makes a satisfying lunch for four to six people.

For best results, cut the vegetables thin so that they wilt and meld into a tender mass. (The vegetables alone make a beautiful side dish.) Cheddar-style raw-milk goat cheese, available in many natural foods markets, is my favorite for this dish.

MAKES 36 WEDGES OR 104 COCKTAIL-SIZE PIECES

2 tablespoons extra-virgin olive oil
3 or 4 medium leeks, white part only, sliced into 2-inch-long thin slivers
    (2 cups) and washed (see Note)
$\frac{1}{2}$ pound carrots, cut into thin 2-inch-long matchsticks (2 cups)
Salt
1 medium red bell pepper, cut into thin lengthwise strips
$\frac{1}{2}$ pound zucchini, green part only, cut into thin 2-inch-long strips
    ($1\frac{1}{2}$ cups; see Note)
Freshly ground black pepper
1 recipe Basil Pesto (page 171)
6 large sprouted-wheat tortillas _or_ 12 whole-wheat chapatis
    (Indian flatbread)
2 cups (6 ounces) grated Cheddar or Cheddar-style cheese,
    preferably raw

Warm the oil in a large skillet. Add the leeks and carrots and a generous sprinkling of salt, and sauté until wilted, a couple of minutes. Add the bell pepper and zucchini strips, and sauté until all the vegetables are softened, about 2 minutes. Sprinkle with black pepper, and add salt if necessary.

Spread a layer of pesto on all of the tortillas. Layer 3 tortillas with equal parts vegetables and cheese. Top with the remaining tortillas, pesto side down. You will have 3 stuffed tortillas.

Warm a heavy-bottomed nonstick or cast-iron skillet or griddle. Add a quesadilla and dry-cook until the cheese is melted and the tortilla is speckled with brown spots, 1 to 2 minutes. Remove it from the heat and use a sharp knife or a pizza cutter to cut the quesadilla into wedges or small squares. Repeat with the remaining quesadillas. Serve warm.

NOTE: *Cut the leeks, the white part only, into 2-inch-long cylinders. Cut them in half lengthwise and thinly slice. Measure the slices and then wash.*

Cut the zucchini into 2-inch-long cylinders. Set a piece upright on a cutting board. Using a sharp knife, cut downward, circling the zucchini as you cut single-layer slabs of the green skin with just a small portion of the white attached. Cut the green slabs into thin strips and discard the seedy white center (or save it for stock).

To freeze the quesadillas: Cut them to the desired size. Arrange the pieces in a single layer on a baking sheet, and freeze for about 2 hours. As soon as the pieces are frozen, place them in a freezer bag. To reheat, defrost them for 30 minutes at room temperature. Then spread them on a baking sheet, cover with aluminum foil, and bake in a preheated 350°F oven for 15 minutes.

Crispy Thai Wontons with Shoyu Dipping Sauce

Filled with Thai-flavored cabbage, mushrooms, and peanuts, these wontons make perfect party fare. They crisp up in seconds. For a wonderful main course, simmer them in water like ravioli and serve them in Porcini Broth (page 158) to which you have added a teaspoon of grated lime zest.

MAKES 120 COCKTAIL PIECES OR 60 FULL-SIZE WONTONS

2 tablespoons sesame oil

2 cups cremini mushrooms, cut into $1/2$-inch dice

Salt

1 tablespoon shoyu

One 14-ounce can light coconut milk

2 teaspoons Thai green curry paste

6 cups shredded Napa cabbage

1 cup mung bean sprouts

$1/4$ cup unsalted roasted peanuts, chopped

1 teaspoon grated lime zest

1 tablespoon fresh lime juice

$1^{1}/2$ pounds wonton wrappers

Coconut or canola oil for frying

Dipping sauce

2 tablespoons shoyu

2 tablespoons water

1 tablespoon mirin

1 tablespoon brown rice vinegar

1 teaspoon toasted sesame oil

Prepare the wonton filling: Warm the sesame oil in a large skillet over medium heat. Add the mushrooms and a sprinkling of salt, and sauté, stirring constantly, until the mushrooms are browned and have released their juices, about 3 minutes.

Add the shoyu, coconut milk, and curry paste. Scrape up any brown bits in the skillet, and stir to combine the ingredients. Raise the heat to high and reduce until syrupy, about 10 minutes.

Add the cabbage and cook, stirring often, until the cabbage wilts and the filling is dry, 3 to 5 minutes. Stir in the bean sprouts and peanuts, and cook just until the sprouts have softened, about 30 seconds. Then stir in the lime zest, lime juice, and salt to taste. Transfer the filling to a bowl and let it cool to room temperature.

Make the dipping sauce: In a small bowl, mix together the shoyu, water, mirin, brown rice vinegar, and sesame oil. Divide among small ramekins.

Line a baking sheet with parchment or wax paper. Have a small bowl of water, a pastry brush, and a fork handy.

For full-size wontons: Place a wonton wrapper on a work surface, dip the pastry brush in the water, and brush water around the edges, forming a $\frac{1}{2}$-inch border. Place a heaping teaspoon of filling in the middle of the wrapper. Fold the wrapper in half, sealing the edges with the tines of a fork. Place the wonton on the prepared baking sheet. Repeat until all the filling is used.

For cocktail-size wontons: Cut the wrappers in half (diagonally if you are using square wrappers), and use just $\frac{1}{2}$ teaspoon of filling for each one.

Pour coconut oil to a depth of $\frac{1}{8}$ inch in a medium skillet. Heat it over medium heat until the oil starts to shimmer, 3 to 4 minutes. Add the wontons, 3 or 4 at a time, and pan-fry, turning once, until golden brown, about 6 seconds per side. Remove the wontons from the oil with tongs or a slotted spoon, and drain on a paper-towel-lined baking sheet.

Serve the wontons warm, with the dipping sauce alongside.

To freeze them, arrange the cooked wontons in a single layer on a baking sheet and freeze for about 2 hours. Once they are frozen, store them in resealable freezer bags. To reheat, spread them out on a baking sheet and bake, uncovered, in a preheated 350°F oven for 15 minutes.

Yuca Cakes with Mango Mojo

These savory mini pancakes are dolloped with a spicy, fruity mango sauce. Ideal party fare, they can be made in advance and frozen.

A light dusting of flour gives the cakes a dry surface, making them brown beautifully in the oil.

MAKES 40 TO 45 MINI PANCAKES

1 1/2 **pounds yuca**
1 **onion, grated (**1/2 **cup)**
1 1/2 **teaspoons salt**
3 **scallions, white and green parts, thinly sliced**
1/4 **cup chopped fresh cilantro**
Freshly ground black pepper
1 **cup unbleached white flour**
Coconut oil or extra-virgin olive oil, for frying
Mango Mojo (recipe follows)

Peel the yuca and cut out the tough central core. (The wider the yuca, the bigger the core.) Cut enough yuca into small chunks to equal 1 cup; set the remainder aside. Bring a small pot of water to a boil, add the yuca chunks, and cook until tender, about 20 minutes. Drain, and mash thoroughly with a fork.

Meanwhile, grate the remaining yuca on the large holes of a grater. You should have 3 cups grated yuca. Place this in a medium bowl and add the onions, salt, scallions, cilantro, and a generous sprinkling of black pepper. Stir in the mashed yuca until the mixture is well combined and holds together. Form the yuca mixture into 1 1/2-inch-wide pancakes.

Spread the flour on a wide plate. Have ready a tray or plate lined with paper towels.

Pour coconut oil to a depth of 1/8 inch in a large skillet, and place over medium-high heat. Heat just until the oil is shimmering and a hand held 4 inches above the skillet feels warm. Dredge the pancakes in the flour, and fry them in the oil until golden, about 2 minutes per side. Place the cooked cakes on the paper towels to absorb any excess oil.

Serve warm, drizzled with the Mango Mojo.

NOTE: *Do not refrigerate the cakes. If you make them earlier in the day, keep them covered at room temperature. You can also freeze them in a single layer on a baking sheet.*

When the cakes are frozen, stack them in resealable bags. Defrost at room temperature for 30 minutes; then bake, uncovered, in a preheated 350°F oven for 15 minutes.

Mango Mojo

This fruity, spicy sauce is also delicious on sautéed tempeh, salmon, or chicken.

MAKES ABOUT 2 CUPS

> **1 tablespoon extra-virgin olive oil**
> **2 garlic cloves, minced**
> **1 teaspoon ground cumin**
> **2 tablespoon fresh lime juice**
> **1/2 cup fresh orange juice**
> **1 large mango, peeled and cut into chunks (2 cups)**
> **1 chipotle chile in adobo sauce**
> **3/4 teaspoon salt**
> **1 teaspoon grated lime zest**

Combine the oil, garlic, and cumin in a small skillet, and sauté over low heat, just until the garlic begins to turn golden, about 3 minutes. Immediately transfer the mixture to a blender or food processor, and add the lime juice, orange juice, mango, chipotle chile, salt, and lime zest. Blend the sauce until smooth. Taste, and add salt if necessary.

Store, covered, in the refrigerator for up to a week. Serve the sauce warm or at room temperature.

About Yuca

Yuca is a starchy tuber with white flesh and a barklike dark brown skin. It ranges dramatically in size, from 4 inches to 2 feet long, and it has a fibrous core that must be removed. I find it easiest to cut the root into 2-inch cylinders, then peel each cylinder with a knife and cut around the hard center core. The pieces are then ready for chopping or grating. If your yuca is narrow in circumference, it may not have a particularly fibrous core.

Yuca can be found at well-stocked supermarkets or Latino grocery stores.

Roasted Eggplant and Pepper Salad

In this recipe, both the eggplant and the peppers are cooked in the traditional Turkish style: roasted over a flame. Your kitchen will smell amazing, and you'll love the resulting smoky flavor. Alternatively, you can broil the eggplant, turning it on all sides until blistered, and then finish cooking it in a 375°F oven until tender.

Make this up to four days in advance and serve it as an appetizer spread or as a side salad.

SERVES 4

1 eggplant (1 to 1¼ pounds)
2 red bell peppers
1 jalapeño pepper
1 tablespoon fresh lemon juice
2 garlic cloves, minced
2 tablespoons extra-virgin olive oil
¾ teaspoon salt
1 tablespoon red wine vinegar
2 tablespoons chopped fresh parsley

One by one, roast the eggplant, bell peppers, and jalapeño directly over a gas burner, turning frequently with tongs, until charred all over (the eggplant should be soft). Place the eggplant and the peppers in a bowl covered with plastic wrap, or in a paper bag, and leave them for about 10 minutes for the skins to steam.

Scrape the charred skin off the eggplant. Slice the eggplant and place the slices in a strainer over a bowl. Sprinkle with the lemon juice, and set it aside while you prepare the peppers.

Scrape the charred skin from the peppers, and remove the tops and seeds. Mince the peppers and set them aside in a bowl.

Press the eggplant flesh against the sides of the strainer to remove excess moisture. Mince the eggplant and add it to the bowl containing the peppers. Stir in the garlic, oil, salt, and vinegar. Taste, and add more salt if necessary. Let the mixture sit for 20 minutes to allow the flavors to marry. Chill. Serve sprinkled with the parsley.

NOTES: *If you have a large eggplant, or if you find your eggplant is not thoroughly cooked after charring it on the burner, you can finish cooking it in a 375°F oven until soft.*

Do not wash the pepper skins off under running water. Instead, have a bowl of water nearby to wet your hands with; this will make it easy to rub off the charred skin.

Soups

Basic Vegetable Stock

Roasted Chicken Stock

Autumn Harvest Red Lentil Soup

Indonesian Corn Chowder

Roasted Red Pepper Soup with Tofu Basil Cream

Butternut Squash Soup with Crispy Shallots and Sage

Smoky Black Bean Soup with Tortillas, Avocado,
  and Lime Cream

Kabocha Squash Soup with Gingery Adzuki Beans

White Bean and Spinach Soup with Rosemary

Moroccan Chickpea Soup

Wild Mushroom Winter Potage

Marrakesh Minestrone with Cilantro Purée

Asparagus Soup with Garlic Cream

Southeast Asian Miso Soup

Greens in Garlic Broth

Mysore Rassam

Honeydew Soup with Cucumber Mint Salsa

Making soup

can be one of the most satisfying experiences in the kitchen. As wonderful aromas waft across, you can conjure up your inner grandma, inner witch, or inner alchemist. Many soups are virtually one-pot meals, so all you need for an accompaniment is a piece of crusty bread and perhaps a salad. Moreover, most soups taste better the day after you make them and are delicious for several days after that. They even freeze well. ◉ Soups are appropriate in all seasons. There's nothing like a steaming bowl of a hearty chowder on a chilly day; it's a way to warm up without being weighted down. As the weather improves, lighter varieties made with spring greens are tonic and refreshing. Make use of summer's bounty with corn and red pepper soups or melon coolers. When autumn returns, it's time for squash and harvest vegetable soups. ◉ Here are soups that are truly worth the effort. A homemade stock is important to have on hand, and I've included two of my favorites. But I've included soups with lots of built-in flavor for those who don't use homemade stock. ◉ The textures vary: some soups are creamy, some chunky, and some a combination of the two. The cream soups here are smooth without the addition of heavy cream: potatoes make the roasted red pepper soup silky, while oats do the same thing for the asparagus soup. ◉ Any dairy garnish is optional. The roasted red pepper soup is delicious with dill yogurt swirled in, but for those wishing to avoid dairy, a tofu sour cream is a fine substitute. ◉ Even if you're not a highly experienced cook, you'll find that soups are easily transformed. Is the texture too thick? Simply thin the soup with additional liquid. Too thin? Simmer the soup a bit longer to reduce and thicken the broth. When reheating a soup, do not recook it; just slowly bring it to a simmer. Make sure to taste it after it's warmed, and add seasoning if needed. Some soups, such as bean soups, thicken when cooled. If you need to add more liquid, you will definitely need to add a pinch of salt as well, to bump up the flavor. ◉ All the soups in this book were made in a heavy-bottomed medium (4-quart) pot or a large (6- to 8-quart) pot. Rather than fill a pot to the brim and risk spilling soup as it cooks, choose a pot that is big enough. The heavy bottom on a good pot prevents vegetables from scorching. Use cold, filtered, or bottled water when you make a stock or soup. Don't use hot tap water—it picks up whatever residue is in your pipes. ◎ After sautéing the vegetables for a soup, I usually cover the pot to bring the liquid to a quick boil. Then I lower the heat and cook the soup partially covered. This allows for minimal evaporation while letting a bit of steam escape, thus eliminating messy spillovers. ◎ Cook your soup at a steady simmer: small bubbles should break the surface regularly. Don't cook at a rolling boil (where large bubbles break the surface and ingredients collide with one another), and don't cook at too low a heat (no bubbles rise). Keep an eye on the soup so you can adjust the heat if necessary. ◎ Don't forget the garnish—the garnishes are an integral part of the design and flavor of the soup.

Stocks

I recommend making a homemade stock occasionally; certain recipes are infinitely better with homemade stock. I've provided two—a basic vegetable stock with a good clear flavor, and a chicken stock made with roasted bones. You can use the chicken stock immediately after cooking it, because most of the fat is rendered during the roasting. When you're cooking chicken for other recipes, keep the bones, such as the backbone, and wings in the freezer until you're ready to make stock. ◎ Making stock is neither difficult nor time-consuming. It usually takes only 10 minutes or so to rough-chop the vegetables. Once the stock is simmering, the cooking time is labor-free. A stock is best made in a pot with high sides so that less water evaporates. Keep the pot uncovered to prevent the stock from clouding. Make a stock while you're prepping soup ingredients, or make one while you're at the stove doing something else; you can always freeze it. A basic stock can be tailored to enhance a specific soup. For example, parsnips, fennel, and sweet potatoes are wonderful additions to a sweet vegetable soup. When I'm making stock for a particular soup, I'll often use the vegetable trimmings and herbs from the soup recipe to enhance the flavor of the stock. Shallots and green beans are suitable for any potage. Avoid spinach, as it makes stock taste grassy, and avoid onion peels, which darken the stock and give it a bitter taste. Also avoid the brassica family, which includes cauliflower, cabbage, brussels sprouts, and broccoli. Beets, while appropriate in some soups, will turn a stock red. And while a stock is a good place to use up bits and pieces of leftover vegetables, do not even think of using anything that is tired or spoiled-looking.

Beans

All beans must be washed before you use them. First, sort through the beans to remove any stones. Then put the beans in a bowl and add cold water to cover. Swish the beans around with your fingers (the sediment will rise to the top), and drain. Refill the bowl with fresh water and rinse again. ◎ Beans fall into two categories: those that need to be soaked and those that do not. Lentils of any variety, and split beans such as moong dhal or yellow split peas, do not. In the the soup recipes here, the chickpeas, black beans, and Great Northern and cannellini beans all need to be soaked. The cooking liquid is essential to the flavor of the soup, so it is important to cook the beans from scratch. These beans should be soaked for 6 to 8 hours before they are cooked. ◎ The easiest method is to soak beans overnight in three times as much water as beans. If there is no time to give beans a 6-hour soak, use the quick-soak method: cover the beans with water in a saucepan and bring to a boil. Remove the pan from the heat and let the beans sit in the water for an hour or two. To make beans most digestible, always drain off the soaking liquid and cook them in fresh water.

A pressure cooker is a fantastic tool for cooking beans. Pressure cookers lock in flavor, give the beans a marvelous soft texture, and create a good, thick broth. Many students have confessed to me that they are afraid of pressure cookers; they fear that they are bombs masquerading as a pot. Truthfully, I have seen a pressure cooker explode only once, and that was an old-style cooker. The new pressure cookers are safe and so efficient that even if you were to use your cooker only for beans and bean soups, it's worth having in the kitchen. The best thing about using a pressure cooker is that the cooking time is reduced drastically. In the case of the Moroccan Chickpea Soup, for instance, the time reduces from 2 hours to a mere 25 minutes. To use a pressure cooker, add the ingredients and liquids to the cooker. Let the liquid come to a boil, and then lock the lid. The pressure will immediately start to rise. When the pressure gauge registers on the second line, it's at full pressure. Adjust the heat so it is low, or just high enough to maintain this pressure. Start counting from the point when the second pressure line goes up. When cooking only beans, add a splash of oil to keep the beans from foaming and clogging. If for any reason your pressure cooker clogs, it will let you know by hissing loudly. Turn it off, let it depressurize by one of the two methods listed below, and then clear out the clog. There are two ways to bring down the pressure. The easiest way is to just remove the cooker from the heat and let the pressure release naturally, which takes about 10 minutes. The food keeps cooking during that time. Or you can hold the cooker under cold running water for an instant release. This is a good choice when you wish to check if your food is done. A word of caution: do not lean your head right over the pressure cooker when you open it, or you'll get a bean steam facial. If I'm cooking something that would suffer from being overcooked, such as beans for a salad, I undercook them in the pressure cooker and finish them off by simmering them on the stovetop for a few minutes. If the beans are for a soup, where a very tender bean is desirable, a few extra minutes of cooking time make no difference at all.

Basic Vegetable Stock

This is an all-purpose flavorful stock, suitable for most soups. Tailor it to individual recipes by adding vegetables and seasonings included in those recipes.

MAKES 6 CUPS

1 tablespoon extra-virgin olive oil
1 leek, white and green parts, *or* greens from 2 leeks, chopped into 1-inch
    pieces and washed
1 medium onion, chopped
2 carrots, roughly chopped
2 celery stalks, roughly chopped
1 zucchini, chopped into 1-inch pieces
1/2 cup roughly chopped shallots
2 garlic cloves, unpeeled, halved
1/4 pound (2 cups) green beans
1/2 cup dry white wine
About 10 thyme sprigs
About 10 parsley stems
10 black peppercorns
1 bay leaf
2 quarts water

Warm the oil in a large pot over medium-low heat. Add the leeks, onions, carrots, celery, zucchini, shallots, garlic, and green beans, and sauté until the vegetables are softened, about 10 minutes.

Add the wine, turn up the heat to medium-high, and reduce for 5 minutes. Then add the thyme, parsley, peppercorns, bay leaf, and water and bring to a boil, uncovered. Lower the heat and simmer for about 45 minutes, or until the flavors develop.

Remove the pot from the heat and strain the stock, pushing the solids against the strainer to extract as much liquid as possible.

Store in the refrigerator for up to 1 week, or in the freezer for up to 2 months.

Roasted Chicken Stock

Any time you cook a cut-up chicken, the neck, back, and wings usually go to waste. But if you throw them in the freezer, you can use them to make a great roasted stock. When you roast the chicken, most of the fat ends up in the roasting pan, so the stock is ready to use as soon as it is cooked—no degreasing necessary. The vinegar in the stock helps draw out the calcium from the bones, making it available in the stock. You can also use leftover roast chicken.

MAKES ABOUT 10 CUPS

1 whole chicken, cut into parts, including back and neck, *or* backs, necks, and wings from 3 chickens, *or* a leftover roast chicken (see Note)
2 leeks, white and green parts, cut into 2-inch pieces and washed, *or* 5 cups chopped leek greens
3 medium carrots, peeled and cut into 2-inch chunks
4 celery stalks, cut into 2-inch pieces
1 bay leaf
About 10 parsley stems
About 10 thyme sprigs
1 tablespoon apple cider vinegar
4 quarts water

Preheat the oven to 400°F.

Lightly salt the chicken pieces and place them on a roasting rack in a baking pan. Roast until the skin is golden brown and the meat is tender, 50 minutes to 1 hour.

Place the back, neck, and wings directly into a large stockpot. Remove the meat from the bones on the remaining pieces and save it for another use. Transfer the bones to the stockpot. Add the leeks, carrots, celery, bay leaf, parsley, thyme, vinegar, and water, and bring to a boil, uncovered. Then lower the heat and simmer until the flavor has developed, about 2 hours.

Strain the stock, pressing the solids against the strainer to extract as much liquid as possible. Use immediately, or refrigerate for up to 4 days (skim off any fat before using the chilled stock). The stock will keep in the freezer for up to 2 months.

NOTE: *If you are using leftover roast chicken, cut the chicken into pieces and place the back, neck, and wings in a stockpot. Remove the breast and leg meat from the bones and reserve it for another use; add the bones to the stockpot. Then add the vegetables, herbs, vinegar, and water, and proceed with the recipe.*

Autumn Harvest Red Lentil Soup

This lentil-vegetable soup is a flirt, with its sweet and warming tastes. Red lentils provide a creamy backdrop for the jewel-like vegetables.

SERVES 4

1 cup red lentils, sorted and rinsed
5 1/2 cups water
1 bay leaf
Salt
2 tablespoons extra-virgin olive oil
2 onions, cut into small dice (2 cups)
4 garlic cloves, minced
One 2-inch piece fresh ginger, minced
2 teaspoons ground cumin
2 teaspoons ground coriander
1/2 pound butternut squash, cut into 1/2-inch dice (2 cups)
1 parsnip, cut into 1/2-inch dice (1/2 cup)
2 carrots, cut into 1/2-inch dice (1 cup)
1 tablespoon fresh lemon juice
1/2 pound spinach, stemmed, washed, and torn into bite-size pieces,
    ***or* one 5-ounce bag baby spinach, rinsed**
Cayenne pepper

Combine the lentils, 4 cups of the water, the bay leaf, and 1 teaspoon salt in a medium saucepan. Cover, and bring to a boil. Then lower the heat and simmer, partially covered, for 20 minutes, or until the lentils are tender.

Discard the bay leaf, and purée the lentils with an immersion blender or in a standing blender. (If you want a little more texture, you can simply whisk the lentils until creamy.) Set the lentils aside.

Meanwhile, warm the olive oil in a medium skillet over medium-low heat. Add the onions and sauté until they are softened, about 7 minutes. Add the garlic, ginger, cumin, and coriander, and sauté for 3 minutes. Add the squash, parsnips, carrots, 1/2 teaspoon salt, and the remaining 1 1/2 cups water. Cover and simmer until the vegetables are soft, about 10 minutes.

Stir the lemon juice and spinach into the lentils. The heat will immediately wilt the spinach. Add the vegetables and simmer for 5 minutes to marry the flavors. Season with a generous pinch of cayenne. Taste, and add salt if necessary. Serve hot.

Indonesian Corn Chowder

Flecks of corn, tomato, and cilantro float on a flavorful creamy corn base in this chowder. The lemon grass, chiles, ginger, and cilantro stems infuse the soup with great flavor.

SERVES 4 TO 6

2 tablespoons extra-virgin olive oil
1 onion, chopped (1 cup)
1 carrot, chopped ($^{1}/_{2}$ cup)
1 celery stalk, chopped
1 garlic clove, minced
6 cups corn kernels (from 6 to 8 ears fresh corn)
2 fresh lemongrass stalks, cut into thirds
10 cilantro stems
2 jalapeño peppers, halved
One 2-inch piece fresh ginger, unpeeled, cut into 4 thin slices
$4^{1}/_{2}$ cups water
Salt
2 medium tomatoes, peeled, seeded, and cut into small dice
1 tablespoon plus 1 teaspoon fresh lime juice
$^{1}/_{4}$ cup chopped fresh cilantro

Warm the olive oil in a medium saucepan over medium-low heat. Add the onions, carrots, and celery, and sauté until softened, 10 minutes. Add the garlic and $4^{1}/_{2}$ cups of corn kernels, and sauté for 2 more minutes.

Tie the lemongrass, cilantro stems, peppers, and ginger in a cheesecloth bundle, and add it to the vegetables. Add the water, cover, and bring to a boil. Stir in 1 teaspoon salt, lower the heat, and simmer, partially covered, for 20 minutes.

Remove the herb bouquet and discard it. Transfer the soup to a blender and blend until smooth. Pour the soup through a strainer into a saucepan, stirring it with a wooden spoon to help push the soup through the mesh. Discard the fibrous pulp left in the strainer.

Add the remaining $1^{1}/_{2}$ cups corn and simmer for a couple of minutes to cook the corn. Stir the tomatoes, cilantro, and lime juice into the soup. Taste, and add up to $^{1}/_{4}$ teaspoon salt if necessary. Serve hot.

NOTE: *To tie a cheesecloth bundle, open the cheesecloth, place the ingredients inside, and roll the parcel into a tube. Pull the ends together to tie the bundle; there's no need for string.*

Roasted Red Pepper Soup with Tofu Basil Cream

This soup is a flexitarian's delight. You'll love the cool green cream swirled into the vibrant red purée. When you're in a hurry, bottled peppers and a boxed stock will provide great results. When you have time, roast your own peppers and use home-made stock for a more luxurious version.

SERVES 4

2 tablespoons olive oil

2 cups diced leeks, white part only (small dice)

Salt

2 garlic cloves, minced

$1/2$ teaspoon hot red pepper flakes

2 tablespoons tomato paste

4 red bell peppers, roasted (see page 19), *or* 2 cups bottled
    roasted red peppers, drained

1 thin-skinned potato ($1/4$ pound), cut into small cubes

$4 1/2$ cups homemade vegetable or chicken stock
    (pages 44 and 45) *or* boxed vegetable broth

Freshly ground black pepper

1 teaspoon red wine vinegar

Tofu Basil Cream (recipe follows) *or* $3/4$ cup sour cream
    or plain yogurt mixed with $1/4$ cup chopped fresh basil

Warm the olive oil in a saucepan over medium-low heat. Add the leeks and $1/2$ teaspoon salt, and sauté for about 8 minutes, or until the leeks are softened. Add the garlic, red pepper flakes, and tomato paste, and sauté for 3 minutes. Then add the roasted peppers, potato cubes, and stock. Cover and bring to a boil. Lower the heat and simmer, partially covered, until the potatoes are tender, about 15 minutes.

Transfer the soup to a blender and purée it. Return the soup to the saucepan and add $1/2$ teaspoon salt along with a sprinkling of black pepper and the vinegar. Taste, and add more salt if necessary. Serve hot, with a dollop of Tofu Basil Cream on each serving.

NOTES: *A 16-ounce jar of roasted peppers, which measures out to 2 cups, is the perfect amount for this soup. I recommend the organic variety, available in every natural foods store.*

Imagine brand vegetable broth is wonderful in this recipe, since the tomato-based stock beautifully complements the roasted red peppers.

Tofu Basil Cream

Dollop some of this bright green cream onto a baked potato or use it as a dip for vegetables.

Boxed tofu is more processed than the tofu found in the refrigerator section, but it works wonderfully here because it has very little soybean flavor and retains its firm silken texture.

MAKES ½ CUP

6 ounces (½ box) firm silken tofu
1 tablespoon extra-virgin olive oil
1 tablespoon fresh lemon juice
¼ teaspoon salt
Freshly ground white pepper
½ cup fresh basil leaves

Place all the ingredients in a food processor or blender and process until smooth. This keeps, covered and refrigerated, for up to 4 days.

Buy tomato paste in a tube so that you can measure out small amounts and store the tube in the refrigerator. Alternatively, measure the remainder of a can of tomato paste in 1-tablespoon mounds onto a parchment- or wax-paper-lined baking sheet. Freeze for about 1 hour, until firm; then pile the mounds in a resealable freezer bag. Pull out a frozen mound any time you need a tablespoon of tomato paste.

Butternut Squash Soup with Crispy Shallots and Sage

Creamy squash soups sing of autumn. With a soup as simple as this one, roasting the squash first to heighten its flavor is what makes it memorable. The silky texture of the soup is offset with a flourish of caramelized shallots and sage. A nonstick skillet provides deep-fried crispiness with a minimum amount of oil. Note that you can prepare the garnish ahead of time, or while the squash is roasting, if you like.

SERVES 6

One 2½-pound butternut squash
2 tablespoons extra-virgin olive oil
6 garlic cloves
1 leek, white part only, chopped (about 1 cup) and washed
1½ teaspoons ground cumin
1 orange sweet potato (¾ pound), cut into rounds (2 cups)
½ cup apple cider or apple juice
5 cups water
Salt
Freshly ground black pepper

Garnish

2 tablespoons extra-virgin olive oil
½ cup sliced shallots
10 fresh sage leaves

Preheat the oven to 375°F.

Cut the squash in half and place the halves, cut side down, on a parchment-covered baking sheet. Bake until tender, about 40 minutes. Remove the squash from the oven and let it cool for a few minutes. Then remove the seeds with a large spoon and discard them. Scoop the flesh into a bowl. You should have about 3 cups.

Warm the oil in a medium skillet over medium-low heat. Add the garlic cloves, leeks, and cumin, and sauté until the leeks are softened, about 10 minutes. Add the squash, sweet potatoes, apple cider, water, and 1 teaspoon salt. Cover the pot and bring the soup to a boil. Then reduce the heat and simmer, partially covered, for about 15 minutes, or until the sweet potatoes are softened. Purée the soup with an immersion blender or in a standing blender until smooth. Return the soup to the pot and add a sprinkling of black pepper. Taste, and add a bit more salt if necessary.

Make the garnish: Line a baking sheet or a large plate with paper towels, and set it aside. Warm the oil in a medium nonstick skillet over medium heat. Add the shallots and cook, stirring frequently, until they are browned and crisp, about 5 minutes. Using a slotted spoon, transfer the shallots to the paper towels. Immediately add the sage leaves to the skillet and cook them for about 5 seconds, just until they are withered and crisp but still bright green. Using tongs, transfer the sage leaves to the paper towels. When they have drained, crumble the sage leaves into a small bowl.

Serve the soup hot, sprinkled with sage and with a mound of shallots in the middle.

NOTE: *You can store the crispy shallots and sage, covered in an airtight container, at room temperature for up to 1 week.*

Smoky Black Bean Soup with Tortillas, Avocado, and Lime Cream

Serve this rich red-brown soup topped with tortilla strips, avocado chunks, and lime cream when you want to dish up a bowl of high drama.

SERVES 6

2 tablespoons extra-virgin olive oil

1 onion, finely diced (1 cup)

1 celery stalk, cut into small dice

1/2 green bell pepper, cut into small dice

2 garlic cloves, minced

2 teaspoons ground cumin

1 teaspoon dried oregano

1 1/2 cups black turtle beans, soaked (see page 42) and drained

6 cups water

1 1/2 teaspoons salt

One 14.5-ounce can diced tomatoes, preferably fire-roasted

2 chipotle chiles in adobo sauce

2 tablespoons dry sherry

Garnish

3 corn tortillas, cut into 1/4-inch strips

1/2 avocado, cut into small dice

Lime Cream (recipe follows) or sour cream

Warm one tablespoon of the olive oil in a medium saucepan over medium-low heat. Add the onions, celery, and green pepper, and cook until the vegetables are softened, about 10 minutes. Add the garlic, cumin, and oregano, and cook for another few minutes, until fragrant.

Add the beans and water, cover, and bring to a boil. Then lower the heat and simmer, partially covered, until beans are tender, 1 to 1 1/4 hours. Stir in the salt.

Using a slotted spoon, remove 1 cup of the beans and place them in a blender. Add the tomatoes and the chipotles, and blend until smooth. Return the purée to the soup pot. Stir in the sherry and bring to a boil. Reduce the heat and let the soup simmer rapidly for about 15 minutes, until it is reduced to the desired consistency. Taste, and add more salt if necessary.

Make the garnish: Warm a nonstick skillet with the remaining tablespoon oil over medium-low heat, and swirl to coat the bottom of the skillet. Add the tortilla strips and sauté, tossing them frequently, until they are evenly browned, about 3 minutes. Remove the tortilla strips from the skillet and gently blot off any excess oil with a paper towel.

Serve the soup hot, garnished with the avocados, a mound of tortilla strips, and a dollop of Lime Cream.

Pressure cooker method

Warm 1 tablespoon of the olive oil in a pressure cooker over medium-low heat. Add the onions, celery, and green pepper, and cook until the vegetables are softened, about 10 minutes. Add the garlic, cumin, and oregano, and cook for another few minutes, until fragrant. Add the beans and 4 cups water, and cover. Bring to a boil, lock the lid, and bring to high pressure. Cook at high pressure for 15 minutes. Then remove from the heat and let the pressure return to normal naturally. Remove the lid and add the salt. Proceed with the recipe, puréeing 1 cup of the beans with the tomatoes and chipotles.

Lime Cream

This cooling cream harmonizes beautifully with the spicy soup. Use it as an all-purpose condiment to liven up beans and grains.

MAKES ABOUT 1 CUP

6 ounces (1/2 box) soft silken tofu
2 tablespoons fresh lime juice
2 tablespoons canola oil
2 teaspoons brown rice vinegar
1/2 teaspoon salt
1 teaspoon grated lime zest
1/4 teaspoon freshly ground white pepper

Combine all the ingredients in a food processor or blender and process until smooth. Transfer to a small container and refrigerate for at least 15 minutes. This will keep, covered and refrigerated, for up to 5 days.

Kabocha Squash Soup with Gingery Adzuki Beans

Dashi, a quick stock, gives this soup a Japanese flair. Kabocha, a squat green squash in the buttercup family, is sweet and dense; you can substitute any squash in that family, such as buttercup, honey delight, or Black Forest. A gingery adzuki topping, easily made with canned beans, provides texture, color, and bright flavor.

SERVES 4 TO 6

Dashi

- **8 dried shiitake mushrooms**
- **One 3- to 4-inch piece kombu**
- **2 scallions, white and green parts, thinly sliced**
- **1 medium onion, thinly sliced**
- **2 tablespoons shoyu**
- **2 tablespoons mirin**
- **6 cups water**

Soup

- **One 3-pound kabocha squash**
- **2 tablespoons plus 2 teaspoons sesame oil**
- **2 teaspoons maple syrup**
- **2 onions, thinly sliced (2 cups)**
- **4 garlic cloves, minced**
- **1 hot red chile pepper, such as serrano, jalapeño, or Thai bird, seeded and minced**
- **1 1/4 teaspoons salt**
- **Hot toasted sesame oil *or* toasted sesame oil plus cayenne pepper to taste**
- **1/4 cup thinly sliced scallions, white and green parts**

Garnish

- **1 tablespoon sesame oil**
- **1 tablespoon minced fresh ginger**
- **2 garlic cloves, minced**
- **1 can adzuki beans, drained and rinsed, *or* 1 1/2 cups cooked adzuki beans**
- **2 tablespoons mirin**
- **1 teaspoon umeboshi vinegar**
- **1/4 teaspoon salt**

Make the stock: Combine the mushrooms, kombu, scallions, onion, shoyu, mirin, and water in a medium pot. Bring the mixture to a boil. Then lower the heat and simmer, uncovered, for 20 minutes. Strain the broth, pushing the solids against the strainer to extract as much liquid as possible. You should have about 6 cups of stock.

Preheat the oven to 375°F.

Prepare the squash: Place the squash in the oven and bake it for about 15 minutes. (This will make the squash much easier to cut.) Remove the squash from the oven and let it cool for a few minutes. Then cut the squash in half and remove the seeds. Rub the 2 teaspoons sesame oil and the maple syrup on the interior of the squash and on the cut side. Roast, cut side down, on a parchment-covered baking dish until tender, about 25 minutes. Remove the baking dish from the oven and let the squash cool for a few minutes. Then scoop out the flesh and set it aside.

Warm the remaining 2 tablespoons sesame oil in a medium pot over medium-low heat. Add the onions and sauté until they are softened, about 10 minutes. Add the garlic and chile pepper and cook for 1 minute.

Add the squash, salt, and 4 cups of the dashi. Cover and bring to a boil. Lower the heat and cook, partially covered, for about 10 minutes to blend the flavors. Transfer the soup to a blender and blend until smooth. Return the soup to the pot and add a few drops of the hot sesame oil, or a few drops of toasted sesame oil and a large pinch of cayenne pepper. Taste, and add more salt or sesame oil if desired. Top with a sprinkling of scallions.

Prepare the garnish: Combine the oil, ginger, and garlic in a medium skillet. Cook over medium-low heat for about 2 minutes, just until the garlic starts to color. Then add the beans, mirin, vinegar, and salt, and stir to heat through.

Serve the soup hot, with ¼ cup of the adzuki beans in each bowl.

NOTE: *Hot toasted sesame oil is available in natural foods stores and Asian markets.*

White Bean and Spinach Soup with Rosemary

Beans and greens are a winning combination for a light but satisfying meal. Sautéed garlic and rosemary, added just before serving, give this soup a fresh burst of flavor. A homemade stock is preferable, but a quality boxed vegetable broth is fine. Canned beans won't work here, but pressure cooking makes this a quick and easy soup.

SERVES 4 TO 6

3 tablespoons extra-virgin olive oil
2 onions, cut into small dice (2 cups)
1/4 teaspoon hot red pepper flakes
1 1/2 cups Great Northern or cannellini beans, soaked (see page 42)
and drained
7 cups vegetable stock
1 bay leaf
1 rosemary sprig, plus 1 tablespoon finely chopped rosemary leaves
Salt
1 1/2 pounds spinach, stemmed and washed
4 garlic cloves, minced
2 teaspoons fresh lemon juice
Freshly ground black pepper

Warm 1 tablespoon of the olive oil in a medium saucepan over medium-low heat. Add the onions and sauté until they are softened, about 8 minutes. Add the red pepper flakes and sauté for another minute. Add the beans, stock, bay leaf, and rosemary sprig. Bring to a boil and stir in 1 teaspoon salt. Reduce the heat and simmer, partially covered, for about 1 hour, or until the beans are tender. Remove the bay leaf and the rosemary sprig.

Place the spinach in a large pot. Cover, and cook over medium heat, stirring frequently or tossing with tongs to push the uncooked leaves to the bottom of the pot, just until the leaves have wilted, about 3 minutes. (You don't have to add water to the pot; the water clinging to the wet leaves is enough to wilt them.) Remove the spinach from the heat and place it in a bowl. As soon as the spinach is cool enough to handle, squeeze out the excess liquid and roughly chop it. You should have about 2 cups.

Combine the remaining 2 tablespoons olive oil and the garlic in a medium skillet, and warm over medium-low heat. When the garlic is just beginning to color, add the spinach and mix to heat it through. Stir in the chopped rosemary leaves.

Add the spinach mixture to the soup, and stir in the lemon juice and a sprinkling of black pepper. Taste, and add more salt if necessary. Serve hot.

Pressure cooker method

Warm 1 tablespoon of the olive oil in a pressure cooker over medium-low heat. Add the onions and sauté until they are softened, about 8 minutes. Add the red pepper flakes and sauté for another minute. Add the beans, 5 cups stock, the bay leaf, and the rosemary sprig. Bring to a boil and stir in 1 teaspoon salt. Lock the lid and cook over high pressure for 15 minutes. Turn off the heat and let the pressure return to normal naturally. Remove the bay leaf and rosemary sprig. Proceed with the recipe.

Moroccan Chickpea Soup

This soup is particularly soothing after a day spent outside in the cold. Half the soup is puréed and half is left chunky; every ingredient is essential for the synergy of flavors. A pressure cooker turns this into a fast and easy meal.

SERVES 4 TO 6

1½ cups chickpeas, soaked (see page 42) and drained
1 bay leaf
1 pinch saffron threads
7 cups water
2 tablespoons extra-virgin olive oil
2 onions, cut into small dice (2 cups)
4 garlic cloves, minced
½ teaspoon hot red pepper flakes
1 teaspoon ground cumin
1 teaspoon ground coriander
½ teaspoon ground ginger
½ teaspoon ground cinnamon
Salt
2 tablespoons fresh lemon juice
½ cup roughly chopped fresh parsley,
    plus additional for garnish

Combine the chickpeas, bay leaf, saffron, and water in a large saucepan. Cover and bring to a boil. Then lower the heat and simmer, partially covered, until the chickpeas are almost tender, about 1½ hours.

Warm the oil in a medium skillet over medium-low heat. Add the onions and sauté until translucent, about 7 minutes. Add the garlic, red pepper flakes, cumin, coriander, ginger, and cinnamon, and sauté until fragrant, 2 minutes. Add the onion mixture to the beans and simmer until the beans are completely tender, 30 minutes. Add 1½ teaspoons salt, and let the soup sit for 5 minutes.

Remove the bay leaf. Transfer half of the soup to a blender and purée until creamy. Pour the purée back into the soup pot. Add water if the soup seems too thick. Stir in the lemon juice, and a sprinkling of salt if necessary. Stir in the ½ cup parsley. Serve hot, garnished with a sprinkling of parsley.

Pressure cooker method

Warm the oil in a pressure cooker over medium-low heat. Add the onions and sauté until translucent, about 7 minutes. Add the garlic, red pepper flakes, cumin, coriander, ginger, and cinnamon, and sauté until fragrant, 2 minutes. Add the chickpeas, bay leaf, saffron, and 4 cups water, and bring to a boil. Lock the lid in place and bring to high pressure. Cook over high pressure for 25 minutes. Remove from the heat and let the pressure reduce to normal naturally. Unlock the lid and add 1½ teaspoons salt. Let the soup sit for 5 minutes before proceeding with the recipe.

Wild Mushroom Winter Potage

This chunky soup features three types of mushrooms in a roasted root vegetable purée. The soup makes its own stock, so it's not necessary to use one, but substituting Basic Vegetable Stock (page 44) or Roasted Chicken Stock (page 45) for the water adds a further dimension of flavor.

SERVES 4 TO 6

6 cups water
1/2 cup dried porcini mushrooms
1/4 pound parsnips
1/4 pound thin-skinned potato, red or white
1/4 pound celery root
2 tablespoons extra-virgin olive oil
Salt
1/2 cup diced shallots
1/2 pound shiitake mushrooms, stems removed, caps thinly sliced (4 cups)
1/4 pound button or cremini mushrooms, thinly sliced (2 cups)
1 carrot, cut into small dice (1/2 cup)
1 stalk celery, cut into small dice (1/2 cup)
2 tablespoons shoyu
1/4 cup dry sherry
2 tablespoons chopped fresh dill or parsley
Freshly ground black pepper to taste

Preheat the oven to 400°F.

While the oven is heating, bring the water to a boil. Pour the boiling water over the porcini mushrooms in a bowl, and let them sit for 20 minutes. Drain the mushrooms, reserving the liquid. Roughly chop the reconstituted mushrooms and set them aside. Pour the liquid into a bowl through a strainer lined with cheesecloth or a damp paper towel, to catch any grit. Set the strained mushroom stock aside.

Peel and cut the parsnips, potato, and celery root into 1-inch cubes. You should have about 2 heaping cups of vegetables. Place them in a medium bowl and toss with 1 tablespoon of the olive oil and 1/4 teaspoon salt. Spread the vegetables out on a parchment-covered baking sheet and roast, stirring once, until they are browned and tender, 30 minutes.

Combine the mushroom stock, the roasted vegetables, and ½ teaspoon salt in a soup pot, and bring to a boil. Lower the heat and simmer, partially covered, for 10 minutes. Purée the soup with an immersion blender, or transfer it to a standing blender and blend until smooth. Return the purée to the soup pot.

Heat the remaining 1 tablespoon oil in a medium skillet over medium heat. Add the shallots and sauté for 3 to 4 minutes. Add the shiitake and button mushrooms, the reserved chopped porcini mushrooms, and the carrots, celery, and a sprinkling of salt. Sauté for 3 to 5 minutes. Add the shoyu and sherry, and scrape up any brown bits on the bottom of the pan. Reduce the heat and simmer, covered, until the vegetables are tender, 15 minutes.

Stir the vegetables into the purée, along with the dill and black pepper. Simmer for 5 minutes to blend the flavors. Taste, and add salt if necessary. Serve hot.

Marrakesh Minestrone with Cilantro Purée

This zesty vegetable and bean soup is a meal in a pot. As the aroma of warming spices wafts across your kitchen, close your eyes and be transported halfway around the world. To save time, dice the other vegetables while the onions and tomatoes simmer.

SERVES 6

2 tablespoons extra-virgin olive oil

1 onion, cut into small dice (1 cup)

3 cloves garlic, minced

1 pinch saffron threads

1 teaspoon ground fennel

1 teaspoon ground coriander

1/4 teaspoon hot red pepper flakes

1/2 teaspoon ground ginger

1/2 teaspoon ground cinnamon

7 canned plum tomatoes, with 1 cup juice from the can,
     or one 14.5-ounce can whole tomatoes, with their liquid

5 cups water

1 cup finely diced sweet potato

1 carrot, finely diced (1/2 cup)

1 small zucchini, finely diced (1 cup)

Salt

2 cups shredded Swiss chard leaves or chopped spinach

1/4 cup couscous

One 15-ounce can cooked chickpeas, rinsed and drained,
     or 1 1/2 cups cooked chickpeas)

Freshly ground black pepper

1 teaspoon fresh lemon juice

Cilantro Purée (recipe follows)

Warm the oil in a medium saucepan over medium-low heat. Add the onions and sauté until they are softened and translucent, about 7 minutes. Add the garlic, saffron, fennel, coriander, red pepper flakes, ginger, and cinnamon. Sauté until fragrant, about 3 minutes.

Add the tomatoes and the juice, breaking up the tomatoes with the back of a spoon. Cook, stirring occasionally to soften the tomatoes and reduce the liquid by half, about 10 minutes.

Add the water, sweet potatoes, carrots, and zucchini. Cover and bring to a boil. Stir in 1 teaspoon salt. Then reduce the heat and simmer, partially covered, until the vegetables are tender, about 15 minutes.

Add the Swiss chard, couscous, and chickpeas, and simmer for 5 more minutes. Add a generous sprinkling of black pepper, and stir in the lemon juice. Taste, and add a sprinkling more salt if necessary.

Serve hot, garnished with a tablespoon of Cilantro Purée.

NOTE: *A quick way to cut tomatoes is to place them in the pot and use kitchen shears to roughly cut them.*

Cilantro Purée

You can make this purée in a blender or mini food processor, or with a mortar and pestle. The warming flavors of the purée are an absolute must for the soup.

MAKES ABOUT ¾ CUP

1 teaspoon whole cumin seeds
2 tablespoons extra-virgin olive oil
1 tablespoon fresh lemon juice
1 cup fresh cilantro leaves, chopped
1 garlic clove
¼ teaspoon salt
½ teaspoon cayenne pepper

Dry-toast the cumin seeds in a heavy-bottomed skillet for about 1 minute, or until fragrant. Transfer the seeds to a blender and whir until crushed. (Alternatively, place the seeds in a mortar and grind until smooth.) Add the oil, lemon juice, cilantro, garlic, salt, and cayenne. Blend (or pound) until smooth. This keeps, covered and refrigerated, for up to 3 days.

Asparagus Soup with Garlic Cream

Local asparagus is one the first harbingers of spring, and this soup is high on my list of springtime favorites.

The garlic cream adds a delicious flavor to soups, sauces, and bean dishes. The garlic mellows while the herbs infuse it with flavor.

Crispy fried shallots (see page 51) would be a scrumptious addition.

SERVES 4 OR 5

1 pound asparagus, 1 1/2 inches of the hard ends removed
Salt
2 tablespoons extra-virgin olive oil
1 1/2 cups minced shallots
1/4 cup rolled oats
5 cups Basic Vegetable Stock (page 44)

Garlic Cream

1 medium head garlic, separated into cloves and peeled
2 tablespoons extra-virgin olive oil
1 cup water
4 thyme sprigs
Freshly ground black pepper
1 to 2 teaspoons fresh lemon juice
1/4 cup chopped fresh flat-leaf parsley, for garnish

Cut 1 1/2 inches off the tip of each asparagus spear, and set the tips and stems aside.

Bring a saucepan of salted water to a boil, add the asparagus tips, and cook until tender, about 4 minutes. Drain and set aside.

Warm the oil in a medium saucepan over medium-low heat. Add the shallots and a pinch of salt, and sauté for 5 minutes, or until they are softened and lightly browned. Add the oats, asparagus stems, and stock, and bring to a boil. Lower the heat and simmer, partially covered, until the oats are tender, about 30 minutes.

Meanwhile, make the Garlic Cream: In a small saucepan, combine the garlic, oil, water, and thyme. Simmer, uncovered, until the garlic is tender, 20 to 30 minutes. Discard the thyme sprigs and transfer the mixture to a blender. Purée, adding a little of the vegetable cooking liquid if needed.

Stir the Garlic Cream into the soup and mix well. Purée the soup in a standing blender or with an immersion blender.

Return the puréed soup to the pot. Add salt to taste, and season with black pepper and lemon juice. Add the reserved asparagus tips, and reheat if necessary. Serve warm, garnished with a sprinkling of chopped parsley.

NOTE: *Although they may seem unusual in a soup, blended oats produce a delicate, creamy consistency; you'll never know they're there.*

Southeast Asian Miso Soup

This light and energizing Asian treat is fierce enough to drive away a cold. Don't be intimidated by the long list of ingredients; the stock takes only minutes to assemble, and the garnishes are a breeze.

SERVES 4 OR 5

Spicy stock

1 leek, white and green parts, roughly chopped and washed

1 medium onion, cut into large dice

1 carrot, roughly chopped

1 celery stalk, roughly chopped

8 dried shiitake mushrooms

2 fresh lemongrass stalks, cut into 4-inch pieces

One 2-inch piece fresh ginger, unpeeled, cut into 6 pieces

4 garlic cloves, unpeeled, cut in half

2 jalapeño peppers, cut in half

About 10 cilantro stems

2 quarts water

Garnishes

2 ounces rice stick noodles, broken into pieces

2 tablespoons dark red miso, such as hatcho miso

4 ounces ($1/3$ box) firm silken tofu, cut into $1/4$-inch dice

1 scallion, white and green parts, thinly sliced

$1/2$ bunch watercress, heavy stems removed (1 cup)

2 tablespoons fresh lime juice

$1/4$ cup fresh cilantro leaves

Salt

1 small fresh chile, such as Thai bird, serrano, or jalapeño,
    cut into very thin rings, optional

Combine all the stock ingredients in a soup pot, and bring to a boil. Then lower the heat and simmer, uncovered, for 35 minutes until the flavor is developed.

While the stock is simmering, bring a small pot of water to a boil. Add the rice noodles and let them boil for 1 minute. Then remove the pot from the heat and let the noodles sit in the hot water for 10 minutes to soften. Drain, and set aside.

Strain the stock. You should have about 5 cups of stock. If you have less than that, add enough water to measure 5 cups. Discard the vegetables and herbs.

Pour the stock into a saucepan and reheat it if necessary. Transfer ¼ cup of the stock to a small bowl and add the miso, stirring until it dissolves. Return the miso mixture to the stock, and add the noodles, tofu, scallions, and watercress. Stir in the lime juice and cilantro leaves. Taste, and add a pinch of salt if necessary. Serve hot, garnished with a few chile rings if desired.

Greens in Garlic Broth

Your body will thank you for this gorgeous tonic after the heavier foods of winter. To make the soup quickly, put the stock on to simmer while you prepare the greens. Once the stock is ready, the soup takes only 20 minutes. You can substitute any greens that you have on hand: mustard greens, spinach, frisée, and sorrel are all delicious. Add a can of white beans to the soup, serve some crusty bread, and you have a nourishing light meal.

SERVES 4 TO 6

Garlic broth

- 2 heads garlic, cloves separated and peeled
- 2 cups sliced leek greens, washed
- 1/4 cup green or brown lentils, sorted and rinsed
- 10 fresh sage leaves
- 10 thyme sprigs
- 1 bay leaf
- 10 cups water
- 1 teaspoon salt

Soup

- 2 tablespoons extra-virgin olive oil
- 2 cups sliced leeks, white part only, washed
- 1 cup diced carrots (small dice)
- 1 bunch watercress, heavy stems removed, chopped into bite-size pieces (about 2 cups)
- 1 bunch arugula, heavy stems removed, chopped into bite-size pieces (about 2 cups)
- 1 bunch escarole, chopped into bite-size pieces (about 2 cups)
- 1 bunch Swiss chard, stems removed, chopped into bite-size pieces (about 6 cups)
- Salt
- 1 teaspoon umeboshi vinegar
- Freshly ground black pepper
- Extra-virgin olive oil
- 1/2 cup grated Parmesan cheese

Prepare the garlic broth: Combine the garlic, leek greens, lentils, sage, thyme sprigs, bay leaf, and water in a soup pot and bring to a boil. Lower the heat and stir in the salt. Simmer, partially covered, until the flavor is rich and garlicky, 30 to 45 minutes.

Remove the pot from the heat and strain the stock, pushing the solids against the strainer to get as much liquid as possible. Measure the broth: you should have 2 quarts. If you don't have that much, add water to measure 2 quarts.

Warm the oil in a large saucepan over medium-low heat. Add the leeks and carrots, and cook until translucent, about 10 minutes. Add the watercress, arugula, escarole, chard, and 1 teaspoon salt, and sauté until wilted, about 5 minutes. Add the broth and bring to a boil. Then lower the heat and simmer, partially covered, for 10 minutes.

Stir in the umeboshi vinegar. Sprinkle with black pepper. Taste, and add salt if necessary. Serve hot, topping each serving with a drizzle of olive oil and 1 to 2 tablespoons Parmesan cheese.

Mysore Rassam

Tomatoes, ginger, and tamarind flavor this piquant South Indian–inspired soup. It's traditionally made as a thin broth, but I prefer it with more body. For the best texture, make sure to cook the split peas until they are meltingly tender. If you're in an Indian store, buy the traditional split yellow pigeon peas called *toor dhal* and use those instead.

SERVES 4 TO 6

1 cup yellow split peas, or *toor dhal*

7½ cups water

1 teaspoon ground turmeric

2½ cups fresh tomatoes, seeded and chopped, *or* one 28-ounce can tomatoes, drained

2 tablespoons minced fresh ginger

½ cup cold water

1 teaspoon tamarind concentrate (see Notes)

1 tablespoon ground coriander

1 teaspoon ground cumin

3 serrano or Thai bird chiles, halved, stems removed

1 teaspoon molasses

2 teaspoons salt

2 tablespoons ghee

¾ teaspoon mustard seeds

⅛ teaspoon ground asafetida (see Notes)

Pinch of cayenne pepper

2 tablespoons finely chopped fresh cilantro

Wash the split peas and place them in a medium pot along with 4 cups of the water and the turmeric. Cover, and bring to a boil over medium-high heat. Then reduce the heat and simmer gently, partially covered, stirring occasionally to prevent sticking, until the split peas are very tender, about 45 minutes. Add another cup of water if the split peas have absorbed all the water and still need additional cooking time.

While the peas are cooking, combine the tomatoes, ginger, and ½ cup of cold water in a blender, and purée. Set the purée aside.

Using a standing or an immersion blender, blend the split peas until smooth. Add the remaining 3 cups water to the peas and return the mixture to the pot. Stir in the tomato purée, tamarind concentrate, coriander, cumin, chiles, molasses, and salt. Cover and bring to a boil over medium-high heat. Reduce the heat and simmer, partially covered, for 15 minutes. Remove from the heat.

Warm the ghee in a small skillet. When it is very hot, carefully add the mustard seeds. (Keep a pot lid handy; the seeds may splatter and sputter.) When the sputtering stops and the seeds turn gray (about 5 seconds), add the asafetida. Immediately pour the spiced ghee over the lentil soup and stir to mix. Cover the pot and let the soup rest briefly, at least 5 minutes. Then stir in the cayenne pepper. Taste, and add a bit more salt if necessary. Serve hot, sprinkled with the cilantro.

NOTES: *Tamarind concentrate, which keeps indefinitely in the refrigerator, is from the fruit of the tamarind tree. It has a tart fruity flavor and is used in Indian and Southeast Asian cooking. If you have tamarind paste, you can soak a 1-inch chunk in 1/4 cup hot water. Strain the seeds, and use the pulp in this recipe in place of the tamarind concentrate.*

Asafetida, also known as hing, *is made from a resin, and can be purchased in Indian stores. It's quite smelly, so close the jar immediately after using. When it is cooked in oil or ghee, however, it emits a pleasant oniony aroma. For this reason, it is often used when onions and garlic are not present in a dish. An ingredient in many dhals, it is considered a valuable digestive aid.*

Honeydew Soup with Cucumber Mint Salsa

A refreshing starter on a hot summer day, this soup is topped with a cooling salsa. Honeydew stars, while avocado lends a luxurious texture. Surprisingly, no additional liquid is needed. For the best results, be sure to get a sweet, ripe melon.

SERVES 6

Soup

One ripe 4-pound honeydew melon, flesh cut into chunks (6 cups)
$1\frac{1}{2}$ ripe Hass avocados
$\frac{1}{4}$ cup fresh lime juice
$\frac{3}{4}$ teaspoon salt

Cucumber Mint Salsa

1 cucumber, peeled, seeded, and cut into small dice ($\frac{3}{4}$ to 1 cup)
$\frac{1}{2}$ jalapeño pepper, stemmed, seeded, and minced
$\frac{1}{4}$ cup chopped fresh mint
1 tablespoon fresh lime juice
2 tablespoons minced red onion
Salt
$\frac{1}{2}$ ripe Hass avocado

Prepare the soup: Working in two batches, combine the honeydew, avocados, lime juice, and salt in a blender, and purée until smooth. Pour the purée through a strainer into a container. Refrigerate the soup until chilled, at least 2 hours and up to 1 day.

Make the salsa: Mix the cucumber, jalapeño, mint, lime juice, and red onion in a medium bowl. Sprinkle with salt. Holding the avocado half in one hand, make $\frac{1}{4}$-inch crosshatch cuts through the flesh with a table knife, cutting down to the skin. Separate the diced flesh from the skin by gently scooping the avocado cubes out with a spoon. Add the diced avocado to the bowl and mix gently. Season with additional salt to taste.

Serve the soup in individual bowls, topped with a spoonful of salsa.

Salads

Baby Greens with Roasted Red Pepper Vinaigrette and
Warm Walnut-Crusted Goat Cheese Medallions

Raspberry Vinaigrette ▪ Reduced Balsamic and
Hazelnut Oil Vinaigrette

Watercress and Grapefruit Salad with
Thai Peanut Dressing

Shredded Romaine Salad with Dill and Scallions

Romaine Salad with Creamy Avocado Dressing

Spinach Salad with Lemon-Rosemary Vinaigrette and
Smoky Shiitakes

Watercress and Hearts of Palm Salad with
Plantain Chips

Green Leaf, Date, and Cashew Salad with
Tamarind Dressing

Green Leaf, Cucumber, and Wakame Salad with
Carrot-Ginger Dressing

Frisée, Endive, and Celery Salad with
Anchovy Vinaigrette

Wilted Arugula with Braised Tempeh, Mango,
and Red Onion

Wilted Spinach Salad with Orange-Curry Dressing

Asian Slaw with Peanuts

Salvadoran Slaw

Beet, Tomato, and Watermelon Salad with
Caramelized Almonds

Gazpacho Salad with Tomato Vinaigrette

Turkish Tomato Salad with Fresh Herbs

There is nothing like a salad

to lighten a meal or accompany a main course. From green salads to cabbage slaws, from warm wilted greens to seasonal tomato combinations, there is a salad that will please everyone's palate. ◉ In this chapter you will find leafy green salads, some with traditional vinaigrettes, often with an unexpected twist. The fruit- and vegetable-based dressings—such as the avocado dressing, roasted red pepper vinaigrette, carrot-ginger dressing, and tomato vinaigrette—are low in oil, so you can pour them on with hedonistic abandon. Many of the salads include ethnic seasonings; others are made up of surprisingly unusual but harmonious mixes of ingredients, such as you'll find in the Beet, Tomato, and Watermelon Salad. ◉ Except for the Frisée, Endive, and Celery Salad and the Watercress and Grapefruit Salad, the recipes are all vegetarian. Any dairy garnish is optional. ◉ For the sake of convenience, I have included a selection of recipes that use romaine, baby spinach, and mesclun. There's no waste, and they come prewashed (although I find it's a good idea to give them an additional quick soak). Although spinach is fairly sweet, it goes well with fruit and sweet dressings as well as savory ones, and it is delicious warm and wilted as well. Mesclun has a slightly bitter taste and goes well with assertive vinaigrettes such as the reduced balsamic or the raspberry. A 5-ounce package of baby spinach measures about 6 cups, perfect for 4 servings. A quarter pound of mesclun measures 6 cups, but I usually buy ½ pound for 6 people. ◉ Crisp romaine is versatile as well; it can be accompanied by a simple lemon–olive oil dressing or a thick creamy dressing. Peppery arugula and watercress are good raw or cooked; just be sure to trim off the heavy stems. Frisée, escarole, endive, and radicchio, all members of the chicory family, are somewhat bitter, with escarole weighing in on the lighter side. Escarole, when used in a wilted salad, is best slightly cooked, whereas crinkly-leaved frisée is tasty either way. Soft and hearty butter lettuce makes a great foil for the more bitter greens. Green leaf, an all-purpose favorite of mine, features in a couple of these recipes. ◉ Napa cabbage (Asian, or Chinese, cabbage), with its football

74

shape and crinkly leaves, makes a wonderfully tender coleslaw. Both red and green cabbage can be eaten raw or cooked and are available year-round. ◎ Wash your greens well. Gritty greens are a sure way to render even a delicious salad inedible. Immerse the greens in a bowl of water or in a sink filled with water. Swish the greens around with your hands to dislodge any dirt. Then lift them out of the water, letting any dirt settle to the bottom. Repeat if necessary with fresh water until no dirt remains. If you have a salad spinner, wash the greens in it: The insert acts as a colander. Lift out the basket, dump the water, and repeat as needed. Spinach and arugula are especially gritty and need to be washed a number of times. ◎ Dry salad greens well in order not to dilute the dressing. The salad spinner is the sure way to eliminate most of the water. If the greens are still a little too damp after a good spin, pat them dry with a kitchen towel or paper towel. ◎ In an ideal world, we wouldn't prepare salad greens until immediately before eating, but that's not always realistic. With a little care, you can prepare your greens in advance: Wash, dry, and cut or tear the leaves; then wrap them in a paper towel (to absorb moisture), and store them in a plastic bag. When you are handling a large quantity of greens, layer them, separated by paper towels, in a covered container. You can store most greens this way for up to 24 hours. ◎ To get an accurate assessment of your dressing, dip a leaf from your salad into the dressing and taste it. If you use a spoon or your finger, the flavor will not be accurate. To enhance the flavor of the salad, lightly salt and pepper the greens before tossing them. Then slowly add some dressing, toss to combine, and taste before adding more dressing.

Baby Greens with Roasted Red Pepper Vinaigrette and Warm Walnut-Crusted Goat Cheese Medallions

I often serve this festive salad for brunch. When you use bottled roasted peppers, it takes only 5 minutes to make the dressing. Sherry vinegar gives it a special flavor, but balsamic and red wine vinegar are fine substitutes.

The walnut-crusted goat cheese medallions make fabulous appetizers on their own. The cheese log can be kept in the refrigerator or freezer, ready to be baked at a moment's notice. If you don't eat cheese, sprinkle the salad with toasted croutons.

SERVES 6

Vinaigrette   (MAKES ⅔ CUP)

1 large red bell pepper, roasted (see page 19), *or* ½ cup bottled
    roasted red peppers, drained
3 tablespoons extra-virgin olive oil
1 tablespoon sherry vinegar
½ teaspoon salt
1 garlic clove
Freshly ground black pepper to taste
½ teaspoon honey

Goat cheese medallions

½ pound goat cheese (soft style, in a log)
1 garlic clove, minced
2 tablespoons fresh thyme *or* 3 tablespoons chopped fresh parsley or basil
1 tablespoon extra-virgin olive oil
1 teaspoon Dijon mustard
½ cup walnuts, toasted and chopped into small pieces
Sixteen ½-inch-thick slices of baguette

Salad greens

½ pound (about 12 cups) mesclun (baby greens)
1 cucumber, peeled
½ cup fresh basil leaves, torn in half

Prepare the vinaigrette: Place all the dressing ingredients in a blender, and blend until smooth. Transfer to a bowl or jar, and set aside.

Make the medallions: In a medium bowl, mix the goat cheese with the garlic, thyme, olive oil, and mustard until well combined. Spread the walnuts on a plate and roll the cheese in the walnuts, pressing the nuts into the sides until you have an 8-inch log. Wrap the log in plastic wrap and freeze it for 10 minutes, or refrigerate it for at least 30 minutes, until it is firm enough to cut.

Preheat the oven to 350°F.

Lay the baguette slices in a single layer on a baking sheet and toast until crispy, about 5 minutes per side.

Slice the goat cheese log into 16 half-inch rounds. Place the rounds on the bread and return the baking sheet to the oven for 5 minutes, just until heated through.

Make the salad: Meanwhile, place the mesclun in a large bowl. Using a Y-shaped vegetable peeler, peel the cucumber into long strips until you get to the center. Discard the seeds. Add the cucumber strips and the basil to the greens. Sprinkle the salad lightly with salt and pepper, and toss to combine.

Toss the salad with the dressing, and serve it with the goat cheese toasts.

NOTES: *The roasted red pepper dressing will keep in the refrigerator for up to 1 week.*

The cucumbers, cut lengthwise with a Y-shaped peeler, blend into the salad like another form of lettuce.

Here are two of my favorite dressings. They're especially good on baby greens salads.

Raspberry Vinaigrette

You can purchase raspberry vinegar, but making your own takes only minutes and the flavor is beyond compare. Defrosted frozen organic raspberries are flavorful when the fresh variety are past their prime. Blackberries can be used also.

This dressing coats about 12 cups of baby greens, enough for 4 to 6 people. Add ½ cup toasted sliced almonds and ½ cup fresh raspberries to the salad. If figs are in season, quarter one, cutting partway through, for each serving and open it like a flower—a fitting garnish to an elegant salad.

MAKES ABOUT ¾ CUP

2 tablespoons balsamic vinegar
½ cup fresh or defrosted frozen raspberries
1 tablespoon minced shallots
½ teaspoon Dijon mustard
¼ teaspoon salt
Freshly ground black pepper
6 tablespoons extra-virgin olive oil

Combine the vinegar with the raspberries in a small bowl. Smash the raspberries into the vinegar with the back of a spoon until they are completely broken up. Let the vinegar-berry mixture sit for at least 5 minutes. Then strain the raspberry vinegar into a small bowl, pressing hard on the berries to extract all the juice. You should have ¼ cup of liquid.

Add the shallots, mustard, salt, and a sprinkling of black pepper. Whisk in the olive oil. Keep this in the refrigerator, covered, for up to 2 weeks.

Reduced Balsamic and Hazelnut Oil Vinaigrette

The reduced balsamic vinegar dressing lacquers green lettuce leaves with a shiny coat. This dressing coats 12 cups of baby greens, enough for 4 to 6 people. Add candied hazelnuts for a salad guaranteed to send your taste buds to seventh heaven.

MAKES ¾ CUP

¾ cup balsamic vinegar
½ teaspoon Dijon mustard
½ cup toasted hazelnut oil
Salt
Candied Hazelnuts (recipe follows), optional

Pour the vinegar into a small saucepan and bring it to a boil. Lower the heat and simmer rapidly, uncovered, until the liquid is reduced to ¼ cup, about 10 minutes.

Pour the reduced vinegar into a small bowl and stir in the mustard. Slowly drizzle the hazelnut oil into the bowl, whisking constantly until the oil and vinegar are emulsified. Keep this in the refrigerator, covered, for up to 3 weeks.

CANDIED HAZELNUTS (MAKES 1 CUP)

1 cup hazelnuts, toasted and skinned (see page 18), roughly chopped
2 tablespoons maple syrup
2 tablespoons natural sugar, preferably maple sugar, Sucanat, or
    evaporated cane sugar

Preheat the oven to 350°F.

Place the hazelnut pieces in a medium bowl and toss them with the maple syrup and sugar. Spread them on a parchment-covered baking sheet, and bake for 15 minutes, stirring once, until the nuts are caramelized. Remove the nuts from the oven and scrape them into a bowl; allow to cool.

The candied hazelnuts will keep, covered, at room temperature for up to 3 weeks.

Watercress and Grapefruit Salad with Thai Peanut Dressing

This salad is a perfect starter to Thai dishes or the Baked Thai Tempeh Triangles (page 228). The dressing is light and complex, with a delicate peanut flavor and a bright citrus edge. It is also delicious over baby greens such as mizuna and arugula. For a delicious vegetarian version, substitute 1 teaspoon white miso for the Thai fish sauce.

SERVES 4 OR 5

3 tablespoons fresh lime juice

1 tablespoon Thai fish sauce

1 tablespoon honey

2 garlic cloves, minced

1 small chile, such as Thai bird chile, minced, _or_ 1/2 jalapeño pepper, minced

1 tablespoon creamy peanut butter

1/3 cup unrefined peanut oil or canola oil

1 tablespoon chopped fresh cilantro

2 tablespoons plus 1/4 cup chopped unsalted roasted peanuts

3 bunches watercress, washed, heavy stems removed (about 6 cups)

1 seedless cucumber, sliced into thin rounds

2 red grapefruits, segmented (see Note)

In a small bowl, whisk together the lime juice, fish sauce, honey, garlic, and chile. In another small bowl, whisk together the peanut butter and the oil. Slowly add the oil mixture to the lime juice mixture in a steady stream, whisking until well combined (emulsified). Stir in the cilantro and the 2 tablespoons peanuts. For maximum flavor, let the dressing sit for 30 minutes to allow flavors to marry.

In a medium bowl, toss the watercress with the dressing just until coated. Mound the salad onto plates, and surround with the cucumbers. Ring the salad with the grapefruit segments. Garnish with the remaining 1/4 cup peanuts, and serve.

NOTE: _To segment the grapefruit, cut a disk off the top and bottom of each grapefruit, slicing through the colored peel and white pith to expose the flesh. Set the grapefruit on one end and cut downward, following the contours of the fruit to remove the skin and pith, exposing the pink flesh. Use a paring knife to lift out each segment._

Shredded Romaine Salad with Dill and Scallions

Because it's so easy to assemble, I probably make this salad more than any other. It has a clean bright taste, and the three shades of green are simply gorgeous. For a delicious brunch, serve this with Cauliflower, Green Bean, and Mushroom *Kuku* (page 234) and *Mujadarrah* (page 210). Or try it with Turkish Stuffed Trout in Parchment (page 250) and Dolma Pilaf (page 196). In autumn, I often sprinkle this salad with fresh pomegranate seeds. Crumbled feta cheese is delicious as well.

SERVES 4

6 cups shredded romaine lettuce
3/4 cup chopped fresh dill
1/2 cup thinly sliced scallions, white and green parts
Salt and freshly ground black pepper
1 garlic clove, minced
2 tablespoons fresh lemon juice
1/4 cup olive oil
Pomegranate seeds, optional
Crumbled feta cheese, optional

In a large bowl, mix the lettuce with the dill and scallions. Sprinkle the greens liberally with salt and pepper.

Whisk the garlic, lemon juice, and oil together in a bowl. Add the dressing to the greens and toss together. Top with pomegranate seeds or crumbled feta if desired.

NOTES: *To shred romaine, use a sharp knife. Keeping the head intact, cut the lettuce into 1/2-inch strips, starting from the loose ends and moving toward the root.*

Snip the dill with kitchen shears or pull it off with your fingers. Then coarsely chop the leaves.

Romaine Salad with Creamy Avocado Dressing

This salad is basically an avocado Caesar. The dressing is creamy and the greens can take quite a lot of it without being overpowered. It's a fairly hearty dish; a big plate alongside a bowl of Smoky Black Bean Soup (page 52) makes a satisfying meal. With the cheese included, it works well as a main-course salad.

SERVES 4 TO 6

Dressing   (MAKES 1 CUP)

1 teaspoon whole cumin seeds

3 tablespoons fresh lime juice

3 tablespoons extra-virgin olive oil

1 ripe avocado

1/2 teaspoon salt

1/4 teaspoon Dijon mustard

1 garlic clove, minced

1/4 to 1/2 cup water

Freshly ground black pepper to taste

Cayenne pepper to taste

Salad

1 tablespoon extra-virgin olive oil

2 corn tortillas, cut into strips

Salt

1 head romaine lettuce, torn into bite-size pieces (12 cups)

1 tomato (6 ounces), seeded and diced small

1/4 cup cheese cubes (small dice), preferably raw-milk Monterey Jack
    cheese, optional

Prepare the dressing: Dry-toast the cumin seeds in a heavy-bottomed skillet over medium-high heat until fragrant, about 2 minutes. Grind to a powder, using a spice grinder or a mortar and pestle. Combine the ground cumin, lime juice, oil, avocado, salt, mustard, garlic, and 1/4 cup of the water in a blender and blend until smooth. Add the remaining water if necessary. Add a pinch of black pepper and a pinch of cayenne. Taste, and add more salt if necessary.

Line a plate with a paper towel. Warm the olive oil in a medium nonstick skillet over medium heat. Add the tortilla strips and sauté, using tongs to move them around constantly, until crisp and lightly golden, about 2 minutes. Transfer the strips to the prepared plate and allow to drain. Sprinkle with salt.

Place the romaine in a salad bowl and toss it with the dressing, tomato, and cheese (if using). Serve topped with the tortilla strips.

Spinach Salad with Lemon-Rosemary Vinaigrette and Smoky Shiitakes

This salad always gets rave reviews for its rich flavor. Serve it as a starter, or with the tempeh croutons as a light lunch. The shiitakes shrivel and crisp as they roast.

SERVES 4

Smoky shiitakes

1/2 pound fresh shiitake mushrooms, stems removed, caps cut into 1/2-inch slices (about 4 cups)

2 tablespoons extra-virgin olive oil

2 tablespoons shoyu

Dressing (MAKES 1/2 CUP)

1 teaspoon minced fresh rosemary

1 teaspoon grated lemon zest

1 tablespoon fresh lemon juice

1 tablespoon balsamic vinegar

1 tablespoon shoyu

1/2 teaspoon Dijon mustard

1 garlic clove crushed with 1/4 teaspoon salt (see Note)

1/4 cup extra-virgin olive oil

Freshly ground black pepper to taste

Salad

1/4 cup pine nuts

3/4 pound spinach, stemmed and washed, *or* 1/2 pound baby spinach, washed (10 cups)

1/2 cup thinly sliced red onion (in half rings)

1 orange, segmented (see Note, page 80)

Tempeh Croutons (recipe follows), optional

Prepare the mushrooms: Preheat the oven to 375°F.

In a medium bowl, toss the mushrooms with the olive oil and shoyu. Place them on a parchment-covered baking sheet and bake, tossing once, until browned and crisp, about 30 minutes. Set aside in a small bowl.

Make the dressing: In a medium bowl, whisk together the rosemary, lemon zest, lemon juice, vinegar, shoyu, mustard, and crushed garlic. Slowly whisk in the oil until thoroughly combined. Sprinkle with black pepper, and set aside.

Dry-toast the pine nuts in a heavy-bottomed skillet, over medium heat until just golden, about 3 minutes. Set aside.

Place the spinach, red onions, orange segments, tempeh (if using), and mushrooms in a large bowl. Add the dressing and toss to coat. Serve the salad sprinkled with the pine nuts.

Tempeh Croutons

One 8-ounce package tempeh
1 tablespoon extra-virgin olive oil
1 tablespoon shoyu
1 1/2 teaspoons molasses
1/2 teaspoon paprika
1 garlic clove crushed with 1/4 teaspoon salt (see Note)

Preheat the oven to 375°F.

Cut the tempeh into 1/2-inch pieces. Place the tempeh pieces in a steamer basket over simmering water, and steam for 7 to 10 minutes. Meanwhile, whisk the oil, shoyu, molasses, paprika, and crushed garlic in a medium bowl. Transfer the steamed tempeh to the marinade and toss to coat. Spread the tempeh on a parchment-covered baking sheet and roast, stirring once, until golden brown, about 20 minutes. Remove from the oven and set aside to cool. Prepare the croutons up to 2 days in advance and store, covered, in the refrigerator.

NOTE: *To crush garlic and salt together, mince the garlic, leave it on the cutting board, and sprinkle the salt on the garlic. Use the flat side of the knife to mash the garlic and salt into a paste. Alternatively, mash the garlic and salt together with a mortar and pestle.*

A Word About Spinach

For a beautiful salad, chop off the stems where they meet the leaves, or for a more elegant look, hold each leaf and pull back on the stem to remove it.

Make sure to wash the spinach properly! There's nothing worse than biting into grit. Even when spinach comes packaged as "thrice washed," in my experience the leaves always need additional washing.

Watercress and Hearts of Palm Salad with Plantain Chips

This unusual salad is fun to eat, with its great variety of colors, flavors, and textures. The crisp plantain chips are also good with any of the appetizer dips or simply by themselves. Serve the salad with Cajun Roasted Sweet Potatoes (page 110), Glazed Brussels Sprouts (page 106), and Seared Sesame-Crusted Tuna (page 252).

SERVES 4 TO 6

1 green plantain
1 tablespoon extra-virgin olive oil
Salt
4 cups torn green-leaf lettuce (bite-size pieces)
4 cups watercress, hard stems removed
1/2 cup roasted red bell pepper (fresh or bottled), in small dice
2 tablespoons capers, drained
One 14-ounce can hearts of palm, drained, cut into 1/4-inch rings (1 1/2 cups)

Dressing (MAKES 1/2 CUP)

1/4 cup fresh orange juice
2 tablespoons red wine vinegar
1 garlic clove crushed with 1/4 teaspoon salt (see Note, page 85)
1 teaspoon Dijon mustard
1/4 cup extra-virgin olive oil
Freshly ground black pepper

Preheat the oven to 350°F.

Peel the plantain. (It's easiest to do this with a paring knife rather than a peeler, since the skin is tough.) Shave the peeled plantain into strips, using a Y-shaped peeler. Try to get the widest, flattest strips possible, although all pieces are usable.

In a medium bowl, mix the plantain strips with the olive oil and a sprinkling of salt. Place the strips in a single layer on a parchment-covered

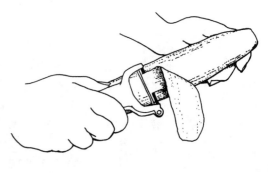

baking sheet and bake, turning them once, until golden and crispy, 20 to 25 minutes. (Check for ones that are crisping more quickly and remove those first.) Set aside.

Mix the lettuce, watercress, roasted peppers, capers, and hearts of palm in a large bowl.

Make the dressing: Whisk the orange juice, vinegar, crushed garlic, mustard, and olive oil in a small bowl.

Sprinkle the salad with salt and black pepper, and stir the dressing into the salad. Serve garnished with the plantains.

Green Leaf, Date, and Cashew Salad with Tamarind Dressing

Here's a healthy way to satisfy a hedonistic sweet tooth: cashews and dates nestled with lettuce in a tangy vinaigrette, in an unusual yet harmonious combination. For a light Indian fusion meal, serve this salad with Indian-Spiced Cauliflower, Chickpeas, Potatoes, and Kale (page 232) and Cardamom and Coconut Basmati Rice (page 201).

SERVES 4 TO 6

1 teaspoon tamarind concentrate (see Note, page 71)
1 tablespoon fresh lime juice
2 tablespoons maple syrup
1 teaspoon minced fresh ginger
1/4 cup extra-virgin olive oil
Salt
Pinch of cayenne pepper
1 head green-leaf lettuce, torn into bite-size pieces
1/4 cup unsalted cashews, chopped
1/4 cup (about 4) dates, chopped into small pieces
Freshly ground black pepper

In a small bowl, whisk together the tamarind concentrate, lime juice, maple syrup, ginger, and olive oil. Stir in 1/4 teaspoon salt and the cayenne.

Mix the lettuce with the cashews and dates in a salad bowl. Sprinkle the greens with salt and pepper. Add the dressing and toss to combine.

Green Leaf, Cucumber, and Wakame Salad with Carrot-Ginger Dressing

This salad is a concert of harmony and contrasts. The sweet lettuce mixes gracefully with the leaflike sea vegetable and crunchy cucumbers, which are then tossed with a tangy dressing. The shoyu sesame seeds round out the flavors nicely.

SERVES 4 TO 6

Dressing (MAKES 1 CUP)

- 1/2 cup roughly chopped carrots
- 2 tablespoons roughly chopped fresh ginger
- 2 tablespoons roughly chopped shallots
- 1/4 cup brown rice vinegar
- 2 tablespoons apple juice or mirin
- 1 teaspoon shoyu
- 1 teaspoon toasted sesame oil
- 1/2 cup sesame oil or canola oil
- Salt
- Freshly ground black pepper

Shoyu sesame seeds

- 2 tablespoons sesame seeds
- 1 teaspoon shoyu

Salad

- Two 4-inch pieces wakame
- 1 large cucumber
- 1 head (about 3/4 pound) green-leaf lettuce, washed and torn into pieces (About 12 cups)

Prepare the dressing: Place the carrots, ginger, shallots, vinegar, juice, shoyu, and toasted sesame oil in a blender and blend until smooth. With the motor running, add the sesame oil in a thin stream. Then add 1/4 teaspoon salt and a sprinkling of black pepper. Pour the dressing into a jar. The dressing will keep for up to 1 week in the refrigerator.

Toast the sesame seeds: In a small bowl, toss the seeds with the shoyu until all the seeds are moistened. Dry-toast the seeds in a heavy-bottomed skillet over medium-high heat, stirring constantly to prevent sticking, until they are dry and fragrant, about 2 minutes. (Alternatively, spread the seeds on a parchment-covered baking sheet and toast in a 350°F oven for about 7 minutes, until dried and toasted.) Set aside.

Soak the wakame in cold water for 10 minutes. Then cut and discard the hard spine, and slice the wakame into thin pieces. Set aside.

Peel the cucumber, cut it in half lengthwise, and scoop out the seeds with a spoon. Cut the cucumber lengthwise into ½-inch-wide spears. Cut each spear into 2-inch-long pieces.

Mix the lettuce, wakame, and cucumber spears in a large bowl. Toss with the dressing, and divide among individual plates. Serve sprinkled with the sesame seeds.

Frisée, Endive, and Celery Salad with Anchovy Vinaigrette

When I visit Rome, I invariably eat a lot of *puntarelle* salads, made of the wild chicory available throughout Italy. My Roman friend Federica tells me she simply gathers it at the roadside. Since wild chicory is not widely available in the United States, I use this combination of frisée, endive, and celery. Thinly sliced celery crisps and curls when it is soaked in cold water, and the toasted almonds also lend a delicious crunch. Even people who aren't wild about anchovies tell me they love this dressing.

SERVES 6

Dressing   (MAKES ⅓ CUP)

6 anchovy fillets
1 tablespoon fresh lemon juice
2 tablespoons red wine vinegar
2 garlic cloves
6 tablespoons extra-virgin olive oil
¼ teaspoon salt
Freshly ground black pepper

Salad

6 tablespoons sliced almonds
4 cups frisée leaves (from 1 large or 2 small heads, ¾ pound)
2 heads (½ pound) Belgian endive
2 celery stalks

Prepare the dressing: Combine the anchovies, lemon juice, vinegar, garlic, olive oil, salt, and black pepper to taste in a blender, and blend until smooth. Set aside.

Dry-toast the almonds in a heavy-bottomed skillet over medium heat, stirring frequently, until golden, about 3 minutes. Set aside.

Pull the tender leaves off the frisée, discarding the thick white stems. Separate the endive leaves and slice them into thin spears. You should have 3 cups endive. Cut the celery stalks crosswise into thirds, making pieces about 3 inches long, and then cut each piece lengthwise into thin strips. You should have about 1 cup.

Soak the frisée and the celery in cold water to cover for at least 15 minutes to crisp. Then drain, pat dry, and place in a large bowl. Toss the greens with the dressing. Divide the salad among six plates, and sprinkle each serving with a tablespoon of toasted almonds.

About Wilted Salads

In late winter and early spring, leafy bitter greens such as escarole, dandelion, and frisée are at their tastiest and most nutritious. These hardy greens act as tonics that help regulate the liver, purify the blood, and improve digestion. While some greens taste delicious raw or cooked, many of them are at their best in wilted salads.

The best greens for warm salads wilt down fast and have enough flavor to stand up to a warm, robust dressing. Kale, collards, and mustard greens aren't good choices because their tough leaves cook too slowly. Instead, I use mellow, tender spinach and Swiss chard, peppery watercress and arugula, and pleasantly bitter escarole, frisée, and dandelion.

The greens in wilted salads are warmed and just lightly cooked, never to the point where they are shriveled. The leaves still have some shape to them and are not totally limp. I tried cooking greens and dressing together in a skillet, but the dressings were liable to burn and the greens reduced unevenly. I prefer the double boiler method described in the recipes here.

The success of a properly wilted salad starts with dried greens: Dry the washed greens thoroughly to prevent the salad from getting watered down. You can even wrap the washed greens in a kitchen towel and place them in a plastic bag in the vegetable bin overnight. Once you have all the elements prepared, the salads cook in less than 2 minutes, so it's a good idea to have everyone at the table before you start tossing.

Wilted Arugula with Braised Tempeh, Mango, and Red Onion

This light and satisfying dish is packed with flavor. It's a great way to eat greens and tempeh. Dandelion makes a delicious alternative to the arugula.

SERVES 4

½ pound tempeh
1½ cups water
¼ cup shoyu
1¼ cups pineapple juice
5 tablespoons fresh lime juice
4 garlic cloves, whole, plus 1 garlic clove, minced
One 2-inch piece fresh ginger, cut into 4 slices
¼ cup minced red onion
1 jalapeño pepper, stemmed, seeded, and minced
½ teaspoon Dijon mustard
½ teaspoon salt
2 tablespoons fresh cilantro, coarsely chopped
1 tablespoon plus 2 teaspoons canola oil
¾ pound arugula, tough stems removed (about 9 cups)
1 ripe mango

Cut the tempeh into 12 equal "fingers." In a medium saucepan, combine the water, shoyu, ¼ cup of the pineapple juice, 2 tablespoons of the lime juice, the whole garlic cloves, the ginger, and the tempeh. Cover and bring to a boil over high heat. Then lower the heat and simmer, covered, for 15 minutes.

Remove the tempeh from the marinade and set it aside. Using tongs or a slotted spoon, remove the ginger and garlic; discard. Add the red onion to the marinade and simmer for 1 minute. Drain, and place the onions in a small bowl. Sprinkle in 1 tablespoon of the lime juice, toss to coat, and set aside.

Simmer the remaining 1 cup pineapple juice in a small saucepan until it is reduced to ¼ cup, 10 to 15 minutes.

Combine the reduced pineapple juice, the remaining 2 tablespoons lime juice, and the minced garlic, jalapeño, mustard, salt, cilantro, and 1 tablespoon oil in a small bowl. Whisk thoroughly and set aside.

Wash and dry the arugula. Place the arugula in a large heatproof bowl, prefer-ably metal. Peel the mango and cut it into ¾-inch-thick slices; set aside.

Warm a medium nonstick skillet over medium heat. Add the remaining 2 tea-spoons oil and swirl to coat the pan. Add the tempeh and sauté, turning once, until browned, about 2 minutes per side. Remove the skillet from the heat and set aside.

Bring several cups of water to a simmer in a wide pot. Toss the arugula with ⅓ cup of the dressing and place the bowl over the simmering water. Using tongs and holding one side of the bowl with a pot holder, toss the greens in the bowl until they are warm and beginning to wilt, about 1½ minutes.

Divide the greens among four plates, and arrange 3 pieces of tempeh over each mound of greens. Place the mango strips between the tempeh fingers. Sprinkle each salad with some red onions. Drizzle the remaining dressing over the salads and around the edges of the plates. Serve immediately.

Wilted Spinach Salad with Orange-Curry Dressing

This vibrant orange dressing looks beautiful on the dark green spinach leaves. Dried fruits, such as apricots, blueberries, and strawberries, are delicious in this salad, and Swiss chard makes a good alternative to the spinach. For a protein boost, toss the salad with roasted chickpea nuts, available in Indian stores, or serve it with Tamarind Chickpeas (page 203).

This dressing is also delicious on a combination of arugula, thinly sliced red onion, and oranges.

SERVES 4

1 cup fresh orange juice
1 garlic clove, minced
1 teaspoon curry powder, preferably hot
1 tablespoon chopped shallots
1/2 teaspoon salt
1 tablespoon extra-virgin olive oil
2 tablespoons dried currants
2 tablespoons dried cherries, halved
3/4 pound fresh spinach, stemmed and washed (6 to 7 cups)

Simmer the orange juice, uncovered, in a small saucepan over medium heat until it is reduced to 1/4 cup, about 10 minutes.

Combine the reduced orange juice, garlic, curry powder, shallots, salt, and olive oil in a small bowl and whisk to combine. Set aside.

Bring several cups of water to a simmer in a wide pot.

Mix the dried fruit and spinach in a large heatproof metal bowl, and toss with 3 tablespoons of the dressing. Set the bowl over the simmering water. Holding the edge of the bowl with a pot holder, use tongs to toss the greens until they are just wilted, about 1 minute.

Divide the salad among four plates. Drizzle the remaining dressing around the plates and over the greens. Serve immediately.

Asian Slaw with Peanuts

This dressing tastes strong at first, but after it sits for 30 minutes or so, the flavors marry and mellow. The peanuts are an absolute must. The slaw makes a delicious accompaniment to Tempeh Burgers (page 128).

SERVES 4

6 cups shredded Napa cabbage
Salt
3 medium garlic cloves, minced
2 tablespoons minced fresh ginger
1 jalapeño pepper, red if available, stemmed, seeded, and minced
1/4 cup chopped fresh mint
2 tablespoons apple cider vinegar
1/4 cup chopped unsalted dry-roasted peanuts

Place the cabbage in a large bowl, sprinkle 1 teaspoon salt over it, and toss to mix. Place a smaller bowl over the cabbage and place a weight—such as a can of beans—in the bowl. Set aside for 30 minutes to let the cabbage wilt; it will shrink considerably. Drain all the excess liquid.

Add the garlic, ginger, japapeño, and mint to the cabbage, and mix well. Add the vinegar and mix again. Taste to see if more salt is needed. Let the slaw sit for at least 30 minutes. Then serve, sprinkling peanuts over each serving. This will keep, covered and refrigerated, for up to 3 days.

Salvadoran Slaw

This recipe comes from my Salvadoran friend Delores Maria Mejía, who makes it on Sundays, when she cooks up a large batch of *pupusas.* It is a must with Bean and Cheese *Pupusas* (page 208) and Tomatillo Salsa (page 175). The pickled jalapeños give it a good kick. This slaw is best made a day in advance, to allow the cabbage to wilt and the flavors to marry.

SERVES 6

1 small head green cabbage, cored and shredded (8 cups)
1 cup grated carrots
1 teaspoon salt
½ cup water
½ cup apple cider vinegar
1 can pickled jalapeño peppers
1 teaspoon dried oregano

Bring a couple of quarts of water to a boil in a kettle or medium pot. Place the cabbage in a colander in the sink, and pour the boiling water over the cabbage to lightly wilt it. Drain it well. Transfer the cabbage to a medium bowl. Stir in the carrots and the salt.

Open the can of pickled jalapeños and set aside 4 pieces jalapeño, 2 pickled carrots, and 2 tablespoons of the pickling juice.

Heat the ½ cup water in a small pot, and stir in the vinegar. Stir this mixture into the cabbage along with the pickled jalapeño, pickled carrots, pickling juice, and oregano. Cover the bowl and refrigerate for several hours, preferably overnight, to allow the flavors to mellow and marry.

Beet, Tomato, and Watermelon Salad with Caramelized Almonds

This unusual combination of fruits and vegetables works surprisingly well. The brilliant color alone is enough to rouse your appetite. The salad goes well with the Butterflied Barbecue Spice–Rubbed Chicken (page 265) or its tofu version (page 225), roasted corn, and sautéed spinach. I like to serve it in a separate bowl so the juice doesn't bleed onto the rest of the plate.

SERVES 4 TO 6

1/2 pound (3 medium-small) beets
1 cup whole almonds
2 tablespoons maple syrup
2 tablespoons maple sugar, Sucanat, or evaporated cane sugar
1/4 cup balsamic vinegar, preferably white
2 tablespoons extra-virgin olive oil
2 cups cherry tomatoes, halved
2 cups cubed watermelon (3/4-inch cubes)
Salt and freshly ground black pepper

Place the beets in a medium saucepan and cover them with water. Cover, and bring to a boil. Lower the heat to a simmer and simmer for about 45 minutes, or until the beets are tender. (Alternatively, place the beets in a pressure cooker, cover with water, and cook at high pressure for 10 minutes. Allow the pressure to reduce naturally, or run water over the top for a quick way to bring down the pressure.

Meanwhile, preheat the oven to 350°F.

In a small bowl, toss the almonds with the maple syrup and sugar. Spread them on a parchment-covered baking sheet and bake, tossing the nuts every 5 minutes to keep them from sticking and to distribute the sugar, until caramelized, 15 to 20 minutes. Remove from the oven and let cool. Chop the almonds by hand into medium pieces and set aside.

Remove the beets from the hot liquid and submerge them in a bowl of cold water to cool. Then remove the skins and cut the beets into 1/4-inch dice. You should have about 1 1/2 cups.

Whisk the vinegar and oil together in a small bowl. Place the beets, tomatoes, and watermelon in a medium bowl. Sprinkle generously with salt and pepper, and toss with the dressing. Serve sprinkled with the caramelized almonds.

Gazpacho Salad with Tomato Vinaigrette

The flavors of gazpacho remind me of southern Spain on a summer day. In this salad, gazpacho meets panzanella, a traditional Italian bread salad, for a zesty and flavorful dish. This salad is best made from July through October, when flavorful ripe tomatoes are at their peak. The dressing can be made up to 4 days in advance. For best results, assemble and toss the salad just before serving.

SERVES 6

Dressing (MAKES ABOUT 1½ CUPS)

- 1 pound (2 to 3 medium) ripe tomatoes
- 1 garlic clove, smashed
- 2 tablespoons red wine vinegar
- 3 tablespoons extra-virgin olive oil
- ¾ teaspoon salt
- 1 teaspoon paprika
- Freshly ground black pepper
- 1 scallion, white and green parts, thinly sliced

Salad

- 2 cups sourdough bread cubes
- 1 tablespoon extra-virgin olive oil
- 1 pound tomatoes
- 1 small red onion, finely diced (½ cup)
- 1 cucumber, peeled, seeded, and cut into ½-inch-thick slices
- ¼ cup fresh basil leaves, torn into pieces
- 1 bunch arugula (¼ pound or 3 cups), washed, large stems trimmed, and torn into pieces
- Salt and freshly ground black pepper

Prepare the dressing: In a blender, purée half of the tomatoes until smooth. Strain the pulp through a fine-mesh sieve, pressing hard on the solids. You should have about ¾ cup juice. Peel and seed the remaining tomatoes, and cut them into small dice; set aside.

Rinse out the blender container and return the tomato juice to it. Add the garlic, vinegar, oil, salt, paprika, and a sprinkling of black pepper. Blend until smooth. Stir in the scallions and chopped tomatoes, and pulse to combine. You should have about 1½ cups of dressing.

Make the salad: Preheat the oven to 350°F.

In a medium bowl, toss the bread cubes with the olive oil. Spread the bread cubes on a baking sheet and bake until crisp, about 15 minutes. Remove them from the oven and set aside.

Remove the stems from the tomatoes. Halve the tomatoes and cut each half into 4 wedges. Cut the wedges in half to make chunky pieces. Place the tomatoes in a large bowl and add the red onion, cucumber, basil, arugula, and bread cubes. Sprinkle the salad generously with salt and pepper, and stir in the dressing. Serve immediately.

Turkish Tomato Salad with Fresh Herbs

This is a flavorful and vibrant salad; the pomegranate syrup goes perfectly with tomatoes. For a Turkish feast, serve this with the Shredded Romaine Salad with Dill and Scallions (page 81), Dolma Pilaf (page 196), Turkish Stuffed Trout in Parchment (page 250), and Baklava (page 304).

SERVES 6

1/4 cup pomegranate syrup

2 tablespoons extra-virgin olive oil

2 pints (1 1/4 pounds) cherry tomatoes, small ones halved, larger ones quartered

2 cups thinly sliced scallions (from 1/2 pound scallions)

1 cup chopped flat-leaf parsley

1 cup pitted kalamata olives, halved

2 jalapeño or serrano chiles, seeded and minced

Salt

1 cup walnuts, toasted and coarsely chopped

Combine the pomegranate syrup and the olive oil in a small bowl, and whisk until blended. Set aside.

In a large bowl, toss the tomatoes with the scallions, parsley, olives, and chiles. Sprinkle generously with salt. Add the dressing and toss well. Serve sprinkled with the walnuts.

NOTE: *The dressing can be prepared and the vegetables chopped several hours ahead. Toss just before serving.*

Vegetables

Delicata, Cauliflower, and Pearl Onion Roast

Coconut Green Beans with Mustard Seeds

Mashed Sweet Potatoes with Chestnuts and Brandy

Glazed Brussels Sprouts

Braised Cabbage with Cranberries

Lacquered Carrots with Coriander

Garlicky Braised Kale with Balsamic Vinegar and Capers

Cajun Roasted Sweet Potatoes

Mashed Sweet Potatoes and Turnips with
   Caramelized Shallots

Cornmeal-Dusted Broiled Vegetable Chips

Celery Root and Red Bliss Smash

Potato Salad with Caramelized Onions

Grilled Potato and Leek Salad with Tarragon Vinaigrette

Zucchini Latkes

Swiss Chard with Corn and Balsamic Vinegar

"Eat your vegetables

or you'll get scurvy!" was my mother's mantra at the dinner table. It didn't matter that scurvy, a disease caused by a vitamin C deficiency, was common among eighteenth-century sailors and was remedied by adding lime juice to their rum rations. I don't quite remember how effective that threat was, but I do know that nowadays I don't need to be coerced into eating my vegetables. Vegetables from dark leafy greens to brightly colored varieties occupy a prominent position on the plate of a healthy hedonist. ◎ Greens make people feel wonderful. Dark leafy greens—such as Swiss chard, collards, and kale—are packed with vitamins and minerals. So is spinach, which unlike the others, can be eaten raw as well as cooked. ◎ If you're not a fan of "true grit," wash your greens. This is one mantra that my mother and I chant together. It's easiest to wash them after they have been trimmed and cut. Wash them as you would salad greens. Spinach, escarole, and arugula are typically *very* gritty and may need to be submerged several times in fresh water. Wash the greens until no more dirt is left at the bottom of the bowl. Unlike salad greens, greens for cooking do not need to be spun dry; the excess liquid will evaporate during the cooking process. Greens wilt dramatically when cooked, so a pound of tender greens, such as spinach or chard, is perfect for 2 people; a pound of firmer greens, such as collards and kale, which wilt down a little less, will do for 4. ◎ Part of the fun of cooking is trying new vegetables or combinations of vegetables. Some of these recipes entail the simplest preparations, while others are more elaborate. Some involve unusual preparations of familiar vegetables, like Cajun Roasted Sweet Potatoes or Coconut Green Beans with Mustard Seeds. Most of the recipes require little prep time. ◎ Start with the freshest, most luscious vegetables you can find. If there is a greenmarket near you, buy your vegetables there. It is a dazzling experience to survey the stalls of multicolored vegetables, displayed in tantalizing piles. ◎ Part of the excitement of vegetables is that they are seasonal, so celebrate the seasons. Although you may be able to buy asparagus in the middle of winter, you'll find that it pales, both in flavor and in price, in comparison to the asparagus available in spring. In the middle of summer you can purchase yellow zucchini, crookneck squash, white, yellow and green pattypan squash, and regular green zucchini. The selection of tomatoes will be colorful and various, turning simple salads into beautiful affairs. Orange squashes come out in full regalia in the autumn. ◉ Grow something yourself. Even if you're a city-dweller, you may be able to grow some herbs or a tomato plant on the windowsill and watch it thrive. Buy organic whenever you can so that you can avoid heavily sprayed and genetically engineered produce. Another advantage to shopping at greenmarkets, cooperatives, or from community-supported agriculture groups is that you can have a relationship with the growers and can ask them about their produce. ◉ Celebrate the glories of vegetables, in all their resplendent shapes, colors, and varieties. Treat them like nature's art box: have fun combining colors and cuts and flavors and textures.

Sometimes the most flavorful results come from the simplest technique . . .

Roasted Corn

Place ears of corn, still in their husks, on a baking sheet and roast in a preheated 400° to 450°F oven until the husks are parched and browned, 40 minutes to 1 hour. Let them cool for a few minutes, and then remove the husks (the silk burns away in the roasting). Serve the corn however you like it—whole, halved, or cut into wheels. The concentrated flavor is extra sweet.

Sautéed Summer Squash

Summer squash caramelizes beautifully if it is salted first, to draw out the moisture: Cut zucchini, crookneck, or pattypan squash into $1/5$-inch-thick slices, and place them in a bowl. Salt the squash generously ($1/2$ teaspoon for $1 1/2$ pounds of squash) and toss. Let sit for 30 minutes. Then pat the squash dry with paper towels. Heat oil or clarified butter in a skillet over medium-high heat, and sauté the squash until golden, about 2 minutes per side. Sprinkle with black pepper, and serve.

Delicata, Cauliflower, and Pearl Onion Roast

This combination of vegetables roasts beautifully, with the cauliflower turning into a golden brown delicacy. Delicata, a beautiful yellow-orange oblong squash with green stripes, has tender skin that doesn't need to be peeled.

SERVES 4

1/4 pound (20 small or 10 large) pearl onions, preferably red
1 pound delicata squash, halved lengthwise and seeded
1/2 medium cauliflower, cut into medium florets (3 cups)
2 tablespoons extra-virgin olive oil
1/2 teaspoon salt

Preheat the oven to 400°F.

Bring a medium pot of water to a boil. Cut off the tip and the root ends of the onions, and blanch them in the boiling water for 1 minute. Then peel the onions and place them in a medium bowl.

Cut each delicata half into triangular wedges, and add them to the bowl. Add the cauliflower, oil, and salt, and toss. Spread the vegetables on a parchment-covered baking sheet, and roast, stirring every 15 minutes, until they are tender and well browned, about 45 minutes. Serve hot or at room temperature.

NOTES: *Many people consider pearl onions too bothersome, but they are not particularly time-consuming to prepare unless you're cooking for a huge crowd. Simply cut off the tips and the roots, and blanch them for a minute in boiling water; the outer skins will peel off easily. Look for red pearl onions, which are particularly pretty in this dish.*

Other good squash choices for this dish include members of the buttercup family, such as kabocha, Honey Delight, and Black Forest, which all have edible skin. Sweet Dumpling squash and Red Kuri pumpkins are also tasty. If you use the reliable standby butternut, peel it before you cook it.

Coconut Green Beans with Mustard Seeds

This is a delectable complement to any of the Indian dishes in this book. Not only does it look and taste great: it's as simple as can be.

SERVES 4 TO 6

³/4 pound (4 cups) fresh green beans
2 tablespoons coconut oil or ghee
2 garlic cloves, minced
¹/4 teaspoon ground turmeric
¹/2 teaspoon whole mustard seeds
1 jalapeño chile, seeded and minced, *or* **¹/4 teaspoon red pepper flakes**
³/4 teaspoon salt
¹/4 cup water
¹/4 cup dried unsweetened coconut

Cut off the ends of the green beans. Then cut the beans in half, so you have 2-inch pieces.

Combine the oil, garlic, turmeric, mustard seeds, chiles, salt, green beans, and water in a large skillet. Cover and cook over medium-low heat until the green beans are just tender, about 5 minutes.

Uncover the skillet and raise the heat to medium-high. Cook, stirring constantly, until the water evaporates and the garlic is light golden, about 3 minutes. Remove the skillet from the heat, and stir in the coconut. Serve hot.

Mashed Sweet Potatoes with Chestnuts and Brandy

This dish is every bit as satisfying a comfort food as plain mashed potatoes, with a splash of brandy lending a sophisticated touch. Dried chestnuts add a mysterious smokiness to the flavor, and a pat of butter sends it over the top. Although these potatoes are appropriate for your Thanksgiving feast, don't limit them to special occasions.

SERVES 4

**2 pounds (2 large) sweet potatoes, cut into 1-inch chunks
(5 to 6 cups)**
**½ cup dried chestnuts, soaked overnight or quick-soaked
(as for beans, page 42)**
Salt
3 cups water
1 tablespoon butter
1 tablespoon brandy
Freshly ground nutmeg
Freshly ground black pepper

Place the sweet potatoes, chestnuts, 1½ teaspoons salt, and the water in a medium saucepan, and bring to a boil. Lower the heat and simmer, partially covered, until the sweet potatoes and chestnuts are softened, about 45 minutes. (Check from time to time to make sure there's still some liquid in the pot. Add a little more water if it seems dry.) Drain.

Transfer the sweet potatoes and chestnuts to a food processor, and add the butter and brandy. Process until smooth. Add a sprinkling of nutmeg and of black pepper. Taste, and add more salt if necessary. Serve hot.

Glazed Brussels Sprouts

These candied morsels are especially dainty when prepared with very small brussels sprouts. For an unusual and striking combination, serve them with the Cajun Roasted Sweet Potatoes (page 110), Watercress and Hearts of Palm Salad (page 86), and Seared Sesame-Crusted Tuna (page 252). Be sure to cut the brussels sprouts in half, so the glaze can permeate the cut sides.

SERVES 4

1 pound brussels sprouts
1 tablespoon extra-virgin olive oil
1/2 teaspoon salt
3 tablespoons maple syrup
1 tablespoon Dijon mustard
1 tablespoon butter
1 teaspoon red wine vinegar
Freshly ground black pepper

Preheat the oven to 400°F.

Peel off the outer leaves of the brussels sprouts. Trim the stems, leaving just enough to keep the leaves intact. Cut the sprouts in half lengthwise, place them in a medium bowl, and toss with the olive oil and salt. Spread the sprouts on a parchment-covered baking sheet, and roast, stirring a couple of times, until tender and browned, about 30 minutes. Remove them from the oven and place them in a shallow baking dish.

Combine the maple syrup, mustard, and butter in a small saucepan or skillet, and bring to a boil over medium heat. Cook until the mixture reduces and thickens slightly, 2 minutes or so. Then remove the pan from the heat and stir in the vinegar. Pour the mixture over the brussels sprouts, and toss to combine. Sprinkle with black pepper. Serve hot.

NOTE: *Brussels sprouts are really miniature cabbages, and assertive condiments like mustard that go well with cabbage also work with sprouts. You don't need to wash brussels sprouts; just peel off the outer leaves and trim the stems. Be careful not to cut too far up the stems or the sprouts will fall apart.*

Braised Cabbage with Cranberries

In this fruit and vegetable braise, the cranberries meld into the cabbage, resulting in a vibrant fuchsia-colored dish. Serve it with the Porcini Mushroom Ragout with Chicken (page 262) or at a holiday feast.

Caraway seeds are generally available only whole. Grind them yourself in a spice grinder or with a mortar and pestle, or use the seeds whole.

SERVE 4 TO 6

1 tablespoon extra-virgin olive oil

1 onion, thinly sliced (1 cup)

1 teaspoon ground caraway seeds

2 sweet apples, such as Golden Delicious, peeled, cored, and thinly sliced

6 cups shredded red cabbage (about 1/2 medium head)

1 cup apple juice or cider

1/2 cup dry red wine

1 cup cranberries, fresh or frozen

2 tablespoons natural sugar, preferably maple sugar or
   evaporated cane sugar

Salt

Freshly ground black pepper

Warm the oil in a medium saucepan over medium-low heat. Add the onions and sauté until they are softened, 7 minutes.

Add the caraway and apples, and cook for 2 minutes. Then add the cabbage, apple juice, wine, cranberries, sugar, and 1/2 teaspoon salt. Cover and bring to a boil. Reduce the heat to a simmer and cook for 5 minutes. Then uncover and simmer, stirring occasionally, until the cabbage is tender and the cranberries have melted into it, 15 minutes. The braising liquid should have reduced and thickened, and the cabbage and apples have become very pink. Stir in a sprinkling of black pepper. Taste, and add more salt if necessary. Serve hot or at room temperature.

Lacquered Carrots with Coriander

These carrots are sweet but not cloying. Everything goes into the pan at once, and the pan is then uncovered to allow the carrots to brown. They are especially beautiful if you keep the cuts fairly long and at least ½ inch thick. This is a good choice to serve with Roast Chicken with Maple Glaze (page 264).

SERVES 4 OR 5

2 tablespoons extra-virgin olive oil
¼ cup maple syrup
¼ cup dry sherry or mirin
1 tablespoon balsamic vinegar
1 pound carrots, cut into 2-inch roll cuts or ½-inch-thick diagonal cuts (4 cups)
½ teaspoon salt
2 teaspoons ground coriander
Freshly ground black pepper

Combine the olive oil, maple syrup, sherry, vinegar, carrots, salt, and coriander in a large skillet. Cover and cook over medium-low heat until the carrots are just tender, 12 to 15 minutes.

Uncover the skillet and cook, stirring constantly, until the carrots caramelize, about 6 minutes. Sprinkle with black pepper to taste, and serve hot.

NOTE: *You can use a 1-pound bag of baby carrots if you prefer. These cook in about 15 minutes. There won't be much liquid left when you uncover the skillet, but keep cooking the carrots for 5 to 6 minutes to brown them, stirring constantly.*

Garlicky Braised Kale with Balsamic Vinegar and Capers

Eat mineral-rich dark leafy greens, like kale and collards, regularly and every cell in your body will thank you. The addition of capers lifts the kale from homey fare to gourmet status.

SERVES 4

10 garlic cloves
2 tablespoons extra-virgin olive oil
4 teaspoons capers, drained
1 pound kale (1 large bunch), stemmed, washed,
  and cut into 1-inch pieces
1/2 teaspoon salt
Freshly ground black pepper
1/2 cup water
1 teaspoon balsamic vinegar

Whack each clove of garlic with the side of a heavy knife to lightly crush it. Slice each smashed piece in half.

Combine the olive oil and the garlic in a medium saucepan and place over medium heat. Sauté, stirring, until the garlic starts to brown, 2 to 3 minutes. Add the capers and sauté for another minute. Then add the kale, salt, a sprinkling of black pepper, and the water. Use tongs to toss the kale, pushing the uncooked leaves to the bottom, until all the greens are wilted. Then reduce the heat, cover, and simmer until the kale is tender, about 10 minutes.

Uncover the pan, turn the heat to high, and boil, stirring frequently, until the liquid has almost evaporated. Remove the pan from the heat and stir in the vinegar. Serve immediately.

Cajun Roasted Sweet Potatoes

These spice-flecked jewels have a *picante* kick and lots of flavor. The crusty outside contrasts with a meltingly tender inside. If you're not in the mood to turn up the heat, feel free to leave out the cayenne pepper.

SERVES 4

2 pounds sweet potatoes, preferably Garnet or Jewel yams,
    cut into large wedges or 1 1/2-inch pieces (5 to 6 cups)
2 tablespoons extra-virgin olive oil
1 tablespoon maple syrup
2 garlic cloves, minced
1/2 teaspoon paprika
1/4 teaspoon freshly ground black pepper
1/4 teaspoon ground cumin
1/4 teaspoon ground mustard
1/4 teaspoon cayenne pepper
1/2 teaspoon dried thyme leaves
1/2 teaspoon dried oregano
1/2 teaspoon salt

Preheat the oven to 400°F. In a large bowl, toss the sweet potatoes, oil, maple syrup, and garlic together.

Mix the spices and herbs together in a small bowl. Sprinkle the spice mixture over the sweet potatoes, and toss to combine evenly.

Arrange the sweet potatoes in a single layer on a parchment-covered baking sheet, and roast, turning twice, until they are caramelized on the outside and very tender, about 45 minutes. Test with a fork to see that they are thoroughly cooked. Serve hot or at room temperature.

NOTE: *I like to cut these potatoes using angular cuts (see illustration), but cubes work very well too; just adjust the cooking time. The sweet potatoes should have a crusty exterior and a soft, tender inside.*

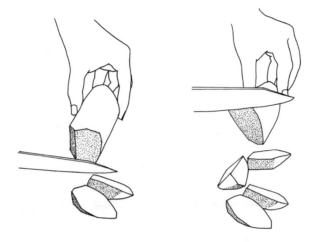

A yam is a large tuber that has starchy, pale yellow flesh. Different varieties grow in tropical and subtropical climates, and it is difficult to find a true yam outside a Latin market. In our markets, sweet potatoes are often confused with yams. The tubers with a dry, mealy flesh are often called sweet potatoes, while the ones with the moister, denser flesh are usually (incorrectly) called yams. Garnet and Jewel yams are two varieties of sweet potato with deep orange-red flesh and skin.

In all my recipes, "sweet potatoes" means the orange-fleshed ones (they may be called yams in your market).

Mashed Sweet Potatoes and Turnips with Caramelized Shallots

Cozy comfort food is given an elegant spin here with caramelized shallots. Turnips take the sweet edge off the potato and give the dish a more complex flavor. Hand-mash the ingredients for the best texture, so you can see the white turnip flecks shining through the orange sweet potatoes.

SERVES 4 TO 6

1 1/2 pounds sweet potatoes, peeled and cut into 1-inch pieces (about 4 cups)
1/2 pound turnips, cut into 1-inch pieces (about 2 cups)
1/4 cup extra-virgin olive oil
1/2 cup shallots, cut into thin rings (from 2 to 3 medium shallots)
Salt
Freshly ground black pepper

Fill a large saucepan with 1 inch of water, and set a steamer basket over it. Bring the water to a simmer. Add the sweet potatoes and turnips, cover the pan, and steam the vegetables until completely softened, about 10 minutes.

Meanwhile, warm the olive oil in a medium skillet over medium heat. Add the shallots and sauté until golden and crisp, about 5 minutes. Immediately strain the shallots, reserving the shallots and the oil separately.

Remove the vegetables and the steamer basket from the saucepan, and discard the water. Return the vegetables to the pan and stir in 2 tablespoons of the reserved olive oil, 1 teaspoon salt, and a sprinkling of black pepper. Mash the vegetables coarsely, so that you can still see white flecks of turnip in the sweet potatoes. Taste, and adjust the seasonings if necessary. Serve sprinkled with the caramelized shallots.

Cornmeal-Dusted Broiled Vegetable Chips

Humble root vegetables turn irresistible when made into crunchy chips. You won't believe how quickly you can make these—and how tasty they are. Use any combination of root vegetables you like; just keep the total weight to 1 pound. Beets make a great addition to the mix, but keep them separate until they're cooked to prevent them from coloring the other vegetables. Serve these as a side dish, with one of the onion dips (see pages 26–27), or on a bed of lettuce.

SERVES 4

Salt
1 small sweet potato
1 small low- to medium-starch potato, such as Red Bliss or
    white creamer (do not use russet)
2 medium carrots
1 small parsnip
2 tablespoons extra-virgin olive oil
Freshly ground black pepper
2 tablespoons cornmeal

Fill a medium saucepan about three-quarters full of water, add 1 teaspoon salt, and bring to a boil.

While the water is heating, cut the potatoes into ¼-inch rounds. Cut the carrots and parsnips into ¼-inch-thick diagonal slices.

Preheat the broiler.

Blanch the vegetables in the boiling water until just barely fork-tender, about 3 minutes; don't overcook. Using a slotted spoon, transfer them to a medium bowl; let them cool for a few minutes.

Toss the vegetables with the oil and a sprinkling of salt and black pepper. Add the cornmeal, and toss to combine. Place the coated vegetables in a single layer on a baking sheet or broiler pan, and place under the broiler. Broil for 3 to 4 minutes on the first side, until lightly browned. Turn the vegetables over and broil the other side for 3 minutes. (You will probably need to do this on two trays.)

Serve hot or at room temperature.

NOTE: *If you are using other root vegetables, just remember to cut oval and round vegetables (beets, celery root, rutabagas) into ¼-inch rounds.*

Celery Root and Red Bliss Smash

Take a break from ordinary mashed potatoes with this lighter version that combines celery root with the potatoes. Celery root is very flavorful, and braising it before mashing heightens the taste even more. The dish is especially delicious when made with stock. Serve this with Butterflied Barbecue-Spice–Rubbed Chicken (page 265) or with Roast Chicken with Maple Glaze (page 264).

SERVES 5 OR 6

> **3 tablespoons extra-virgin olive oil**
> **1 pound celery root, cut into 1-inch pieces (3 cups)**
> **1 pound thin-skinned potatoes, such as Red Bliss,**
>   **cut into 1-inch pieces (2 cups)**
> **Salt**
> **Freshly ground black pepper**
> **1 cup chicken stock, vegetable stock, or water**
> **1½ teaspoons fresh lemon juice, plus more to taste**
> **1 tablespoon butter, optional**

Warm 2 tablespoons of the olive oil in a large skillet over medium heat until shimmering. Add the celery root and the potatoes, sprinkle with 1½ teaspoons salt and black pepper to taste, and sauté until beginning to brown, 5 to 7 minutes. Add the stock and scrape up any brown bits that have stuck to the skillet; there may be a lot.

Cover, and simmer until the vegetables are completely tender, 10 to 12 minutes. Mash the vegetables in the skillet, stirring to soak up the pan juices. Then stir in the lemon juice and the remaining 1 tablespoon oil. Taste, and add more salt and pepper if desired, and a splash of lemon juice if necessary. Stir in the butter (if using). Serve hot.

Potato Salad with Caramelized Onions

In this flavorful salad, the aromatic oil from cooking the onions becomes the base of the dressing. Serve it with Red Snapper Provençale (page 244) or Fish in *Charmoula* (page 255). Try to buy similar-size potatoes so they cook evenly.

SERVES 6

1½ pounds Red Bliss or white creamer potatoes, or any
**   small thin-skinned potatoes, unpeeled**
Salt
6 tablespoons extra-virgin olive oil
2 onions, thinly sliced (2 cups)
2 tablespoons red wine vinegar
1 tablespoon fresh lemon juice
2 tablespoons chopped fresh rosemary
6 tablespoons chopped fresh parsley
Freshly ground black pepper

Place the potatoes in a medium saucepan and cover with cold water by 1 inch. Bring to a boil, add 1 teaspoon salt, and lower the heat to a simmer. Cook until tender, 15 to 20 minutes, depending on their size. Drain the potatoes and set aside.

Meanwhile, warm the olive oil in a medium skillet. Add the onions and cook, stirring occasionally, until they are golden brown, about 15 minutes. Immediately strain the onions, reserving the onions and the oil separately.

When the potatoes are just cool enough to handle, slice each one into 4 rounds. Remove only the loose skins that are falling off. Put the potatoes in a large bowl.

In a small bowl, whisk together the vinegar, lemon juice, reserved oil, and 1 teaspoon salt. Pour this over the warm potatoes. Add the caramelized onions, rosemary, parsley, and a sprinkling of black pepper. Stir gently to combine. Let the potatoes sit for at least 30 minutes at room temperature. Taste, and add more salt if necessary. Serve at room temperature. The salad can be made up to 2 days ahead. (If refrigerated, bring to room temperature before serving.)

Grilled Potato and Leek Salad with Tarragon Vinaigrette

These grilled potatoes, accompanied by grilled leeks and a lively tarragon-infused vinegar, are bursting with flavor. Even an indoor grill pan will yield excellent results. The chives and cherry tomatoes enliven the salad with vibrant color.

SERVES 6

Salt

1 1/2 pounds small red or white thin-skinned potatoes, unpeeled

1/4 cup white wine vinegar

About 4 tarragon sprigs, plus 1/4 cup roughly chopped
    fresh tarragon leaves

3 tablespoons extra-virgin olive oil, plus more for grilling the leeks

Freshly ground black pepper

3 medium (1 1/2 to 2 pounds) leeks, white and light green parts,
    halved and washed

1 celery stalk, cut into small dice (1/2 cup)

1 teaspoon Dijon mustard

2 tablespoons chopped fresh chives

1 cup cherry tomatoes, halved

Bring a medium pot of water to a boil. Add 1 teaspoon salt, and then add the potatoes. Cook the potatoes until just tender, about 10 minutes, depending on their size. Drain, and set aside until cool enough to handle.

Meanwhile, combine the vinegar and the tarragon sprigs in a small saucepan, and bring to a boil. Immediately remove the pan from the heat and let it sit for 10 minutes. Drain, discarding the tarragon and reserving the vinegar.

Preheat a grill or stovetop grill pan to medium.

Cut the potatoes into 1/2-inch slices (3 or 4 slices per potato). Toss the potatoes in a bowl with 1 tablespoon of the olive oil, or just enough to coat the potatoes, 1/2 teaspoon salt, and a sprinkling of black pepper. Grill the potatoes on both sides until they have pronounced grill marks and are cooked through, about 3 minutes per side. Transfer the potatoes to a medium bowl.

Pull at the center few layers of each leek, making each leek become two. This enables the outer part to flatten against the grill. Brush all the leeks with olive oil, and sprinkle with salt and black pepper. Grill until tender, about 4 minutes per side. Transfer the leeks to a cutting board and cut them into ½-inch pieces. Add the leeks to the potatoes, along with the chopped celery.

In a small bowl, whisk the reserved tarragon vinegar with the mustard. Then whisk in the remaining 2 tablespoons olive oil. Add 1½ teaspoons salt and a sprinkling of black pepper.

Add the dressing, chopped tarragon, chives, and tomatoes to the potatoes. Stir together gently, and set aside for at least 15 minutes to let flavors marry before serving.

Serve warm or at room temperature. You can prepare this up to 2 days in advance.

Zucchini Latkes

These crisp Turkish-inspired zucchini pancakes make a wonderful start to a sumptuous meal. Even finicky eaters savor green vegetables when they're prepared this way. These latkes are lighter than the potato version and not at all greasy. You can make them ahead and freeze them, or you can make them early on the same day—in which case there's no need to refrigerate them; just pop them in a 350°F oven to heat them before serving.

MAKES 8 PANCAKES; SERVES 4

1 pound (4 small or 2 to 3 medium) zucchini
1 teaspoon salt
1/2 cup chopped fresh dill
1/4 cup thinly sliced scallions, white and green parts (see Notes)
1/4 cup unbleached white flour
1 egg, lightly beaten
Freshly ground black pepper
1 cup bread crumbs, preferably fresh
Extra-virgin olive oil, for sautéing
Yogurt (see Notes), for garnish
1/2 pound (2 medium) tomatoes, cut into small dice

Using the largest hole on a box grater or the grating disk on a food processor, shred the zucchini. Transfer the zucchini to a strainer, sprinkle the salt over it, and stir to combine. Let it sit for 30 minutes. Then grab handfuls of the zucchini and squeeze out the water. Repeat twice with each handful to squeeze out as much liquid as possible. Transfer the zucchini to a medium bowl. Stir in the dill, scallions, flour, egg, and a liberal sprinkling of black pepper. The mixture should be fairly moist.

Spread the bread crumbs on a plate. Divide the zucchini mixture into 8 portions. Spoon each portion onto the bread crumbs and coat with the crumbs.

Cover the bottom of a medium skillet, either conventional or nonstick, with oil and warm it over medium heat. When the oil is hot, add 4 pancakes and sauté them, pressing with a spatula to flatten them, until golden brown, about 2 minutes on each side. Transfer the pancakes to a plate, and keep warm. Repeat with the remaining pancakes.

Serve hot, topped with yogurt and chopped tomatoes.

NOTES: *Don't waste your time washing dill. I've never found dill to be dirty or bug-laden, and water will only make it limp.*

You can skip the scallions and add ½ cup finely chopped red onion and 1 cup grated parsnip.

To make your yogurt thick and delicious, place 2 cups whole or low-fat yogurt in a cheesecloth-lined strainer set over a bowl. Place it in the refrigerator and let the yogurt drain for at least 2 hours and up to overnight. Two cups yogurt will become about 1 cup thickened.

Swiss Chard with Corn and Balsamic Vinegar

This is a fun way to eat greens. The shallot-balsamic-corn bits infuse these quick-cooking greens with texture, color, and great flavor. This summery dish is perfect with Smokin' Drunken Chili (page 229) or Salmon Medallions with Lime-Mustard Teriyaki (page 248).

SERVES 4

2 tablespoons extra-virgin olive oil
1/4 cup minced shallots
1 cup fresh corn kernels (from 2 ears)
Salt
3 teaspoons balsamic vinegar
2 pounds (2 bunches) Swiss chard
Freshly ground black pepper

Warm the olive oil in a large skillet over medium heat. Add the shallots, corn, and 1/4 teaspoon salt. Sauté until the corn has released its liquid and the shallots have started to brown, about 4 minutes. Stir in 2 teaspoons of the balsamic vinegar, scrape up the brown bits with a spatula, and remove from the heat. Remove the corn mixture from the pan and set aside. Set the pan aside for cooking the chard.

Use a sharp knife to cut the chard leaves off the stems. Cut the leaves into large bite-size pieces, and place them in a large bowl of cold water. Swish to loosen any dirt, then lift the chard out of the bowl. Spin the chard to remove excess water, but don't worry if there's a bit of moisture clinging to the leaves. Place the chard in the skillet and cook over medium heat stirring frequently or tossing with tongs to push the uncooked leaves to the bottom of the skillet, until it is wilted and bright green, 3 to 4 minutes. Toss in the corn mixture and the remaining 1 teaspoon vinegar, along with a sprinkling of salt and black pepper, and stir well to combine. Serve immediately.

NOTE: *If you're making this dish during the fall or winter, use 1 cup of frozen corn kernels.*

Burgers and a Sandwich

Salmon Burgers with Cucumber Mustard Sauce

Halibut Burgers with Basil Mayonnaise

Tuna Burgers with Teriyaki Ketchup

Tempeh Burgers

Black Bean Burgers with Bell Pepper–Avocado Sauce

Red Lentil–Chickpea Burgers with Two Sauces

   Spicy Peanut Sauce

   Sauce Taratour

Tempeh Reubens with Caramelized Onions

My childhood idea

of a perfect sandwich was peanut butter and jelly on store-bought white bread with no crust, and no filling spilling out over the edge. Although fresh, non-hydrogenated peanut butter remains comfort food for me, thankfully my culinary cravings have expanded considerably. Nowadays I love good crusty bread, and I do not object if a delicious filling pokes out the sides. As I became aware of the variety of great-tasting burgers that can be made with wholesome and satisfying ingredients, the burger has also become an important part of my diet.

A burger or a sandwich filling should be tasty enough to stand alone, without the bread, so the fillings here are big on flavor. I've included six of my favorite burgers and one of my favorite sandwich fillings, a succulent tempeh Reuben. The salmon, halibut, and tuna burgers are quick meals. For the best texture, chop the fish by hand instead of grinding it in a food processor. You can cook the tuna and salmon burgers as you would a plain piece of salmon or tuna: seared, medium, or cooked all the way through. The halibut, like any white-fleshed fish, needs to be cooked thoroughly.

I've included three vegetarian burgers as well. The red lentil–chickpea burger can be topped with two different sauces, each one giving the dish a distinctive flavor. The Southwest-style tempeh burger is a great way to introduce someone to protein-packed tempeh. The vegetarian burgers are wonderful stuffed into pita bread or served on top of a tortilla. The black bean and tempeh burgers are a little *picante*, so feel free to turn down the heat. Unfortunately, these days bread is getting a bad rap from certain fad-diet gurus. And it's true that the super-refined white pillowy stuff that permeates supermarket shelves is nutritionally valueless. Whole-grain bread, with texture and flavor, on the other hand, is the kind that nourishes. There are a lot of options nowadays on the average grocery shelf. Look for bread whose first ingredient is "whole," as in whole-wheat flour or whole-rye flour. Look for at least 2 grams of fiber per serving, preferably 3.

Salmon Burgers with Cucumber Mustard Sauce

You don't see salmon burgers on restaurant menus very often, but they are a fabulous way to eat this rich and healthful fish. Subtle with fresh herb flavor, this quick and easy burger is equally delicious with or without a bun. The sauce is wonderful on poached salmon as well.

SERVES 4

Burgers

1 1/2 **pounds fresh salmon, skinned**
3 **tablespoons chopped fresh tarragon**
1/4 **cup chopped fresh dill**
2 **tablespoons minced shallots**
1/4 **teaspoon salt**
Freshly ground black pepper

Cucumber Mustard Sauce

1/4 **cup Dijon mustard**
1 **tablespoon minced shallots**
2 **tablespoons chopped fresh dill**
2 **teaspoons white wine vinegar**
1/4 **cup extra-virgin olive oil**
1/2 **cucumber, peeled, seeded, and cut into small dice (5 to 6 tablespoons)**

Olive oil, for sautéing
4 **whole-grain buns, optional**

Prepare the burgers: Chop the salmon by hand into very small pieces. Place it in a bowl, and stir in the tarragon, dill, shallots, and salt, and black pepper to taste. Form the mixture into 4 patties, cover, and refrigerate until ready to cook. You can prepare these up to 1 day ahead.

Make the sauce: In a small bowl, mix together the mustard, shallots, dill, vinegar, olive oil, and cucumbers. Set aside.

Warm about 1 tablespoon olive oil, or enough to coat the bottom of a large nonstick skillet, over medium heat. Add the burger patties and sauté until they are cooked through with a little pink in the middle, about 3 minutes per side, or to desired doneness. Serve with or without the bun, slathered with the Cucumber Mustard Sauce.

Halibut Burgers with Basil Mayonnaise

The small amount of Thai green curry paste in this dish packs a lot of flavor. Halibut burgers require an egg white to help bind them together, and they need to be cooked all the way through. The Tofu Basil Cream from the Roasted Red Pepper Soup (page 49) is an equally tasty alternative to the Basil Mayonnaise.

SERVES 4

Burgers

$1\frac{1}{2}$ **pounds halibut, skinned**
1 teaspoon Thai green curry paste
1 tablespoon Thai fish sauce
$\frac{1}{2}$ cup bread crumbs, preferably fresh
2 tablespoons finely chopped fresh chives
$\frac{1}{4}$ teaspoon salt
1 egg white

Basil Mayonnaise (MAKES ¾ CUP)

1 egg yolk
1 teaspoon Dijon mustard
$\frac{1}{4}$ cup canola oil
6 tablespoons extra-virgin olive oil
1 teaspoon fresh lemon juice
Salt
$\frac{1}{2}$ cup chopped fresh basil

Extra-virgin olive oil, for sautéing
4 burger buns, preferably whole-wheat, optional
Cucumber slices, for garnish

Prepare the burgers: Chop the halibut by hand into very small dice. Transfer it to a bowl and stir in the curry paste, fish sauce, bread crumbs, chives, and salt. Stir in the egg white. Form the mixture into 4 patties and refrigerate, covered, for at least 20 minutes or until ready to serve.

Make the mayonnaise: In a small bowl, whisk together the egg yolk and mustard. Slowly drizzle in the canola and olive oils, whisking constantly to emulsify the mixture. Then stir in the lemon juice, a sprinkling of salt, and the basil. The mayonnaise will be very green. (You can also make the mayonnaise in a food processor or blender: Pulse the egg yolk and mustard together. Then slowly drizzle in the oils through the feed tube while the machine is running, stopping to scrape down the sides a couple of times. Stir in the lemon juice, salt, and basil.)

Warm about 1 tablespoon oil, or enough to coat the bottom of the pan, in a large nonstick skillet over medium-high heat. When the oil is hot (so you can hold an outstretched hand 1 inch above the pan for only a few seconds), lower the heat and add the burgers. Sauté over medium heat until the fish is cooked through, about 4 minutes on each side. (Sneak a peek with the tip of a knife to check that they are cooked through. They should feel firm, like the tip of your nose.) Serve with or without the bun, slathered with the Basil Mayonnaise.

Homemade mayonnaise is a snap to make—by hand or in a food processor or blender—and tastes much better than the bottled variety. If you make it by hand, anchor the mixing bowl by arranging a damp kitchen towel in a circle on your work surface and then placing the bowl in the middle to fit snugly. This way you can drizzle the oil with one hand while you whisk with the other and your bowl won't go anywhere. You can make any other herbed mayonnaise using the method described in this recipe. For a garlic mayonnaise, crush a couple of garlic cloves and mix them with the mustard and egg yolk. Homemade mayonnaise keeps for up to a week in the refrigerator. Raw eggs can contain salmonella (although it is very uncommon in organic eggs), so be careful when you are preparing mayonnaise for high-risk groups such as the elderly, small children, and pregnant women.

Bread crumbs are best when made by hand. I always keep a supply in the freezer to use at a moment's notice (see page 18).

Tuna Burgers with Teriyaki Ketchup

The exotic ketchup lends an Asian twist to this juicy burger. The burger itself takes just minutes to prepare, and you can serve it as cooked through or as rare as you like. The tuna keeps on cooking after you take it out of the pan, so you might want to take the burgers off the heat a minute or so before they are cooked to the desired doneness.

SERVES 4

Burgers

1½ pounds fresh tuna

1 cup minced scallions, white and green parts (from 6 to 8 scallions)

4 garlic cloves, minced

2 tablespoons minced fresh ginger

2 tablespoons shoyu

2 tablespoons Dijon mustard

½ teaspoon salt

Freshly ground black pepper

Teriyaki Ketchup

2 tablespoons shoyu

¼ cup sake, mirin, or dry sherry

2 tablespoons maple syrup

2 teaspoons tomato paste

1 teaspoon Dijon mustard

Extra-virgin olive oil, for sautéing

4 whole-grain buns

½ cup pickled ginger, optional

Prepare the burgers: Chop the tuna by hand into small pieces with a sharp knife. (Do not be tempted to put it in a food processor—it will shred the tuna.) Place the tuna in a medium bowl and mix in the scallions, garlic, ginger, shoyu, mustard, salt, and a sprinkling of black pepper. Form the mixture into 4 patties. Cover with plastic wrap, and refrigerate for at least 20 minutes or up to overnight.

Make the ketchup: Combine the shoyu, sake, maple syrup, and tomato paste in a small skillet and bring to a boil. Then lower the heat and simmer, uncovered, until the ketchup is reduced and thickened, 6 to 7 minutes. Remove the skillet from the heat and immediately whisk in the mustard.

Warm about 1 tablespoon oil, or enough to coat the bottom of the pan, in a large nonstick skillet over medium-high heat. Hold your hand 1 inch above the skillet, and when it feels uncomfortably hot, add the burgers. Lower the heat and sauté for a couple of minutes on each side, or until cooked to your preference.

Spread the Teriyaki Ketchup on each bun, add the burgers, and serve topped with the pickled ginger (if using).

NOTE: *Right before the ketchup thickens, the reduced liquid foams into a thick, bubbly layer. Remove the skillet from the heat at that point, and let the bubbles settle. It should be the perfect consistency. If it is still not thick enough, heat it for another minute or so and check again.*

Tempeh Burgers

These flavorful high-protein burgers are a favorite in my household. The patties can be shaped up to 3 days in advance; they freeze well; and they can even be cooked on a grill. A little dark miso adds depth of flavor. If you like, serve the burgers topped with salsa or Designer Guacamole (page 176). The Asian Slaw with Peanuts (page 95) makes a great accompaniment.

MAKES 7 BURGERS

Burgers

1/2 cup unsalted sunflower seeds
1/2 cup rolled oats
1 dried ancho chile, stemmed and seeded
1 dried chipotle chile, stemmed and seeded
1/4 cup (about 8) sun-dried tomatoes
1 pound tempeh
2 tablespoons coconut oil or olive oil, plus more for sautéing
1 1/2 cups water
3 tablespoons shoyu
1 onion, cut into small dice (1 cup)
2 garlic cloves, minced
2 teaspoons ground cumin
1 teaspoon ground coriander
1 tablespoon red, barley, hatcho, or dark miso
Salt and freshly ground black pepper
1/4 cup chopped fresh cilantro
1 scallion, white and green parts, thinly sliced

Topping

1 ripe Hass avocado
1/4 cup Dijon mustard

7 whole-wheat buns or tortillas
Sliced red onion, for garnish
Sliced tomato, for garnish

Dry-toast the sunflower seeds in a heavy-bottomed skillet over medium heat, stirring to prevent burning, until golden, about 3 minutes. Remove the seeds and place them in a small bowl.

Dry-toast the oats in the same skillet until fragrant, about 2 minutes. Place them in a separate small bowl.

Place the chiles and the sun-dried tomatoes in a small pot, and cover with water. Bring to a boil. Then remove the pot from the heat and allow to soak for at least 10 minutes, or until the chiles and tomatoes are softened.

Crumble the tempeh by hand into a medium bowl.

Warm 1 tablespoon of the coconut oil in a large nonstick skillet over medium-high heat. Add the tempeh and cook, stirring frequently to brown evenly, until lightly golden, 2 to 3 minutes. Add the oats, water, and shoyu. Simmer, stirring occasionally, until all the liquid is absorbed and the mixture is dry, about 10 minutes. Transfer the tempeh to a medium bowl.

Warm the remaining 1 tablespoon oil in a medium skillet over medium-low heat. Add the onions and cook until they are soft, about 10 minutes. Add the garlic, cumin, and coriander, and cook an additional 2 minutes.

Drain the chiles and tomatoes, and place them in a food processor. Add the onion mixture and the miso, and process until smooth. Add the paste to the tempeh mixture, and stir in the sunflower seeds. Taste for seasoning, and add about $1/4$ teaspoon salt and a sprinkling of pepper. Stir in the cilantro and scallions. Set aside until cool enough to handle.

Form the mixture into 7 equal patties. Wrap the patties in plastic wrap and chill them in the refrigerator for at least 30 minutes, and up to overnight, to firm up. If you're going to grill them, chill them for at least a few hours.

Shortly before serving, prepare the topping: Mash the avocado and mustard together in a small bowl. Set it aside.

Lightly coat a medium nonstick skillet with oil, and place it over medium-high heat. When the oil is hot (so you can hold an outstretched hand 1 inch above the pan for only a few seconds), add the burgers (you should hear a sizzling sound). Lower the heat and cook until golden, 3 to 4 minutes. Turn the burgers over and cook for another 3 to 4 minutes.

Spread the tortillas or buns with the dressing, and top with the red onions and tomato. Add the burgers and serve hot.

(CONTINUED NEXT PAGE)

NOTES: *You can keep these burgers for up to 3 days in the refrigerator before cooking them, and you can freeze them for up to 1 month. Simply defrost and then sauté until golden on each side.*

The dried chiles are brittle, so crack them open and pour out the seeds; it doesn't matter if they end up in pieces. Chipotles are smoked red jalapeños with a hot, smoky flavor; ancho chiles, with a mild fruit flavor, are dried poblanos. Blending the two chiles creates a delicious, rich flavor.

There are so many kinds of miso, you could try a different kind every day. I like to have at least two types in my refrigerator: An aged dark variety, such as red (rice), barley, or hatcho (pure soybean), adds a mysterious depth to hearty dishes. I also keep a light miso on hand, such as sweet white, mellow barley, or chickpea, which has no soybeans in it at all. I use the lighter misos when I want a more delicate flavor.

To take the edge off the red onion, soak the sliced onion in cold water for 15 minutes.

Black Bean Burgers with Bell Pepper–Avocado Sauce

These spicy burgers are always a favorite in my cooking classes. The ground pumpkin seeds help bind the ingredients and add a delicious flavor. Serve the burgers tucked into whole-wheat tortillas, slathered with the sauce and topped with shredded romaine.

SERVES 4

Burgers

1/2 cup unsalted pumpkin seeds

2 tablespoons extra-virgin olive oil, plus more for sautéing

1 cup diced onion

Salt

2 garlic cloves, minced

1 chipotle chile in adobo sauce, minced

1 teaspoon ground cumin

1/2 teaspoon dried oregano

One 15-ounce can black turtle beans, rinsed and drained, *or* 1 1/2 cups cooked beans

2/3 cup water or bean cooking liquid

3/4 cup bread crumbs, preferably fresh

Bell Pepper–Avocado Sauce

1 tablespoon extra-virgin olive oil

1 green bell pepper, seeded and cut into 1-inch cubes

1/4 cup thinly sliced scallions, white and green parts

Salt

1/4 cup water

2 tablespoons fresh lime juice

1 jalapeño pepper, stemmed and seeded

1/2 ripe avocado

1 cup fresh cilantro

4 large tortillas, preferably sprouted wheat

Shredded romaine lettuce

Dry-toast the pumpkin seeds in a heavy-bottomed skillet over medium heat until they color and start to pop, about 3 minutes. Finely grind the pumpkin seeds in a blender or food processor, and set aside. (CONTINUED NEXT PAGE)

Warm the olive oil in the same skillet over medium-low heat. Add the onions and ½ teaspoon salt, and sauté until softened, 7 to 10 minutes. Add the garlic, chile, cumin, and oregano and sauté for 1 minute. Then add one third of the beans and ⅓ cup of the water, and mash the beans with a potato masher or fork. When the liquid is absorbed, continue with another third of the beans and the remaining ⅓ cup water. Continue mashing until most of the beans are broken up and the mixture is chunky. Stir in the last third of the beans and mash them lightly. Cook, stirring constantly, until the liquid is absorbed and the beans are very thick and mostly dry. A spoon run across the beans should leave track marks. It's fine if not all of the beans are mashed thoroughly.

Transfer the beans to a medium bowl and let them cool for about 15 minutes. Then stir in the ground pumpkin seeds and ¼ cup of the bread crumbs. Taste, and add a pinch more salt if necessary. Spread the remaining ½ cup bread crumbs on a plate. Using a spoon, drop one fourth of the bean mixture onto the bread crumbs. Sprinkle the top of the beans with crumbs to make the burger easy to handle, and form it into a 4- to 5-inch patty. Place the burger on a clean plate and repeat with the remaining bean mixture and bread crumbs. Refrigerate the burgers for at least 30 minutes to firm up.

Make the sauce: Warm the olive oil in a medium skillet over medium heat. Add the green peppers and sauté until softened, about 7 minutes. Add the scallions and sauté for 1 minute. Transfer the mixture to a blender, and add ¾ teaspoon salt, the water, lime juice, jalapeño, avocado, and cilantro. Blend until smooth. Taste, and add a pinch more salt if necessary.

Warm 1 tablespoon olive oil, or enough to coat the bottom of the pan, in a medium nonstick skillet over medium-high heat. When the oil is hot (so you can hold an outstretched hand 1 inch above the pan for only a few seconds), add the patties. Lower the heat and sauté until golden, 2 to 3 minutes on each side.

Warm the tortillas by passing them briefly over a hot skillet. Spread each one with Bell Pepper–Avocado Sauce and top with lettuce. Fold the tortillas over the burgers, and serve.

Red Lentil–Chickpea Burgers with Two Sauces

This textured burger acts as a tasty canvas for either Spicy Peanut Sauce or Sauce Taratour. I couldn't decide which I liked better, so I'm including both. The spicy curried peanut sauce lends an Indian flair and is also delicious over rice and vegetables, while the Sauce Taratour gives the burgers a Middle Eastern flavor. Sauce Taratour is also good with the chopped Middle Eastern salad from the *Mujadarrah* (page 210).

SERVES 6

Burgers

3/4 cup red lentils, sorted and rinsed

1 3/4 cups water

Salt

One 15-ounce can chickpeas, drained and rinsed, *or* 1 1/2 cups
   cooked chickpeas

1 tablespoon extra-virgin olive oil, plus more for sautéing

1/2 cup minced shallots

3/4 pound carrots, cut into small dice (1 cup)

1 teaspoon ground cumin

1 teaspoon ground coriander

1 cup peas, fresh or frozen

1/2 cup chopped fresh parsley

1 teaspoon fresh lemon juice

Pinch of cayenne pepper

1/4 cup bread crumbs, preferably fresh from whole-grain bread

Spicy Peanut Sauce or Sauce Taratour (recipes follow)

6 whole-wheat pita breads

Shredded romaine lettuce

Chopped fresh tomatoes

Combine the lentils and the water in a medium saucepan, and bring to a boil. Add 1 teaspoon salt, reduce the heat, and simmer, stirring occasionally, until the lentils are tender, about 20 minutes. The lentils should lose their individual shape and cook into one mass. Cook them as dry as they can go without sticking. If you find the water has evaporated before the lentils are cooked, add a small amount of water and continue cooking.

Stir the cooked lentils with a spoon to break them up, and pour them into a medium bowl. Stir in the chickpeas. (CONTINUED NEXT PAGE)

Warm the olive oil in a medium skillet over medium heat. Add the shallots, carrots, and ¼ teaspoon salt, and cook until the carrots are tender, about 3 minutes. Add the cumin, coriander, and peas, and cook until the peas are tender, 2 minutes. Stir the vegetables into the lentils along with the parsley, lemon juice, and cayenne. Stir in the bread crumbs. Taste, and add a pinch more salt if necessary. Let the mixture sit for 10 minutes, or until it is cool enough to handle.

Using your hands, form the lentils into 6 tight patties and place them on a plate. Cover and chill in the refrigerator until very firm, at least 30 minutes.

Sauté the burgers: Warm a tablespoon of oil, or enough to coat the bottom of the pan, in a large nonstick skillet over medium heat. Hold your hand about 4 inches above the pan, and when it feels uncomfortably hot, add the burgers. These burgers are a bit delicate, so do not crowd the pan. Sauté until golden, about 2 minutes. Turn the burgers over and sauté on the other side until golden, 2 minutes. Serve each burger in a pita with Spicy Peanut or Taratour sauce, topped with shredded lettuce and chopped tomatoes.

Spicy Peanut Sauce (MAKES ¾ CUP)

Make this up to a week in advance.

⅓ cup smooth peanut butter
1 teaspoon curry powder
½ teaspoon salt
1 tablespoon maple syrup
1 tablespoon chopped fresh ginger
⅓ cup water
1 tablespoon fresh lemon juice
¼ teaspoon cayenne pepper
1 tablespoon thinly sliced scallions, white and green parts, or chives

Combine the peanut butter, curry powder, salt, maple syrup, ginger, water, lemon juice, and cayenne in a blender and blend until smooth. If it seems too thick, add a little water. Stir in the scallions. Taste and add more salt if necessary. Store covered and refrigerated.

NOTE: *It's easiest to peel ginger with a knife. Cut the skin off the ginger, and cut the ginger lengthwise into thin slabs. Cut the slabs into matchsticks, and mince the matchsticks.*

Sauce Taratour (MAKES ¾ CUP)

Make this up to a week in advance.

½ cup tahini
⅓ cup water
1 garlic clove, minced
3 tablespoons fresh lemon juice
¼ teaspoon salt
¼ cup minced scallions, white and green parts

Whisk the tahini, water, garlic, lemon juice, and salt together in a bowl until smooth. Stir in the scallions. Add more water, 1 tablespoon at a time, if needed to thin the sauce. Store, covered, in the refrigerator for up to a week.

Tempeh Reubens with Caramelized Onions

This is one of the most satisfying vegetarian lunch choices around. Layers of tempeh, sauerkraut, and caramelized onions give the warm sandwich a rich, well-integrated flavor. You can simmer the tempeh in the marinade in advance and then keep it in the refrigerator before sautéing it. Brush the tempeh with oil and grill it before serving. I serve this sandwich open-faced and eat it with a knife and fork; it's also delicious topped with a second slice of bread.

SERVES 4 TO 6

1 pound tempeh
1½ cups water
¼ cup mirin, dry sherry, or apple juice
2 tablespoons shoyu
One 2-inch piece fresh ginger, unpeeled, cut into 5 large pieces
1 teaspoon ground cumin
1 teaspoon ground caraway
Pinch of cayenne pepper
2 tablespoons extra-virgin olive oil, plus more for sautéing
4 cups thinly sliced onions (from 2 large onions)
Salt
1½ cups prepared sauerkraut
6 slices hearty whole-wheat bread
Russian Dressing (recipe follows)
1 bunch arugula (¼ pound), washed, dried, heavy stems removed

Prepare the tempeh: Holding the knife at a 45-degree angle, cut the tempeh along its width into twelve ¾-inch-thick angled diagonal slices. Place the tempeh slices in a medium pot or a large skillet, and add the water, mirin, shoyu, ginger, cumin, caraway, and cayenne. Bring to a boil. Then lower the heat and simmer, covered, for 15 minutes. Drain the tempeh and set aside. At this point, you can refrigerate the tempeh until you are ready to sauté it.

Caramelize the onions: Warm the 2 tablespoons olive oil in a medium skillet over medium-low heat.

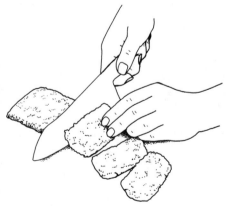

Add the onions and a sprinkling of salt, and sauté until soft, about 10 minutes. Raise the heat and sauté, stirring frequently, until well browned, 5 minutes or so. Set aside.

Warm the sauerkraut in a small saucepan.

Sauté the tempeh: Coat a large nonstick skillet with olive oil and heat it over medium-high heat. Hold your hand about 4 inches above the skillet, and when it is uncomfortably hot, reduce the heat to medium and add the tempeh. Sauté until golden brown, about 3 minutes per side.

Meanwhile, toast the bread. Spread each piece of toast with a heaping tablespoon of Russian dressing. Layer the arugula, tempeh, sauerkraut, and onions on top, and serve.

NOTE: *Caraway usually comes only in the form of whole seeds. Grind the seeds, or you may use them whole.*

Russian Dressing (MAKES ½ CUP)

¼ cup mayonnaise or Nayonaise (eggless mayonnaise)
1 tablespoon tomato paste
¼ cup minced dill pickle
2 tablespoons minced red onion
1 teaspoon Dijon mustard

Mix all the ingredients together in a small bowl until thoroughly combined. This keeps, covered and refrigerated, for up to 5 days.

Pizza, Wonton Ravioli, and Crêpes

Pizza

WHOLE-GRAIN PIZZA CRUST:

MULTIGRAIN, WHOLE-WHEAT, SEMOLINA-RYE, AND SPELT

THREE FAVORITE VEGETABLE TOPPINGS

MUSHROOM SAUTÉ

SAUTÉED FENNEL

SAUTÉED BROCCOLI RABE WITH GARLIC AND
RED PEPPER FLAKES

PIZZA COMBINATIONS

PISSALADIÈRE (PROVENÇAL ONION TART)

Wonton Ravioli

PUMPKIN-PECAN WONTONS WITH SAGE BUTTER

VALENTINE WONTONS

SPINACH-TOFU WONTONS

SOUTHWEST WONTONS

PORCINI BROTH

Crêpes

WHOLE-GRAIN CRÊPES: CORNMEAL, RICE, AND BUCKWHEAT

CORNMEAL CRÊPES WITH REFRIED BLACK BEANS

RICE CRÊPES WITH VEGETABLE STIR-FRY

BUCKWHEAT CRÊPES WITH MEDITERRANEAN BRAISE

BUCKWHEAT CRÊPES WITH ROASTED ASPARAGUS

This chapter

includes some favorite fun foods: pizza, crêpes, and wonton ravioli. All of the recipes can be prepared with a minimum of effort. Each of the four whole-grain pizza doughs, for instance, can be made in a food processor in about a minute, and the toppings can be prepared in a snap. ◎ There's also a selection of whole-grain crêpes: cornmeal, rice, and buckwheat, each of which has a dairy-free and a vegan version. I've included a selection of appropriate fillings, but of course you can use your imagination and stuff the crêpes with just about anything you like. Crêpes are easy to make—and you can prepare them days ahead, making them perfect party fare. ◎ Although I love making my own pasta, sometimes I'm just not inclined to go through the process of rolling out the dough. The ravioli recipes here all call for wontons, which act as ready-made wrappers. You can simmer them, like ravioli, or fry them; the choice is yours. ◎ All these dishes are suitable for starters, light bites, and main courses. You can make these foods in advance for easy entertaining. Better yet, invite some friends over, have them roll their own pizza dough, and top it with their favorite toppings. Or invite them to flip crêpes and fill wontons. This kid-friendly food is comforting for the kid in all of us. Enjoy the playful process and reap the tasty rewards.

Pizza

I love thin-crust pizza—especially if it's whole-grain. In this section you'll find a variety of whole-grain pizza crusts that are fast and easy to make; the food processor is the key. After the ingredients are pulsed together, the dough is processed for a mere 15 seconds. Then it rises for 1 to 1½ hours, leaving ample time to prepare the topping. To simplify shaping the dough, stretch it on a piece of parchment paper; just stretch and flatten the dough until you have a 10-inch round. If you like, you can finish the dough with one quick turn of a rolling pin. Leave the dough on the parchment and add your choice of topping. Then slip the parchment onto a pre-heated pizza stone placed on the bottom rack of the oven. I leave my stone in the oven at all times; that way I don't have to drag it in and out, it's ready when I need it, and it regulates the heat in the oven. When you're not baking directly on the stone, treat it as if it's an extension of the oven rack. (If you don't have a stone, an upturned rimmed baking sheet works well.) A pizza peel simplifies the job of sliding the pizza into the oven; however, sliding it in from the back of a baking tray works also. Bake the pizza at 500°F. The parchment darkens at such a high temperature, but that's not a problem. The pizza is ready after only 10 minutes. Pull the parchment with tongs, or slide a peel under the parchment, to remove the pizza from the oven. Strip away the parchment paper, and your pizza is ready to be sliced and eaten. For the best results, don't be heavy-handed with the toppings. If you use mozzarella, slice just a few medallions off a fresh round and scatter them over the pizza. The cheese melts and spreads quite a bit, and putting too much cheese on a pizza will make it heavy and gooey. I've included some suggestions for topping combinations that work well. They're just suggestions. Remember, you're the chef.

Whole-Grain Pizza Crust

I'm certain you'll be as enthusiastic as I am about these easy-to-make doughs—it takes less than 1 minute to mix and knead them in a food processor. While the dough rises, prepare the sauce and topping. If the dough is ready before you are, just punch it down. You can even refrigerate the dough, covered, overnight; then bring it to room temperature before shaping. For the multigrain cereal variation, use any variety of hot cereal and grind it to a flour in a spice grinder or a food processor.

MAKES TWO 10-INCH PIZZAS

Multigrain Crust

1 cup unbleached white flour
1/2 cup whole-wheat flour
1/2 cup ground multigrain breakfast cereal
1 teaspoon instant yeast
3/4 teaspoon salt
1 tablespoon extra-virgin olive oil, plus extra for oiling the bowl
3/4 cup warm water (105°F)

Whole-Wheat Crust

1 cup whole-wheat flour
1 cup unbleached white flour
1 teaspoon instant yeast
3/4 teaspoon salt
1 tablespoon extra-virgin olive oil
3/4 cup warm water (105°F)

Semolina-Rye Crust

1 cup whole-wheat flour
3/4 cup semolina flour
1/4 cup rye flour
1 teaspoon instant yeast
3/4 teaspoon salt
1 tablespoon extra-virgin olive oil
3/4 cup warm water (105°F)

(CONTINUED NEXT PAGE)

Spelt Crust

2 cups spelt flour
1 teaspoon instant yeast
3/4 teaspoon salt
1 tablespoon extra-virgin olive oil
3/4 cup warm water (105°F)

Choice of Sauces

Fire-Roasted Tomato Sauce (page 169)
Basil Pesto (page 171)
Herbed Olive Tapenade (page 170)
Caramelized onions (see page 136)

Choice of Toppings

Sliced fresh mozzarella
Crumbled goat cheese
Mushroom Sauté (page 144)
Sautéed Fennel (page 144)
Roasted red peppers (see page 19)
Sliced anchovies
Sautéed Broccoli Rabe with Garlic and Red Pepper Flakes (page 145)
Olives

Fit a food processor with the plastic blade. Place all the dry ingredients—flour(s) yeast, and salt—in the processor and pulse to combine. With the motor running, gradually add the olive oil and the warm water through the feed tube. Then turn off the machine, and scrape the bottom and sides of the container with a rubber spatula to loosen the flours. Cover again and process until the dough forms a ball, 15 seconds.

Lightly dust a board with flour. Turn the dough out onto the board and knead it for 30 seconds or so, just until it is smooth and manageable. Place the dough in a well-oiled bowl and turn the dough so that it is covered with oil. Cover the bowl with a damp kitchen towel, and set it in a draft-free place. Let the dough rise until doubled, 1 to 1½ hours. The dough is ready when a fingerprint pressed into it fills in slowly.

Set a pizza stone or an overturned rimmed baking sheet on a rack on the lowest position in the oven. Heat the oven to 500°F.

Set a 15-inch piece of parchment paper on your work surface. Divide the risen dough into 2 balls. Work with one piece at a time, keeping the other one covered. Using oiled fingers, hold the dough and stretch it out to form a 6-inch round. Place it on the parchment paper, and push and flatten the dough until you have a 10-inch round. You can use a rolling pin if you like. Gently dimple the dough with your fingers. Repeat with the second ball of dough.

Spread a thin layer of your choice of sauce over the dough, leaving a 1/2-inch border all around. Add your toppings of choice, being careful not to overload the pizza. Slip the pizza-topped parchment onto a pizza peel or the back of a cookie sheet, and slide it onto the stone. Bake for 10 minutes, or until the pizza is golden around the edges.

Remove the pizza from the oven by using tongs to pull the parchment onto a peel or cookie sheet. Slide the pizza off the parchment onto a cutting board. Use a pizza wheel to cut the pizza into even slices.

NOTE: *Instant yeast is subjected to a gentler drying process than conventional yeast, and it can be mixed directly with recipe ingredients without first being dissolved in water. It is a stronger yeast, which means that, in general, you can use less of it. Brand names include SAF Perfect Rise Gourmet Yeast, Red Star Quick Rise Yeast, Fermipan Instant Dry Yeast, and Fleischmann's Rapid Rise Yeast.*

Three Favorite Vegetable Toppings

Mushroom Sauté (MAKES 2 CUPS)

Use any combination of mushrooms. This is also delicious stuffed into phyllo triangles.

  2 tablespoons extra-virgin olive oil
  3/4 pound wild mushrooms, such as shiitakes, chanterelles,
      or portobellos, or a mixture, thinly sliced
  1/4 cup dry white wine
  1 tablespoon shoyu
  2 shallots, minced (1/2 cup)
  Salt and freshly ground black pepper

Warm the olive oil in a large skillet over medium-high heat. Add the mushrooms and sauté until any liquid evaporates and the mushrooms smell fragrant, about 10 minutes. Add the wine and shoyu, and scrape up any brown bits on the bottom of the pan. Sprinkle with the shallots and cook for a couple of minutes more. Sprinkle with salt and pepper to taste and remove from the heat. You can prepare the mushrooms up to 2 days ahead.

NOTE: *Make sure to remove the stems of shiitake mushrooms. Discard or save them for stock. Remove the stems and the gills (the feathery part underneath the cap) of portobellos by scraping them with a spoon. Wipe the caps clean with a damp paper towel.*

Sautéed Fennel (MAKES 3 TO 4 CUPS)

The licorice taste of fennel is mellowed by a slow sauté. It is delicious mixed with the onions for a variation of the pissaladière.

  2 fennel bulbs (about 2 pounds)
  2 tablespoons extra-virgin olive oil
  Salt and freshly ground black pepper

Cut off any protruding tops from the fennel bulb. Shave off any discolored or bruised parts. Cut the bulb in half from stem to stem, and remove the hard core with a paring knife. Lay the fennel halves cut side down on a cutting board, and thinly slice. (A mandoline makes this task easy.)

Warm the olive oil in a medium skillet over medium-low heat. Add the fennel and sauté, stirring frequently, until it is completely tender, about 20 minutes. Season with salt and black pepper to taste, and remove from the heat. You can prepare this up to 3 days in advance.

Sautéed Broccoli Rabe with Garlic and Red Pepper Flakes (MAKES 2½ CUPS)

This is one of those indispensable basics to have in your repertoire. I often serve this as a vegetable dish on its own. A quick dip in a pot of boiling water takes the bitter edge off the broccoli rabe. For a tasty variation, mix half broccoli rabe with half escarole.

2 bunches (1½ pounds) broccoli rabe
Salt
2 tablespoons extra-virgin olive oil
4 garlic cloves, sliced
½ teaspoon dried red pepper flakes
Freshly ground black pepper

Bring a large pot of water to a boil. Fill a bowl with ice water and set it aside.

While the water is heating, cut off the tough stems of the broccoli rabe. When the water comes to a boil, add 1 teaspoon salt and the broccoli rabe. Blanch until bright green, 3 to 4 minutes. Then quickly drain the broccoli rabe and plunge it into the ice water to stop the cooking.

Drain the cooled broccoli rabe and cut it into bite-size pieces. (You can do this up to 1 day in advance.)

Combine the olive oil, garlic, and red pepper flakes in a medium skillet over medium heat. Cook just until the garlic begins to turn light gold, 2 to 3 minutes. Then immediately add the broccoli rabe and stir until heated through, 1 to 2 minutes. Sprinkle with salt and black pepper, and remove from the heat. Serve immediately as a side vegetable, or make it up to a day in advance to top a pizza.

Pizza Combinations

The most appealing pizzas are both attractive and tasty. Here are some suggestions for combinations that go together beautifully. For the best flavor, use fresh mozarella, not the packaged kind.

Pesto Pizza with Mushrooms and Peppers

Basil Pesto (page 171)
Mushroom Sauté (page 144)
Roasted red bell peppers (see page 19)

Olive Pizza with Fennel and Goat Cheese

Herbed Olive Tapenade (page 170)
Sautéed Fennel (page 144)
Crumbled goat cheese

Cheese and Tomato Pizza with Olives and Broccoli Rabe

Fire-Roasted Tomato Sauce (page 169)
Fresh mozzarella
Sliced olives
Sautéed Broccoli Rabe with Garlic and Red Pepper Flakes (page 145)

Two-Cheese and Tomato Pizza with Mushrooms and Anchovies

Fire-Roasted Tomato Sauce (page 169)
Mushroom Sauté (page 144)
Mozzarella
Goat cheese
Anchovies

Green and Red Pizza

Fire-Roasted Tomato Sauce (page 169) alternated with Basil Pesto (page 171)
Sautéed Broccoli Rabe with Garlic and Red Pepper Flakes (page 145)
Roasted red bell peppers (see page 19)
Sliced olives

Green and White Pizza

Basil Pesto (page 171)
Sautéed Fennel (page 144)
Sautéed Broccoli Rabe with Garlic and Red Pepper Flakes (page 145)
Goat cheese

Caramelized Onion and Fennel Pizza with Peppers and Olives

Roasted garlic (see page 19)
Caramelized onions (see page 136)
Sautéed Fennel (page 144)
Roasted red bell peppers (see page 19)
Sliced olives

Pissaladière (Provençal Onion Tart)

Caramelized-onion pizzas are served all over the south of France, from corner shops that sell them as street food to fine restaurants that serve them as elegant starters. The onions are piled high in a saucepan and slow-cooked until they release their juices and become meltingly tender and sweet. On the tart, the onions are traditionally crisscrossed with strips of red bell peppers and anchovies and studded with black olives. If you're not a fan of anchovies, omit them—the vegetarian version is still delicious. The caramelized onions pair well with any of the whole-grain pizza crusts.

MAKES TWO 10-INCH PIZZAS

3 tablespoons extra-virgin olive oil

4 pounds (about 9) onions, thinly sliced (about 12 cups)

3 garlic cloves, minced

2 bay leaves

5 thyme sprigs

Salt

Freshly ground black pepper

1 recipe Whole-Grain Pizza Crust dough (page 141)

1 small (3.5-ounce) jar anchovies, optional

1 red bell pepper, roasted (see page 19) and cut into thin slices (1 cup)

20 black olives, such as niçoise or kalamata

Warm the olive oil in a large skillet or a large shallow pot over medium-low heat. Add the onions, garlic, bay leaves, thyme sprigs, ¾ teaspoon salt, and a sprinkling of black pepper. Cover and cook gently, stirring occasionally, until the onions have completely wilted down, 50 minutes to 1 hour.

Uncover the skillet, raise the heat to medium, and stir until most of the liquid has evaporated and the onions have started to brown, about 10 minutes. Remove the skillet from the heat and discard the thyme sprigs and the bay leaves. Taste, and add more salt if necessary.

Preheat the oven to 500°F. Shape the dough into two 10-inch pizzas as directed in the pizza crust recipe.

Spread the onions over the dough, leaving a ¾-inch border all around. Slice the anchovies (if using) into thin lengthwise pieces. Arrange the red pepper slices and the anchovies in a crisscross pattern. Place the olives inside the crisscross pattern. Bake for 10 minutes, or until the bottom of the crust is golden and crisp. Cut into slices and serve hot.

Wonton Ravioli

Ravioli are easy to love. Maybe it's the surprise filling inside each little package, or the variety of textures and tastes. Or maybe it's because you can make them in advance and freeze them, so a quick, delicious dinner for your family or an impressive entrée for guests is just minutes away. Making ravioli from scratch takes time. I prefer a simplified version that is practical and easy enough for everyday cooking: wonton wrappers, also known as dumpling skins. Available in the refrigerator section in Asian grocery stores and in many supermarkets, wonton wrappers come in 4-inch rounds or squares. The best wrappers contain only four ingredients: flour, water, salt, and a dusting of cornstarch to keep them from sticking together. Well-wrapped packaged wonton skins will last for a week in the refrigerator or 2 months in the freezer. To prevent a soggy wrapping, cool the filling to room temperature before using it. Don't overstuff the wontons, or the filling may burst through the sides as they cook. Cook the wontons in salted water at a gentle simmer; boiling water can also cause the ravioli to burst. Be sure not to overcrowd the wontons in the pot. Uncooked filled wontons can be covered and refrigerated for 2 days on a baking sheet that has been lined with parchment paper to prevent sticking. Or you can freeze them in a single layer on a baking sheet for about 2 hours and then stack them in freezer bags. Frozen wontons need only about an extra minute of cooking time. Each of these wonton ravioli recipes yields between 60 and 70 pieces, enough for 6 to 8 main-course servings. I always keep a few extra wrappers on hand, in case the filling goes further than expected. Buy two packages of wrappers to ensure that you have enough for these recipes, and then just freeze the extra.

Pumpkin-Pecan Wontons with Sage Butter

Serve a few of these wontons as an elegant autumn starter. I like kabocha squash best, but any winter squash, including the standby butternut, will be fine.

SERVES 6 TO 8

**1 medium squash, such as kabocha or butternut
(2 to 2½ pounds)**
3 tablespoons extra-virgin olive oil
1 tablespoon maple syrup
Salt
1 onion, finely chopped (1 cup)
½ cup chopped pecans
2 tablespoons minced fresh sage, plus more for garnish
Freshly ground black pepper
1 pound wonton wrappers

Sage Butter

½ cup (1 stick) unsalted butter
20 fresh sage leaves, stems removed
Grated Parmesan cheese, for serving

Preheat the oven to 400°F.

Make the filling: Peel and seed the squash, and cut it into 1-inch chunks. You should have about 4 cups of squash. Place the squash in a medium bowl and toss with 2 tablespoons of the olive oil, the maple syrup, and ½ teaspoon salt. Spread the squash on a parchment-covered baking sheet. Roast, stirring once or twice, until the squash is tender and the exterior is beginning to caramelize, about 25 minutes. Transfer the squash to a bowl, and mash it. You should have about 2 cups of mashed squash.

Warm the remaining 1 tablespoon oil in a medium skillet over medium heat. Add the onions and sauté until browned, about 10 minutes. Add the pecans and sauté for 2 more minutes. Then add the mashed squash and cook, stirring constantly, until heated through, about 1 minute. Remove the skillet from the heat and stir in the sage. Add salt to taste and add a sprinkling of black pepper. Allow the filling to cool to room temperature.

Line a baking sheet with parchment. Have a small bowl of water, a pastry brush, and a fork handy.

Fill the ravioli: Place a wonton wrapper on your work surface and brush ½ inch around the edges with water. Place a heaping teaspoon of filling in the middle of the wrapper. Fold the wrapper in half, sealing the edges by pressing them together with the tines of a fork. Press the edges again to make sure wonton is tightly closed. Place the wonton on the prepared baking sheet. Repeat until all the filling is used. (The ravioli can be covered with plastic wrap and refrigerated for up to 2 days.)

Make the Sage Butter: Combine the butter and the sage leaves in a small pan and bring to a boil. Then lower the heat and simmer until the butter is fragrant, 5 minutes. Keep warm.

To cook the ravioli: Bring 4 quarts salted water to a boil in a large, wide pot such as a Dutch oven. Lower the heat to a simmer (do not let water boil again), and add half of the ravioli; they should not be crowded. Cook until the wontons look translucent around the edges, 3 to 4 minutes. Use a slotted spoon to remove the wontons from the pot, and shake off any excess water. Transfer the wontons to individual serving bowls and keep warm. Repeat the process, cooking the remaining wontons. Top each serving with a spoonful of the Sage Butter and a sprinkling of Parmesan. Serve immediately, garnishing each bowl with minced sage.

NOTES: *You can roast the squash whole for 20 minutes to make it easier to peel and cut. Then cut it into chunks, toss with the oil, maple syrup, and salt, and caramelize as described.*

Instead of the Sage Butter, ladle Porcini Broth (page 158) over the cooked wontons for a lighter dish.

Filled wontons make wonderful appetizer bites. Cut the wonton wrappers in half. Fill with ½ teaspoon of filling, and press the edges together. Pour oil to a depth of ⅛ inch in a skillet, and heat over medium-high heat until it is shimmering but not smoking. (Test the heat by laying 1 wonton in the pan: in just seconds it should bubble, brown, and puff). Cook all the wontons, browning them on both sides. If you want to freeze these morsels, cook them first. Freeze in a single layer for a couple of hours, and then stack them in freezer bags. To reheat, spread them on a baking sheet and cook in a preheated 350°F oven for 15 minutes.

Valentine Wontons

This gorgeous beet filling is delicious with the poppy-seed butter. Serve the wontons with the Porcini Broth (page 158) for a dairy-free dish.

SERVES 5 OR 6

2 tablespoons extra-virgin olive oil
1 cup chopped fresh fennel (from 1/2 medium bulb)
1/2 cup minced shallots
Salt
1/4 teaspoon ground ginger
1/2 pound (about 3 small) fresh beets, cooked
1/2 cup walnuts, toasted
1/4 cup dry bread crumbs
Freshly ground black pepper
2 teaspoons fresh lemon juice
1 1/2 pounds wonton wrappers

Poppy-seed Sauce

1/2 cup (1 stick) unsalted butter
2 tablespoons poppy seeds

Grated Parmesan cheese, for serving

Warm the olive oil in a medium skillet over medium-low heat. Add the fennel, shallots, and 3/4 teaspoon salt, and sauté until tender, about 10 minutes. Add the ginger and sauté for another minute or so.

Transfer the fennel mixture to a food processor, and add the beets and walnuts. Process until finely chopped. Add the bread crumbs and process to combine. Add a sprinkling of black pepper and the lemon juice. Taste, and add a pinch more salt if necessary.

Line a baking sheet with parchment. Have a small bowl of water, a pastry brush, and a fork handy.

Place a wonton wrapper on your work surface and brush 1/2 inch around the edges with water. Place a heaping teaspoon of filling in the middle of the wrapper. Fold the wrapper in half, sealing the edges by pressing them together with the tines of the fork. Place the ravioli on the prepared baking sheet. Repeat until the all filling is used. (The ravioli can be covered with plastic and refrigerated for up to 2 days.)

Make the Poppy-seed Sauce: Combine the butter and the poppy seeds in a small pot, and heat until the butter has melted. Keep warm. Set aside.

To cook the ravioli: Bring 4 quarts salted water to a boil in a large, wide pot such as a Dutch oven. Lower the heat to a simmer (do not let the water boil again) and add half of the ravioli. They should not be crowded. Cook until the wontons look translucent around the edges, 3 to 4 minutes. Use a slotted spoon to remove the ravioli from the pot, and shake off any excess water. Transfer the ravioli to individual serving bowls, and keep warm. Repeat the process, cooking the remaining wontons. Top each serving with a generous drizzle of poppy-seed butter and a sprinkling of Parmesan, and serve immediately.

Spinach-Tofu Wontons

The bright flavor of basil really comes through in this recipe. The wontons are perfect topped with Fire-Roasted Tomato Sauce.

SERVES 6 TO 8

**2 large bunches (about 1$\frac{1}{2}$ pounds) fresh spinach,
    stemmed and washed**
2 teaspoons white miso
1 tablespoon fresh lemon juice
2 tablespoons mirin or dry sherry
1 pound firm tofu, drained and rinsed
3 tablespoons extra-virgin olive oil
4 garlic cloves, minced
Salt
2 tablespoons chopped fresh basil
Freshly ground black pepper
1$\frac{1}{2}$ pounds wonton wrappers
1 recipe Fire-Roasted Tomato Sauce (page 169)

Place the spinach in a large pot. Cook over medium heat, stirring frequently or tossing with tongs to push the uncooked leaves to the bottom of the pot, until wilted, about 3 to 4 minutes. (You don't have to add water to the pot, because the water clinging to the leaves from washing is enough to cook them.)

Transfer the spinach to a colander and drain, pressing out any excess liquid. Let the spinach cool slightly; then chop fine and set aside. You should have about 1$\frac{1}{2}$ cups.

Combine the miso, lemon juice, and mirin in a small bowl. Add the tofu and mash with a fork to form small curds.

Combine the olive oil and the garlic in a large skillet, and cook over medium heat just until the garlic begins to color, about 1 minute. Add the tofu mixture and $\frac{1}{2}$ teaspoon salt, and cook until the filling is almost dry, about 5 minutes. Add the spinach and cook, stirring constantly, until the mixture is dry, about 1 minute. Stir in the basil, and add salt and pepper to taste. Transfer the filling to a bowl and let it cool to room temperature.

Line a large baking sheet with parchment. Have a small bowl of water, a pastry brush, and a fork handy.

Place a wonton wrapper on your work surface and brush ½ inch around the edges with water. Place a heaping teaspoon of filling in the middle of the wrapper. Fold the wrapper in half, sealing the edges by pressing them together with the tines of the fork. Place the filled wontons on the prepared baking sheet. Repeat until all the filling is used. The filled wontons can be covered with plastic wrap and refrigerated for up to 2 days.

To cook the ravioli: Bring 4 quarts salted water to a boil in a large, wide pot such as a Dutch oven. Lower the heat to a simmer (do not let water boil again) and add half of the ravioli. They should not be crowded. Cook until the wontons look translucent around the edges, about 3 minutes. Use a slotted spoon to remove the wontons from the pot, and shake off any excess water. Transfer the wontons to individual serving bowls and keep warm. Repeat the process, cooking the remaining wontons. Top each serving with a spoonful of tomato sauce, and serve immediately.

Southwest Wontons

Make this roasted corn, black bean, and red pepper filling in the middle of summer and top the ravioli with Fire-Roasted Tomato Sauce. The colorful mixture is a snap to make if you use roasted peppers from a jar.

SERVES 6 TO 8

3 ears fresh corn
2 tablespoons extra-virgin olive oil
2 garlic cloves, minced
One 15-ounce can black turtle beans, rinsed and drained,
    or **1 1/2 cups cooked beans**
1/2 teaspoon chile powder, preferably chipotle
Salt
1/2 cup vegetable broth
1/2 cup finely diced roasted red pepper
1 teaspoon fresh lime juice
1/4 cup chopped fresh cilantro, plus more for garnish
1 1/2 pounds wonton wrappers
2 3/4 cups Fire-Roasted Tomato Sauce (page 169), made without basil

Husk the corn and remove the kernels. Heat a heavy-bottomed skillet (cast iron is perfect) over medium heat. Add the corn kernels in one layer (you will have to do this in two batches) and dry-roast, shaking the pan from time to time, until the kernels are golden, softened, and cooked through, about 3 minutes. Transfer the corn to a bowl and repeat with the remaining kernels. Set aside.

Combine the olive oil and garlic in a medium skillet and cook over medium heat just until the garlic starts to color, about 1 minute. Add the beans, chile powder, 1/2 teaspoon salt, and vegetable broth. Cook the beans, lightly mashing them with a potato masher, until they are thickened, about 3 minutes. Add the reserved corn and the roasted red pepper. Cook, lightly mashing the ingredients, until the liquid is absorbed, about 1 minute. Add the lime juice and add salt if needed. Stir in the cilantro. Transfer the filling to a bowl and allow it to cool to room temperature.

Line a large baking sheet with parchment. Have a small bowl of water, a pastry brush, and a fork handy.

Place a wrapper on your work surface and brush 1/2 inch around the edges with water. Place a heaping teaspoon of filling in the middle of the wrapper. Fold the wrapper in half, sealing the edges by pressing them together with the tines of the fork. Repeat until all the filling is used. The ravioli can be covered with plastic and refrigerated for up to 2 days.

To cook the ravioli: Bring 4 quarts salted water to a boil in a large, wide pot such as a Dutch oven. Lower the heat to a simmer (do not let water boil again) and add half of the wontons. They should not be crowded. Cook until the wontons look translucent around the edges, 3 to 4 minutes. Use a slotted spoon to remove the ravioli from the pot, and shake off any excess water. Transfer the ravioli to individual serving bowls and keep warm. Repeat the process, cooking the remaining ravioli. Top each serving with a spoonful of tomato sauce, and serve immediately, garnishing each bowl with chopped cilantro.

Porcini Broth

This potent mushroom broth is a perfect alternative to richer butter sauces. Serve it with Pumpkin-Pecan Wontons (page 150), Valentine Wontons (page 152), and Crispy Thai Wontons (page 34) (for the Thai wontons, stir a teaspoon of grated lime zest into the broth at the end).

MAKES 2½ CUPS

1 cup dried porcini mushrooms

6 cups hot water

2 tablespoons extra-virgin olive oil

1 pound button mushrooms, quartered (about 5 cups)

Salt and freshly ground black pepper to taste

½ cup Marsala or Madeira

2 shallots, sliced (½ cup)

2 garlic cloves, cut in half

¼ cup chopped fresh parsley

1 tablespoon shoyu

One 2-inch piece fresh ginger, cut into 5 rounds

Place the porcinis in a medium bowl, cover with the hot water, and soak until softened, about 20 minutes. Use a fork to remove the mushrooms from the liquid, and reserve the mushrooms and the soaking liquid separately.

Meanwhile, warm the olive oil in a large skillet over medium heat. Add the button mushrooms, sprinkle with salt and black pepper, and cook, stirring often, until the mushrooms are deep brown and have caramelized, 15 to 20 minutes. Add the wine and scrape up any brown bits from the bottom of the pan. Simmer until the wine has become syrupy, about 2 minutes.

Add the porcinis to the skillet and slowly pour in the reserved soaking liquid, stopping when you reach grit at the bottom of the bowl. Add the shallots, garlic, parsley, shoyu, and ginger. Bring the mixture to a boil and cook over medium heat until the liquid has reduced to 2½ cups, about 25 minutes.

Strain the broth through a fine-mesh strainer, pressing the solids against the sides to squeeze out as much liquid as possible. Discard the solids. Season with additional salt and pepper to taste. The broth can be refrigerated for up to 3 days or frozen for up to a month.

Crêpes

I fell in love with crêpes on a trip to Paris. When I smelled a delicious aroma wafting out from one of the crêperies on the Left Bank, I would look on with hungry Parisians as the crêpe maker ladled batter onto a huge cast-iron griddle and then spread it over the large surface. After a minute or two, the crêpe maker deftly flipped the pancake with a long wooden spatula and slathered it with filling. Extra crêpes piled up on a side plate, ready to be warmed and filled to a customer's request. In Paris the batters and choices of fillings were essentially the same everywhere: buckwheat crêpes for the savory fillings and wheat crêpes for sweet. Back home, I decided to come up with a variety of whole-grain crêpes that had a full flavor and a delicate texture. I wanted the batter to be versatile enough to satisfy different eating habits, including dairy-free with eggs, and vegan. I use coconut milk for dairy-free crêpes and soy milk for the vegan version. Coconut milk leaves no discernible flavor, yet provides the body and creaminess needed to hold the crêpe together. In the vegan alternative, full-fat soy milk, plus a couple of tablespoons of arrowroot, helps to bind the batter. Make the crêpe batter in a blender; it won't get smooth enough if you whisk it by hand. The blender action also helps to develop the gluten, which is desirable in a crêpe, again to help bind it. The batter needs to sit for at least 30 minutes so that the flour can be completely absorbed by the liquid. The consistency of the batter should be about that of heavy cream. Different flours absorb different amounts of liquid; you can always add a little more liquid if the batter needs it. The buckwheat crêpe typically needs a little extra liquid. Although there are long-handled pans designed especially for making crêpes, a 10-inch nonstick skillet works just as well, if not better. The diameter at the bottom of the pan is 7 inches, an ideal crêpe size, and the nonstick surface means fewer torn pancakes. The key to a good crêpe is having your pan at the right temperature. You will quickly discover the right heat: too high and the crêpes will burn, too low and they will take too long to cook, resulting in a crêpe that never browns. If your pan gets too hot between crêpes—if the pan is smoking—remove it from the heat and set it aside for a moment or two. ◎ The basic procedure for making crêpes is simple: Heat the skillet over medium-high heat. Moisten a paper towel with a little oil, and rub it over the surface—this browns the crêpe nicely. With a ladle or a measuring cup, pour the batter into the skillet (¼ cup for a 10-inch skillet). Immediately lift the skillet and tilt it in all directions so that the batter covers the entire bottom. You have to work fast to spread the batter. If there are a few holes quickly add a little batter to fill them in. ◎ The crêpe is ready to be turned when the top is completely dry and the edges are beginning to brown, about 1 minute. It is important to cook crêpes to this point; otherwise they may break when you flip them. (The vegan crêpes begin to bubble when they are ready to be flipped.) Lift a side to ensure that the crêpe is nicely browned. A pancake turner is great for turning crêpes, or you can use your fingers if you're careful. Cook the crêpe on the second side for about 10 seconds, until it is lightly flecked with brown. Repeat with the remaining crêpes, stacking them on a plate as you go. ◎ The best-looking side of the crêpe, known as the face side, is generally the side that was cooked first and is most evenly browned. This side should face out when the crêpes are filled. ◎ Crêpes are great as a tasty snack, a casual supper, or an elegant starter.

Storing Crêpes

If you are serving the crêpes immediately, stack them and keep them covered with foil in a 200°F oven. ◎ Crêpes are also handy to have on hand in your refrigerator or freezer: Store them, covered, for up to 3 days in the refrigerator. To reheat, cover them with foil and heat in a preheated 325°F oven for 10 to 15 minutes. ◎ Store crêpes, covered in plastic wrap, for up to 2 months in the freezer. It's a good idea to bundle them in amounts you wish to serve. If you want to be able to peel off just one crêpe at a time, layer parchment paper between the crêpes. You can thaw the crêpes in the refrigerator or at room temperature; they take only about 15 minutes to defrost. Do not try to separate them while frozen. Remove the plastic, wrap them in foil, and heat in a preheated 325°F oven for 10 to 15 minutes. Once warmed, they separate easily.

Whole-Grain Crêpes

MAKES 10 TO 12 CRÊPES

Cornmeal Crêpes

$3/4$ cup milk or coconut milk

$3/4$ cup water

2 eggs

$1/2$ cup cornmeal

$1/2$ cup unbleached white flour

$1/2$ teaspoon salt

2 tablespoons melted butter or extra-virgin olive oil

$1/4$ cup chile powder

2 tablespoons finely chopped scallions, white and green parts

Rice Crêpes

$3/4$ cup milk or coconut milk

$3/4$ cup water

2 eggs

$1/2$ cup whole-wheat pastry flour

$1/2$ cup rice flour

$1/2$ teaspoon salt

2 tablespoons toasted sesame oil

Pinch of cayenne pepper

2 tablespoons finely chopped scallions, white and green parts

Buckwheat Crêpes

$3/4$ cup milk or coconut milk

$3/4$ cup water

2 eggs

$1/2$ cup buckwheat flour

$1/2$ cup unbleached white flour

$1/2$ teaspoon salt

2 tablespoons melted butter or extra-virgin olive oil

(CONTINUED NEXT PAGE)

1 cup cooked wild or other dark rice, optional
¼ cup finely chopped scallions, white and green parts

Coconut oil, ghee, canola oil, or sesame oil, for the skillet

Combine the milk, water, eggs, flours (including cornmeal), salt, and butter or oil in a blender and blend until smooth. Let the batter rest for 30 minutes; there is no need to refrigerate it. Then test the consistency: it should have the consistency of heavy cream and should coat your finger. If necessary, add a couple of tablespoons of water to thin the batter.

Stir in the chile powder and scallions for the cornmeal crêpes, the cayenne and scallions for the rice crêpes, and the scallions and rice (if using) for the buckwheat crêpes.

Lightly oil a 10- to 12-inch nonstick skillet, using a paper towel. Warm the skillet over medium-high heat. Pour ¼ cup batter into the skillet, tipping it in a circular motion so that the batter covers the entire surface. Cook until the crêpe bubbles and turns golden around the edges, about 45 seconds. Loosen the edges with a spatula, and then flip it over with the spatula or with your fingers. Cook for 5 to 10 seconds on the second side. Transfer the crêpe to a plate and cover it with a kitchen towel. Continue to cook the crêpes over medium-high heat, lightly oiling the skillet between crêpes, until all the batter is used. If at any time the batter feels as if it has thickened, add a tablespoon or so of water to thin it out.

Vegan version

Omit the eggs and add 2 tablespoons arrowroot. Use 2 cups of original-flavor full-fat soy milk in place of the water and coconut milk.

Cornmeal Crêpes with Refried Black Beans

Serve refried black beans with Fish Tacos (page 258) or tucked into cornmeal crêpes and topped with Designer Guacamole and Red and Yellow Tomato Salsa, and sprinkled with *queso fresco*. To cook the beans from scratch, start with 1½ cups dry beans and reserve 1 cup of the bean cooking liquid for the recipe.

SERVES 4 TO 6

Refried Black Beans

> **2 tablespoons extra-virgin olive oil**
> **2 onions, cut into small dice (2 cups)**
> **3 garlic cloves, minced**
> **1 jalapeño pepper, seeded and minced**
> **2 teaspoons chile powder, preferably chipotle**
> **1 teaspoon ground cumin**
> **Two 15-ounce cans black turtle beans, drained and rinsed, *or* 3 cups cooked beans**
> **1 cup vegetable broth or bean cooking liquid**
> **Salt**
> **2 tablespoons fresh lime juice**
>
> **8 Cornmeal Crêpes (page 161)**
> **½ cup Designer Guacamole (page 176)**
> **1 recipe Red and Yellow Tomato Salsa (page 179)**

Warm the oil in a medium skillet over medium-low heat, and add the onions, garlic, and jalapeño. Sauté until the onions are softened, 7 to 10 minutes. Add the chile powder and cumin, and sauté until fragrant, another minute or so.

Raise the heat to medium and add 1 cup of the beans, ⅓ cup of the broth, and 1¼ teaspoons salt. Using a potato masher or the back of a spoon, mash the beans into the liquid. Continue cooking until the liquid is absorbed, about 3 minutes. Add 1 more cup of the beans and ⅓ cup of the broth, and mash and cook again, stirring. Repeat one more time, mashing and cooking and stirring, until all of the liquid has been absorbed and the beans hold together in the pan without sticking to it. (This process will take 8 to 10 minutes.) Stir in the lime juice and add salt to taste.

Place 1 crêpe, good side down, on a plate. Spoon ⅓ cup of the refried beans in the center. Fold up all four edges toward the center, forming a square with an open center. Repeat with the remaining crêpes and filling. Dollop each crêpe with a tablespoon of guacamole and some salsa, and serve.

Rice Crêpes with Vegetable Stir-fry

This crêpe is given an Asian twist with a vegetable stir-fry filling. It would be a lovely starter for any of the Asian-inspired dishes, such as the Seared Sesame-Crusted Tuna (page 252) or Broiled Miso Black Cod (page 254). Or try these crêpes with Teriyaki Tofu (page 221) and Sea Vegetable Braise (page 181).

SERVES 4

Vegetable Stir-fry

2 tablespoons sesame oil

1/4 pound fresh shiitake mushrooms, stems removed, caps
    thinly sliced (2 cups)

2 tablespoons minced fresh ginger

2 tablespoons shoyu

5 cups shredded Napa cabbage

2 carrots, cut into matchsticks (1 cup)

1/4 pound snow peas, cut into 2-inch-long thin diagonal slices (1 cup)

Salt and freshly ground black pepper

8 Rice Crêpes (page 161)

Set a large skillet over high heat. Add the sesame oil and immediately add the shiitakes and ginger. Stir-fry for 1 minute. Add the shoyu and cook for another minute or two, until the shiitakes are cooked. Add the cabbage and carrots, and stir-fry until the cabbage is tender, about 2 minutes. Stir in the snow peas and cook for 1 minute. Season with salt and pepper to taste, and remove the pan from the heat.

Place 1 crêpe, good side down, on a plate. Spoon 1/3 cup of the vegetable filling in the center. Fold the two sides in, then roll the crêpe up like an egg roll. Repeat with the remaining crêpes and filling. Serve immediately.

Buckwheat Crêpes with Mediterranean Braise

This filling is like a simple ratatouille without the eggplant. The tapenade adds a taste explosion.

SERVES 4

Mediterranean Braise

> 2 tablespoons extra-virgin olive oil
> 2 onions, cut into thin slices (2 cups)
> 1 yellow bell pepper, seeded and cut into 1-inch squares
> 1 red bell pepper, seeded and cut into 1-inch squares
> 3 medium (about 1 pound) zucchini, cut into $\frac{1}{2}$-inch diagonal slices
> Salt
> 3 cloves garlic, minced
> One 14-ounce can diced tomatoes, with juice
> Freshly ground black pepper
> $\frac{1}{2}$ cup fresh basil, cut into chiffonade
>
> 8 Buckwheat Crêpes (page 161)
> $\frac{1}{2}$ cup Herbed Olive Tapenade (page 170)

Warm the olive oil in a large skillet over medium-high heat. Add the onions, peppers, and zucchini, and sauté, turning occasionally, until the zucchini is golden, about 20 minutes. Add a sprinkling of salt. Add the garlic and tomatoes, and scrape up any brown bits on the bottom of the pan. Simmer, uncovered, until most of the tomato liquid has evaporated, about 10 minutes. Sprinkle with black pepper, and stir in the basil. Taste, and add more salt if necessary. Remove from the heat.

Place 1 crêpe face down on a plate. Place a spoonful of filling in a line down the center of the crêpe. Fold over one side and then the other. (The filling should show on each end.) Repeat with the remaining crêpes and filling. Dollop each crêpe with a spoonful of tapenade, and serve immediately.

Buckwheat Crêpes with Roasted Asparagus

Roasted asparagus make a delectable side dish, but they take on a new dimension when wrapped in a folded crêpe.

SERVES 4

Roasted asparagus

**2 pounds asparagus, preferably thick, 1$\frac{1}{2}$ inches of
the hard ends removed
2 tablespoons extra-virgin olive oil
Salt and freshly ground black pepper**

**8 Buckwheat Crêpes (page 161)
$\frac{1}{2}$ cup Herbed Olive Tapenade (page 170)**

Preheat the oven to 400°F.

In a large bowl, lightly toss the asparagus with the oil. Sprinkle with salt and black pepper.

Spread the asparagus on a parchment-covered baking sheet, and roast until the spears are tender and beginning to brown, about 20 minutes, depending on their size.

Place a crêpe face down on a plate, and fold the bottom up to meet the top. Place one fourth of the asparagus spears in the center, and wrap the crêpe around them so that the tops and bottoms of the asparagus are showing. Repeat with the remaining crêpes and asparagus. Spoon a tablespoon of tapenade over each folded crêpe, and serve immediately.

NOTE: *For extra flavor, add 1 tablespoon chopped fresh tarragon or chives to the crêpe batter.*

Sauces and Condiments

Fire-Roasted Tomato Sauce

Herbed Olive Tapenade

Basil Pesto

Thai Double Dynamite

    Spinach-Basil Sauce

    Yellow Pepper–Coconut Milk Sauce

Roasted Red Pepper Sauce

Tomatillo Salsa

Designer Guacamole

Cranberry-Chestnut Relish

Grilled Pineapple–Mango Salsa

Red and Yellow Tomato Salsa

Cucumber, Peanut, and Yogurt Raita

Sea Vegetable Braise

Cranberry-Lime Chutney

Crispy Rice Sticks

Here's an ensemble of sauces, condiments, and flavor enhancers, each one simple and delicious. The Fire-Roasted Tomato Sauce, Basil Pesto, Herbed Olive Tapenade, and Roasted Red Pepper Sauce are fundamentals. They are tasty with pizzas, pastas, and polentas. ◎ But don't stop there. The Yellow Pepper–Coconut Milk Sauce is a delicious basic sauce for Southeast Asian–style dishes. The Grilled Pineapple–Mango Salsa can top Thai dishes and grilled foods, and the Cucumber, Peanut, and Yogurt Raita is a cooling accompaniment to Indian dishes. The Sea Vegetable Braise is a mineral-packed accompaniment to Asian dishes, and the cranberry chutney and relish are both suited for autumn and winter holiday festivities as well as everyday fare. The Tomatillo Salsa and the Designer Guacamole are essential complements to a couple of dishes in this book, but they can embellish any Latin-inspired dish as well. ◎ There is no need to limit these sauces and condiments to specific recipes in this book. Keep a few stashed in your refrigerator, and you can individualize even the simplest dish. It is a breeze to orchestrate the rest of the meal if you have a few luscious embellishments readily available. The sauces and condiments are wonderful pick-me-ups for bean, grain, fish, and chicken dishes, and they can all turn ordinary fare into hedonistic delights.

Fire-Roasted Tomato Sauce

Perhaps the most versatile recipe in this book, this humble sauce takes just minutes to put together. The combination of ingredients makes a great basic tomato sauce, and using fire-roasted tomatoes sends it over the top. Make it with crushed tomatoes for a pizza sauce, and with diced tomatoes for pasta and polenta, where you might want a little more texture. Either way, don't skimp on the oil, the secret for transforming canned tomatoes into a tasty sauce.

MAKES 1¼ CUPS

One 28-ounce can crushed or diced tomatoes,
    preferably fire-roasted
3 tablespoons extra-virgin olive oil
2 garlic cloves, minced
1 teaspoon dried basil
Salt
Freshly ground black pepper

Combine the tomatoes, olive oil, garlic, basil, and ½ teaspoon salt in a medium saucepan. Bring to a boil, reduce the heat, and simmer, partially covered, until the sauce has thickened considerably, about 25 minutes. (If the sauce remains watery, remove the cover, raise the heat, and simmer briskly for several minutes.) Stir in a sprinkling of black pepper. Taste, and add more salt if necessary. The sauce keeps, covered and refrigerated, for up to a week.

Herbed Olive Tapenade

What a treat for olive lovers! Like the pesto and the tomato sauce, this tapenade is fabulous on pizza. Try it in Roasted New Potato Cups (page 29) or over Easy Polenta (page 192).

MAKES 1 CUP

1 cup olives, preferably kalamata, pitted
1 garlic clove
2 tablespoons extra-virgin olive oil
1 tablespoon fresh lemon juice
Pinch of salt
1 cup roughly chopped fresh parsley, chives, and basil, mixed in fairly
   equal portions
1/2 teaspoon grated lemon zest

Combine the olives, garlic, olive oil, lemon juice, salt, herbs, and zest in a food processor and process until smooth, scraping down the sides as necessary.

Store, covered and refrigerated, for up to 3 weeks.

NOTES: *The easy way to pit an olive is to press down on the olive with your thumb or the flat side of a chef's knife. The olive will split, making it easy to remove the pit.*
   Thinly sliced scallion greens can be substituted for the chives.

Basil Pesto

Sometimes you want a pesto with cheese, and sometimes you want a lighter version like this one, where light miso lends depth of flavor. Try it on pizza—with or in place of the tomato sauce—and layer it in Vegetable Quesadillas (page 32) or thin it out with a little of the cooking liquid and serve it with pasta.

MAKES 1½ CUPS

3/4 cup pine nuts
2 cups firmly packed fresh basil
1 garlic clove
2 tablespoons fresh lemon juice
1/3 cup extra-virgin olive oil
1 teaspoon mellow barley miso or other light miso
1/2 teaspoon salt
1/4 teaspoon freshly ground black pepper

Preheat the oven to 350°F.

Spread the pine nuts out on a baking sheet and toast them in the oven until lightly golden, 6 to 7 minutes. Transfer the nuts to a food processor, and add the basil, garlic, lemon juice, olive oil, miso, salt, and pepper. Process until smooth, scraping down the sides as necessary.

Store the pesto, covered and refrigerated, for up to 4 days. You can also freeze it in ice cube trays, then stack the cubes in a freezer bag and freeze for up to a month. The pesto cubes defrost in about 15 minutes.

Thai Double Dynamite

Here are two gorgeous sauces to invigorate a meal: a spinach-basil sauce and a yellow pepper–coconut milk sauce. The colors are stunning together and the flavors are complementary, but they can also stand alone. For an eye-popping presentation serve the sauces together with grilled salmon or Baked Thai Tempeh Triangles (page 228), topped with Crispy Rice Sticks (page 182).

Spinach-Basil Sauce (MAKES 3 CUPS)

To preserve the lively green color of this sauce, heat only the amount you are going to use. If you can't find galangal or Thai chiles, ginger and serrano chiles are delicious substitutes.

> 1 pound fresh spinach, stemmed and washed
> 1$\frac{1}{2}$ teaspoons whole cumin seeds
> 1$\frac{1}{2}$ teaspoons whole coriander seeds
> 1$\frac{1}{2}$ cups fresh basil
> Salt
> $\frac{3}{4}$ cup water
> $\frac{1}{2}$ cup unsweetened coconut milk
> $\frac{1}{4}$ cup canola oil
> 3 tablespoons fresh lime juice
> 2 Thai bird chiles *or* 1 serrano chile, stemmed and finely chopped
> 1 tablespoon chopped galangal or chopped fresh ginger
> 1 tablespoon chopped lemongrass

Place the spinach in a medium skillet. Cover, and cook over medium heat, stirring frequently or tossing with tongs to push the uncooked leaves to the bottom of the skillet, just until the leaves have wilted, about 5 minutes. (You don't have to add water to the pot; the water clinging to the wet leaves is enough to cook them.) Remove the spinach from the skillet and set it aside in a strainer to drain.

Dry-toast the cumin and coriander seeds in a medium skillet over medium heat until fragrant, 2 minutes. Transfer the toasted seeds to a blender and grind until powdered.

Add the spinach, basil, $\frac{3}{4}$ teaspoon salt, the water, coconut milk, oil, lime juice, chiles, galangal, and lemongrass to the blender and blend until smooth. Taste, and add more salt if necessary. Place only the amount you are going to serve in a small saucepan, and heat it gently.

Refrigerate, covered, for up to 4 days.

NOTES: ■ *Cross-sections (little rings) of Thai bird chiles make a beautiful garnish.* ■ *Galangal looks a lot like ginger but has a distinctive flavor. It is often found frozen in Asian grocery stores. It can be chopped or puréed unpeeled because its skin is so thin.* ■ *I usually blend spices in a spice grinder. However, since the rest of the sauce is going to be blended, giving the spices a head start in the blender is more efficient.*

Yellow Pepper–Coconut Milk Sauce (MAKES 3½ CUPS)

This mellow sauce comes alive when heated with the chiles and all the flavors meld together.

> **2 tablespoons coconut oil**
> **3 shallots, minced (³⁄4 cup)**
> **3 yellow bell peppers, seeded and cut into 1-inch cubes**
> **Salt**
> **One 14-ounce can unsweetened coconut milk**
> **2 tablespoons fresh lime juice**
> **1 Thai bird chile, minced, *or* 1⁄2 serrano chile, seeded and minced**

Warm the coconut oil in a medium skillet over medium-low heat. Add the shallots and sauté until translucent, about 4 minutes. Then add the peppers and ³⁄4 teaspoon salt, and sauté until the peppers are softened, about 10 minutes. Transfer the peppers and shallots to a blender, add the coconut milk, and blend until smooth. Stir in the lime juice.

Pour the sauce into a medium saucepan, and heat just until warm. Stir in the minced chiles. Remove the pan from the heat and let the sauce sit for a few minutes to allow the flavors to marry. Then taste, and add more salt if necessary.

The sauce keeps covered and refrigerated, for up to 1 week.

NOTE: *If you are making the sauce in advance, add the chiles a few hours before serving. Chiles become more potent the longer they sit in the sauce.*

Roasted Red Pepper Sauce

This red pepper sauce is a vital addition to your cooking repertoire. It's great over vegetables, delicious with poached salmon, and perfect swirled into soups. Serve heated or at room temperature.

MAKES 2 CUPS (4 SERVINGS)

Pulp from 2 heads roasted garlic (see page 19)
1/4 cup extra-virgin olive oil
4 red bell peppers, roasted (see page 19),
   ***or* 2 cups bottled roasted red peppers, drained**
2 teaspoons red wine vinegar
3/4 teaspoon salt
Freshly ground black pepper
Cayenne pepper

Place the garlic, olive oil, peppers, vinegar, salt, black pepper to taste, and a pinch of cayenne in a blender and blend until smooth. Taste, and add more salt if necessary. If you are serving the sauce heated, pour it into a small saucepan and heat just until warm.

The sauce will keep, covered and refrigerated, for up to 5 days.

Tomatillo Salsa

This tart Mexican condiment is lovely with Bean and Cheese *Pupusas* (page 208). Try it also over Easy Polenta (page 192), Cornmeal Crêpes with Refried Black Beans (page 163), and Barbecue Spice–Rubbed Tofu or Chicken (pages 225 and 265).

MAKES ¾ CUP

½ pound (10 medium) tomatillos
1 serrano chile
¼ cup chopped fresh cilantro
1 tablespoon fresh lime juice
½ avocado
¾ teaspoon salt

Remove the stems and husks from the tomatillos and rinse them. Place the tomatillos and the chile in a heavy-bottomed skillet (such as cast iron), and place it over medium heat. Lightly blister the tomatillos to soften them, turning them frequently. You will hear popping sounds as they blister. Or you can blister the tomatillos in a broiler: Place them on a broiler pan and set it 6 inches from the heat source. Broil the tomatillos, turning them frequently to soften all sides.

Remove the tomatillos from the heat, cut off any black spots, and place them in a blender. Slice the chile, discarding the seeds and stem. Add the chile to the blender along with the cilantro, lime juice, avocado, and salt. Blend until smooth. Serve at room temperature or gently heated. Store, covered and refrigerated, for up to 5 days.

NOTE: *Tomatillos last for several weeks in the refrigerator. Although they can be used raw in a salsa, they are usually simmered or dry-roasted.*

Designer Guacamole

Although this extra-green "designer" version of guacamole is good on just about any Mexican dish, it's a must with Fish Tacos (page 258) and Cornmeal Crêpes with Refried Black Beans (page 163). Make it creamy by whirling it in the food processor or extra-chunky by roughly chopping the chiles, scallions, and cilantro.

MAKES 2 CUPS (4 SERVINGS)

2 ripe avocados, preferably Hass,
pitted and peeled
3 tablespoons fresh lime juice
2 to 3 serrano or jalapeño chiles, stemmed,
seeded, and minced
1/2 cup thinly sliced scallions, white and green parts
(from 3 to 4 scallions)
Salt
1 cup chopped fresh cilantro

Mash the avocados with the lime juice in a medium bowl. Stir in the chiles, scallions, ¾ teaspoon salt, and the cilantro. Taste, and add more salt if necessary. Store, covered and refrigerated, for up to 2 days.

Cranberry-Chestnut Relish

Chestnuts give this relish its creamy richness. Serve it alongside the turkey at your Thanksgiving feast, or try it with Thanksgiving Stuffing Timbales (page 212). For a complete Thanksgiving feast, try the whole menu on page 333.

MAKES 2½ CUPS (6 SERVINGS)

½ cup port
½ cup plus 2 tablespoons maple syrup
1 cup peeled chestnuts (bottled or vacuum-packed)
3 cups fresh cranberries
½ cup dried cranberries
½ cup pecans, toasted and chopped
2 tablespoons chopped fresh mint, optional

Combine the port, maple syrup, and chestnuts in a blender, and blend until smooth. Transfer the mixture to a small saucepan, and add the fresh and dried cranberries. Cover, and bring to a boil over medium heat. Keep an eye on the relish, especially in the beginning, to make sure it does not boil over. Uncover, lower the heat, and cook at a rapid simmer, stirring occasionally, until the cranberries have burst and the mixture has thickened, 15 to 20 minutes.

Remove the relish from the heat and stir in the pecans. Transfer it to a bowl and refrigerate until cool. Serve sprinkled with the mint. This keeps, covered and refrigerated, for up to a week.

Grilled Pineapple–Mango Salsa

Serve this tropical delight with Salmon Medallions with Lime-Mustard Teriyaki (page 248) or with the whole Southeast Asian menu on page 333. You can use an outdoor grill or a stovetap grill pan to cook the pineapple (grilling concentrates the flavor). Alternatively, you can heat a tablespoon of olive or coconut oil in a skillet and sear the strips.

MAKES 3 TO 4 CUPS (8 TO 10 SERVINGS)

1/2 pineapple, cut into 1/2-inch-thick lengthwise slabs
1 mango, peeled and cut into small dice
1 tablespoon fresh lime juice
2 tablespoons chopped fresh cilantro
2 teaspoons minced fresh ginger
1/4 teaspoon cayenne pepper
Salt

Preheat a grill or indoor grill pan until hot. Grill the pineapple slabs (without oil) until marked with grill marks, 3 to 5 minutes per side. Allow to cool, and then cut the slabs into 1/2-inch dice.

Place the pineapple chunks in a medium bowl, and add the mango, lime juice, cilantro, ginger, cayenne, and 1/2 teaspoon salt. Let the mixture stand for about 20 minutes at room temperature to allow the flavors to marry. Then taste, and add more salt if necessary. Store, covered and refrigerated, for up to 4 days.

NOTE: *To cut a pineapple for the grill: Cut off the top and bottom of the pineapple, exposing the flesh. Stand the pineapple upright, and use your knife to cut down the side of the pineapple in the same way you cut a piece of citrus. Quarter the pineapple, and cut away the fibrous core. Cut each quarter into slabs.*

Red and Yellow Tomato Salsa

This basic salsa is elevated from ordinary to distinguished when two different types of tomatoes are used. Serve it with Refried Black Beans (page 163) or as a topping on Bean and Cheese *Pupusas* (page 208). It's fun to make this salsa with a variety of heirloom tomatoes from a farmer's market.

MAKES 1½ CUPS (4 SERVINGS)

2 medium (¾ pound) tomatoes, preferably 1 yellow and 1 red, seeded and cut into small dice
1 garlic clove, minced
1 jalapeño pepper, stemmed, seeded, and minced
¼ cup scallions, white and green parts, thinly sliced on the diagonal
¼ cup chopped fresh cilantro
¼ cup chopped red onion (small dice)
2 tablespoons fresh lime juice
Salt

Combine the tomatoes, garlic, jalapeño, scallions, cilantro, red onions, and lime juice in a medium bowl and stir together. Sprinkle with salt to taste, and let the salsa sit for at least 15 minutes at room temperature to allow the flavors to marry. Taste, and add more salt if necessary. Store, covered and refrigerated, for up to 3 days.

Cucumber, Peanut, and Yogurt Raita

This is a great cooling accompaniment for hot and spicy dishes, and the peanuts give it a satisfying crunch. Serve it, for example, with Indian-Spiced Cauliflower, Chickpeas, Potatoes, and Kale (page 232) or with any of the other Indian dishes on page 333.

MAKES 4 CUPS (6 SERVINGS)

2 cups plain full-fat yogurt, preferably organic
1 teaspoon whole cumin seeds
3 cucumbers
2 serrano chiles, stemmed, seeded, and finely chopped
2 tablespoons finely chopped fresh cilantro or mint
Salt
1 to 2 tablespoons fresh lemon juice
½ cup dry-roasted peanuts, chopped into small pieces

Place a cheesecloth-lined strainer over a bowl, pour the yogurt into the strainer, and let sit for at least 30 minutes to drain out the liquid. Transfer the thickened yogurt to a medium bowl.

Dry-toast the cumin seeds in a small heavy-bottomed skillet, stirring frequently, until fragrant, about 2 minutes. Do not allow them to darken too much. Transfer the seeds to a spice grinder or a mortar and pestle, and grind to a powder. Stir the ground cumin into the yogurt.

Peel the cucumbers, cut them in half lengthwise, and seed them. Slice them into thin half-rounds and add them to the yogurt.

Stir in the chiles, cilantro, ½ teaspoon salt, and 1 tablespoon lemon juice. Taste for seasoning, adding more lemon juice or salt as needed. Set aside for about 30 minutes at room temperature to allow the flavors to marry.

Just before serving, stir in ¼ cup of the peanuts. Sprinkle the remaining peanuts on top.

Store, covered and refrigerated, for up to 3 days.

Sea Vegetable Braise

This is a delightful way to eat your sea vegetables—the gingery broth is assertive enough to tame the hijiki and arame. The braise is delicious atop Rice Crêpes with Vegetable Stir-fry (page 164), Kabocha Squash Soup with Gingery Adzuki Beans (page 54), Seared Sesame-Crusted Tuna (page 252), Tofu and Vegetable Stir-fry (page 224), and Broiled Miso Black Cod (page 254).

MAKES 1½ CUPS (6 SERVINGS)

½ cup (½ ounce) dry hijiki
½ cup (½ ounce) dry arame
1 tablespoon oil, preferably sesame or coconut oil
1 cup thinly sliced onions
2 tablespoons shoyu
¼ cup mirin
2 tablespoons rice syrup
1 tablespoon grated fresh ginger
Salt
1 tablespoon brown rice vinegar
¼ cup thinly sliced scallions (white and green parts)

Place the hijiki and arame in separate bowls. Cover with cold water by at least 2 inches, and soak for at least 20 minutes, or until soft.

Drain the sea vegetables. If the hijiki is long-stranded, roughly chop it.

Warm the oil in a medium skillet over medium-low heat. Add the onions and cook until they are softened, about 10 minutes. Then add the arame and hijiki, and cook, stirring frequently, for 5 minutes.

Add the shoyu, mirin, rice syrup, ginger, and water to cover (about 2 cups). Raise the heat and bring the liquid to a boil. Then lower the heat and simmer rapidly, uncovered, until most of the liquid has evaporated and the flavors have melded, about 30 minutes.

Sprinkle a couple of pinches of salt over the mixture, and stir in the brown rice vinegar and scallions. Serve hot or at room temperature. This keeps, covered and refrigerated, for up to a week.

NOTE: *Hijiki and arame are loaded with minerals (often said to be one of the reasons that Japanese people have lustrous, shiny hair). They are an especially good mineral balance to soy foods.*

Cranberry-Lime Chutney

This chutney pairs well with Butterflied Barbecue Spice–Rubbed Chicken (page 265). Even though they're both tart, the lime juice and the cranberries complement each other beautifully.

MAKES 2 CUPS (6 SERVINGS)

3 cups fresh or frozen cranberries
3/4 cup plus 2 tablespoons maple syrup, plus more if necessary
1/2 teaspoon salt
1 serrano chile, stemmed, seeded, and minced
3 tablespoons fresh lime juice
6 tablespoons chopped fresh cilantro

Place the cranberries, maple syrup, salt, and chile in a small saucepan. Cover, and bring to a boil, making sure the mixture does not boil over. Then uncover and cook at a rapid simmer, stirring occasionally, until the cranberries have burst and the mixture has thickened, 15 to 20 minutes.

Stir in the lime juice and transfer the mixture to a medium bowl. Let it cool to room temperature. Then stir in the cilantro. Taste, and add an additional tablespoon or two of maple syrup if necessary.

Crispy Rice Sticks

These are as fun to make as they are to eat.

MAKES 4 CUPS

1/2 cup coconut or canola oil
2 ounces rice sticks (rice vermicelli)
Salt

Line a plate or baking sheet with paper towels, and set it aside.

Heat the oil in a medium skillet over medium-high heat. When the oil starts to shimmer, grab a small clump of rice stick strands and drop them into the skillet. Within a couple of seconds they will expand and puff. Using tongs, flip them over to crisp the other side. Transfer them to the paper-towel plate to drain, and sprinkle with salt. Repeat with the rest of the strands. You can make these up to 3 days ahead. Serve at room temperature. Store, covered, at room temperature.

Grains and Legumes

Asparagus, Leek, and Barley Risotto

Wild Mushroom and Farro Risotto

Easy Polenta

Quinoa-Grits Polenta

Quinoa Primavera

Dolma Pilaf

Forbidden Black Rice

Thai Jasmine Rice with Chinese Black Beans

Wild Rice with Porcini Mushrooms, Pecans, and
Dried Cranberries

Wild Rice and Spelt Berry Salad with Grapes and
Orange-Cumin Dressing

Cardamom and Coconut Basmati Rice

Moong Dhal

Tamarind Chickpeas

Spicy Baked Beans

Chickpeas with Charmoula Vinaigrette

In this chapter you'll find grain and legume dishes that serve as sides to round out a meal or make satisfying main courses. There are rice dishes featuring wild, black, basmati, and jasmine rice. Quinoa makes an appearance in a polenta, where it's combined with grits. The bean dishes range from American-style baked beans to chickpeas marinated in Moroccan spices. The flavors are global while the techniques are simple. ◉ Many types of grains can be cooked in a number of different styles. Use the exact amount of liquid to steam the grain and you have a fluffy pilaf; use substantially more, and you have a polenta or possibly even a risotto-style dish. The two whole-grain risottos—barley and farro—are baked in the oven rather than stirred at length in a saucepan, making them low-labor dishes. ◉ Inexpensive and versatile, beans and grains lend themselves to interesting flavors and textures. There are so many, it's like opening a box of crayons. The variety is fun and the possibilities are endless.

About Grains

Grains have sustained many cultures for thousands of years. Complex carbohydrates consisting of bran, germ, and endosperm, grains are a good source of fiber, minerals, and the B-complex vitamin. Store grains in a cool, dry place, preferably in sealed glass jars or tightly sealed plastic bags, and try to use them within 6 months of purchase. To make grains more digestible and to neutralize the phytic acid, soak them overnight before cooking and cook them with a small amount of salt. Chew grains well to allow your body to digest them. ◉ Except for the tiniest ones like teff, grains should be washed before cooking. Cover the grain with water in a large bowl. Stir the submerged grains with your hand, and then let the water settle for a moment. Any dust, bugs, or loose particles will float to the surface when the grains settle. Pour off the water, holding back the grains at the last moment with a strainer. Repeat until the runoff water is clear. ◉ Some grains benefit from being toasted before cooking; it enhances their taste, imparting a light nuttiness, and helps them to soften while they cook. To toast, simply warm the grains over medium-low heat in the pot you're going to cook them in. Stir them as they toast until any residual washing water has evaporated. (Or you can sauté the grains in a little oil. The oil coats the individual grains and helps to keep the cooked grains separate.) ◉ All the grains used in this book can be found in natural foods markets: most are also available at supermarkets and specialty stores. ◉ **Rice** can be white or brown, and long grain, medium grain, or short grain. While white rice is stripped of its hull, bran, and germ, thus containing fewer nutrients, sometimes its light texture is appropriate in the context of the meal. White and brown basmati, with their nutty aroma and fluffy texture, double in length when cooked. Thai jasmine rice is another white rice with a distinct, fragrant bouquet. Red Bhutan rice is like a short-grain brown rice, with a deep reddish brown color and a sweet nutty taste. Wild rice is not technically a rice; it is the seed of an aquatic grass found mostly around lakes, although now it is cultivated. It splits open and becomes fluffy when cooked. Wild rice is high in protein, and its wild flavor and aroma make it a favorite gourmet food. Forbidden black rice was once reserved for the emperors of China. It has a naturally sweet taste that is enhanced with a low-key sweetener such as rice syrup. ◉ **Quinoa**, which is not actually a true cereal grain but is used like one, has the highest protein content of any grain. It is a small round grain, about the size of a sesame seed. Light and easily digested, it must be washed well, not only to clean it but to remove the bitter saponin coating that grows on the outer surface of the grain. A fine-mesh strainer is helpful for rinsing quinoa, as the grains are very light and float elusively in water. I like to cook quinoa in combination with other grains—for example, with grits in a polenta. ◉ **Barley** comes in two forms, hulless (only the outer hull is removed) and pearled (the bran is polished off as well). Pearled barley (sometimes called "pearl" barley) has lost all its fiber and half its protein, fat, and minerals. The pearled barley found in natural foods stores has undergone fewer pearlings than the supermarket counterpart, and therefore is a better choice. It is often called "hulled," not to be confused with "hulless." Barley is fairly starchy, making it a natural thickener in soups and great for risotto. It is soothing to the digestive tract and the liver. ◉ **Spelt berries** come from an ancient red wheat that is mentioned in the Old Testament. Spelt has excellent flavor and can often be tolerated by people who are allergic to wheat. Both the whole berries and the flour are delicious. It is more readily soluble in water than wheat is, so it is possible to use 100 percent whole-grain spelt in pizza and pie crusts and breads without making the product overly heavy. The berry softens beautifully and gives great texture to the Wild Rice and Spelt Berry Salad. ◉ **Farro** is a spelt-like grain, well loved in Italy. It is now increasingly available here and makes a wonderful risotto. ◉ **Bulgur** is wheat kernels that have been steamed, dried, and cracked. With a nutty flavor, it comes in a number of different grinds. The coarse grain needs to cook only a short time, while the fine needs no cooking at all, just a soak in hot liquid.

About Beans

High in protein and fiber, beans are versatile, inexpensive, and delicious. They have been an important part of the diet in almost every traditional culture. ◉ Although I usually favor cooking dry beans from scratch, sometimes there simply isn't time. If you opt for canned beans, I highly recommend the organic variety, which are far superior in flavor and quality. Most 15-ounce cans contain 1½ cups cooked beans, equivalent to ¾ cup dried. ◉ **Cannellini beans**, also known as **white kidney beans**, have a creamy texture and an earthy taste, and are used often in Italian cooking. They are similar to Great Northern beans and are longer and plumper than navy beans. ◉ **Navy beans** are smaller than Great Northern beans but have a similar flavor; the two are usually interchangable in recipes. ◉ **Great Northern beans** are the standard bean used in baked bean recipes. ◉ **Lentils** are shaped like discs. In India there are more than fifty varieties. The most familiar ones in the United States are brown and green lentils. Lentils have an earthy flavor and they cook quickly, so they are always used dried. They tend to get a little mushy, although the tiny, elegant lentilles du Puys (French lentils) hold their shape very well. Red lentils cook quickly (in about 20 minutes), and easily turn to mush. For this reason, they are good in soups and sauces. **Moong dhal** is the hulled and split dried mung bean. The whole mung bean is dark green, but when split, the interior is golden yellow. Available in Indian markets, the split mung bean is the most widely used variety in Indian cooking. It is an easily digestible legume, often combined with spices such as asafetida to make it even more digestible. **Split peas** are split dried field peas, available in green or yellow. Their consistency becomes creamy when cooked, so they are perfect for soups and sauces. **Adzuki beans** are small reddish-brown beans with a white stripe along one edge and a sweet, almost nutty flavor. In China, adzuki beans are served on New Year's Eve to bring courage and good fortune in the coming year. **Chickpeas** are creamy, round, beige beans. Versatile, mild, and sweet-flavored, they are popular in many cuisines, especially in Middle Eastern and Mediterranean cooking. They are also ground to form chickpea flour. **Black beans** hold up well against the assertive, hot seasonings found in Mexican and Latin American food. Members of the kidney bean family, they can be substituted for pinto beans in any recipe. Black beans are sweet and hearty, and their deep color contrasts beautifully with other foods. **Pinto beans** have a beige to pink color with mottled splotches—thus the name *pinto*, or "painted." They turn solid pink when cooked. Pintos are synonymous with Southwestern cooking and are the most cultivated bean in the United States. The deep red **kidney bean** is named for its shape and is a member of the same family as pinto beans and anasazi beans. It is the most common bean used in chili. **Fermented black beans**, which are fermented black soybeans, are used in Chinese cooking. They have a distinctive flavor that most people know from Chinese black bean sauce. They need to be rinsed briefly to remove excess salt. Fermented black beans come in plastic bags and will keep indefinitely at room temperature.

Asparagus, Leek, and Barley Risotto

Barley makes for a surprisingly light risotto, perfect for spring. This baked version, with asparagus and peas, requires just a few minutes of actual labor and no stirring. Use semi-pearled barley, called "hulled" barley in natural foods stores, for the best texture, although the other varieties will do in a pinch.

SERVES 6 AS A SIDE DISH

1 tablespoon extra-virgin olive oil
2 cups thinly sliced leeks, white and light green parts
(from 2 medium leeks)
2 garlic cloves, minced
$\frac{1}{2}$ cup thinly sliced scallions, white and green parts
Salt
1 cup barley, hulled or semi-pearled, washed
$\frac{1}{2}$ cup dry white wine
$5\frac{1}{2}$ cups Roasted Chicken Stock (page 45), Basic Vegetable Stock
(page 44), or canned chicken broth
$\frac{1}{2}$ pound asparagus
1 cup green peas, fresh or frozen
$\frac{1}{2}$ cup grated Parmesan cheese
1 tablespoon butter, optional
1 teaspoon fresh lemon juice
Freshly ground black pepper
$\frac{1}{4}$ cup chopped fresh parsley

Preheat the oven to 350°F.

Warm the olive oil in a medium ovenproof pot or Dutch oven over medium-low heat. Add the leeks, garlic, scallions, and a sprinkling of salt, and sauté until softened, about 5 minutes. Add the barley and stir to combine. Add the wine, raise the heat, and simmer, uncovered, until the wine has evaporated, about 5 minutes. Then add the stock and $\frac{1}{4}$ teaspoon salt, and bring to a boil. Cover the pot with a lid or with a piece of aluminum foil, and transfer it to the oven. Bake for about 1 hour, until the barley is tender and the liquid is absorbed.

When the barley is almost cooked, remove the hard ends (about $1\frac{1}{2}$ inches) of the asparagus. Cut the spears into 1-inch pieces; you should have about 1 cup. Set the asparagus and peas in a steamer basket and steam over simmering water until tender, about 5 minutes.

Remove the pot from the oven, uncover it, and place it over low heat. Simmer for a couple of minutes if necessary to absorb any remaining liquid.

When the risotto is ready, stir in the Parmesan, butter (if using), lemon juice, and a sprinkling of black pepper. Stir in the steamed vegetables. Taste, and add salt if necessary. Serve hot, sprinkled with the parsley.

Wild Mushroom and Farro Risotto

This no-stir baked risotto is at its best when made with farro, but short-grain rice will do as well. Farro, a spelt-like whole grain that is common in Italy, is available in Italian and gourmet markets. Serve this with Baby Greens with Roasted Red Pepper Vinaigrette (page 76) for a delicious meal.

SERVES 4 AS A SIDE DISH OR 2 AS A MAIN COURSE

3 tablespoons extra-virgin olive oil
1/2 cup finely diced onion
Salt
1 cup farro or short-grain brown rice
1 cup dry white wine
1/2 cup roasted red bell pepper, fresh or bottled (small dice)
3 1/2 cups Roasted Chicken Stock (page 45), Basic Vegetable Stock (page 44),
    or canned chicken broth
1 shallot, finely minced (1/4 cup)
1/2 pound mixed wild mushrooms such as chanterelle, shiitake, and
    cremini, cleaned and cut into 1/4-inch slices (about 3 cups)
1 garlic clove, minced
1 cup cherry tomatoes, halved
1/4 cup thinly sliced fresh basil
Freshly ground black pepper
1/4 cup grated Parmesan cheese, optional
1 tablespoon butter, optional

Preheat the oven to 350°F.

Warm 1 tablespoon of the olive oil in a medium ovenproof saucepan over medium-low heat. Add the onions and a pinch of salt, and sauté until translucent, about 7 minutes.

Add the farro and stir to coat. Add 1/2 cup of the wine, and scrape up any bits that have stuck on the bottom of the pan. Simmer, uncovered, until nearly dry, 2 to 3 minutes. Add the peppers and stock, and bring to a boil. Cover the pan and transfer it to the oven. Bake until the farro is just tender, 50 minutes to 1 hour.

Meanwhile, warm the remaining 2 tablespoons oil in a medium skillet over medium-low heat. Add the shallots and a pinch of salt, and sauté until they are translucent, about 5 minutes. Add the mushrooms and sauté until the moisture has nearly evaporated, 5 to 10 minutes. Add the garlic and the remaining ½ cup wine. Scrape up any bits that have stuck to the bottom of the pan. Raise the heat and simmer, uncovered, until dry, about 3 minutes. Remove the pan from the heat and set it aside.

When the farro is ready, remove it from the oven and return the pan to the stovetop. Simmer for another minute or so if necessary to evaporate any remaining liquid. Gently stir in the mushrooms, tomatoes, basil, and a sprinkling of salt and black pepper. Stir in the Parmesan and the butter (if using). Serve immediately.

Easy Polenta

This simple way to make polenta involves very little stirring and no risk of burning. It will stay soft in the double boiler.

Mix in whatever you like as the polenta finishes cooking, or cook it in any variety of flavorful liquids. To serve it soft-style, make a hollow in the middle of each serving and mound the sauce in the hollow. Spicy Baked Beans (page 204), Roasted Red Pepper Sauce (page 174), Fire-Roasted Tomato Sauce (page 169), and Porcini Mushroom Ragout with chicken or tempeh (pages 262 and 263) are all delicious accompaniments.

SERVES 6 AS A SIDE DISH

4$\frac{1}{2}$ cups water or vegetable stock
Salt
1$\frac{1}{2}$ cups cornmeal, either fine, medium, or coarsely ground
1 tablespoon butter or extra-virgin olive oil, optional
1 cup grated Parmesan cheese, optional
$\frac{1}{4}$ cup chopped fresh herbs, optional (parsley, thyme, basil, rosemary, tarragon)

Fill a 4-quart saucepan two-thirds full with water and bring it to a simmer.

While the water is heating in the pan, whisk the 4$\frac{1}{2}$ cups water, $\frac{1}{2}$ teaspoon salt, and the cornmeal together in a medium-size metal bowl. Cover the bowl with aluminum foil. (You can also use a double boiler.)

Set the bowl over the simmering water and cook, stirring three or four times, until the polenta is thick and stiff, about 40 minutes; if necessary, add water to the saucepan under the bowl.

Stir in the butter, cheese, and herbs (if using). Taste, and add a pinch more salt if needed. Serve hot, topped with sauce; you can keep the polenta warm in the double boiler for an hour; check it occasionally, and if it is getting too stiff, stir in some water or stock to loosen it.

Polenta can be firmed up and then baked or sautéed and served hot, over your choice of sauce: Spread the warm cooked polenta in an oiled 9 by 13-inch baking dish, smoothing it evenly with a spoon, an offset spatula, or moistened hands. Let it sit for about 30 minutes or until firm. It will keep, covered and refrigerated, for up to 4 days.

To bake the firmed polenta, cut it into triangles or squares. Brush the top with olive oil, and bake in a preheated 400°F oven until browned on top, about 30 minutes, or brush the top with oil, place cut pieces in a broiler pan, and broil until browned on top.

To sauté the polenta, cut it into triangles or squares. Warm about 1 tablespoon olive oil in a nonstick skillet over medium heat. Sauté the pieces until browned and crisp, 3 to 4 minutes per side.

Quinoa-Grits Polenta

This is not your grandmother's polenta! Here, quinoa is mixed with corn grits and cooked polenta-style. It's a perfect combination with zesty Roasted Red Pepper Sauce (page 174). Serve it with roasted asparagus (page 166) and Chickpeas with *Charmoula* Vinaigrette (page 205) for a vegetarian meal. Make sure to rinse the quinoa well to remove the bitter saponin that coats it.

SERVES 4 AS A SIDE DISH

3 cups water
½ teaspoon salt
2 tablespoons plus 2 teaspoons extra-virgin olive oil
½ cup quinoa, well rinsed and drained
½ cup corn grits
3 thyme sprigs
½ cup unsalted sunflower seeds, toasted

Bring the water to a boil in a medium saucepan. Add the salt and the 2 tablespoons olive oil. Add the quinoa, grits, and thyme sprigs, and reduce the heat to a simmer. Cook, covered, stirring occasionally, until the quinoa is cooked, about 15 minutes; uncover the pan and stir frequently during the last few minutes of cooking.

Discard the thyme sprigs and stir the sunflower seeds into the mixture. Spread the polenta out in an oiled 8 by 8-inch baking dish. Let it cool until firm, about 20 minutes.

Cut the firm polenta into quarters, and cut each section into 4 triangles.

Warm the remaining 2 teaspoons oil in a medium nonstick skillet over medium heat. Add the polenta triangles and sauté until golden, about 2 minutes per side. Serve hot.

NOTE: *Quinoa has a Saturn-like ring surrounding each grain, which becomes translucent when the grains are cooked. Since quinoa is so small, it's best to wash it by putting it in a strainer and dipping it in water.*

Quinoa Primavera

Here's a light pilaf, studded with jewel-like flecks of colorful vegetables. For the best flavor and fluffiest texture, dry-toast the quinoa in the pot first. The ginger adds a zesty accent; for milder Mediterranean flavor, substitute minced garlic. This is delightful served with Black Bass in Leek-Saffron-Tomato Broth (page 246).

SERVES 4 AS A SIDE DISH

1 cup quinoa
2 cups water
Salt
2 tablespoons extra-virgin olive oil
1 tablespoon minced fresh ginger *or* 3 garlic cloves, minced
1 small carrot, cut into $1/4$-inch dice ($1/2$ cup)
1 celery stalk, cut into $1/4$-inch dice ($1/2$ cup)
$1/2$ red bell pepper, finely diced ($1/2$ cup)
$1/2$ green bell pepper, finely diced ($1/2$ cup)
$1/2$ cup peas, fresh or frozen
2 scallions, white part only, thinly sliced
Freshly ground black pepper
$1/4$ cup parsley, chopped

Wash the quinoa and drain it well.

Heat a small saucepan over medium-low heat. Add the quinoa and cook, stirring constantly, until the grains are dry and fragrant, about 5 minutes. Then add the water and $1/2$ teaspoon salt, scraping up any grains that have stuck to the bottom. Cover, and simmer until the quinoa is tender, about 15 minutes. Do not stir the quinoa while it is cooking, to allow it to cook evenly and steam holes to form.

Combine the olive oil and the ginger in a large skillet, and place it over medium-high heat. When the oil is hot and the ginger is aromatic but has not yet colored (about 2 minutes), add the carrots and sauté for 1 minute. Stir in the celery, peppers, peas, and scallions. Sauté just long enough for the vegetables to heat through, about 1 minute. Stir in the hot quinoa, and season to taste with salt and black pepper. Stir in the parsley, and serve immediately.

Dolma Pilaf

After spending two days making *dolmades* (stuffed grape leaves), I realized that I liked the filling much more than the grape leaves. So I dispensed with the leaves and substituted bulgur for its fluffy, nutty quality and quick cooking time. Serve this pilaf with the Pecan-Crusted Trout (page 256) or with Chickpeas with *Charmoula Vinaigrette* (page 205). For an unusual variation, use dried blueberries in place of the currants. Leftovers are delicious eaten cold as a salad.

SERVES 4 AS A SIDE DISH

¾ cup coarse-grained bulgur, rinsed

Salt

1½ cups water

¼ cup dried currants or dried blueberries

2 tablespoons extra-virgin olive oil

1 medium onion, cut into small dice (1 cup)

2 garlic cloves, minced

1 tomato, seeded and chopped (½ cup)

¼ cup pine nuts, toasted

¼ teaspoon ground allspice

2 tablespoons finely chopped fresh parsley

2 tablespoons chopped fresh mint

Freshly ground black pepper

Combine the bulgur, ¾ teaspoon salt, and the water in a small saucepan. Cover, and bring to a boil. Then lower the heat and simmer for 15 minutes. Remove the pan from the heat and let the bulgur sit for 5 minutes.

Meanwhile, soak the currants or blueberries in hot water to cover until plump, 15 minutes. Drain, and set aside.

Warm the olive oil in a medium skillet over low heat. Add the onions and cook, stirring occasionally, until translucent and tender, about 10 minutes. Add the garlic and cook a few minutes more. Add the tomatoes, pine nuts, currants, allspice, parsley, mint, and a sprinkling of black pepper. Stir to heat through.

Stir the onion mixture into the bulgur, and mix until combined. Taste, and add more salt if necessary. Serve hot.

Forbidden Black Rice

What was once restricted to the table of the emperor of China is now widely available in natural foods stores and gourmet markets. This flavorful short grain is a beautiful purple-black color and has a savory yet sweet edge.

SERVES 4 AS A SIDE DISH

1 cup forbidden black rice
2 tablespoons rice syrup
1/4 cup mirin
2 1/2 cups water
Salt
1 teaspoon brown rice vinegar

Wash the rice, drain it, and place it in a small heavy-bottomed saucepan. Whisk the rice syrup and mirin together in a small bowl and add to the rice. Stir in the water. Bring to a boil, add 1/4 teaspoon salt, lower the heat and simmer rapidly, uncovered, until the water level is even with the rice, about 45 minutes. Do not mix or disturb the rice while it is cooking. If the water evaporates too quickly, add a little more to keep cooking the rice for the full time.

Cover the pan and simmer for another 5 minutes. Then remove the pan from the heat and let the rice rest for 5 minutes. Stir in the vinegar. Taste, and add more salt if necessary. Serve hot.

Thai Jasmine Rice with Chinese Black Beans

This is a striking black-and-white pilaf combining Chinese black beans with jasmine rice, a fluffy, fragrant rice similar to basmati. For a pan-Asian feast, serve this with Grilled Pineapple–Mango Salsa (page 178) and Baked Thai Tempeh Triangles (page 228).

SERVES 6 TO 8 AS A SIDE DISH

1 1/2 cups Thai jasmine rice

3 cups water

Pinch of salt

1/2 cup fermented black beans

2 tablespoons sesame oil or canola oil

1/2 cup thinly sliced scallions, white and green parts

Rinse the rice and drain it. Combine the rice, water, and salt in a medium saucepan. Cover, and bring to a boil over medium heat. Then lower the heat and simmer until the water has been absorbed, 15 minutes. Remove the pan from the heat and let the rice sit for 5 minutes.

While the rice is resting, rinse the black beans in several changes of water (to reduce the saltiness).

Warm the oil in a medium skillet over medium heat. Add the scallions and cook for about 1 minute. Add the beans and cook for another minute, until heated through. Gently fold the black bean mixture into the rice, and serve.

Wild Rice with Porcini Mushrooms, Pecans, and Dried Cranberries

Here's a festive pilaf for your holiday table. Serve this with Porcini Mushroom Ragout with chicken or tempeh (pages 262 and 263) and Cranberry-Chestnut Relish (page 177).

SERVES 6 TO 8 AS A SIDE DISH

1 cup wild rice, rinsed
4 cups water
Salt
1 ounce ($^3/_4$ cup loosely packed) dried porcini mushrooms
2 tablespoons extra-virgin olive oil
$^1/_2$ cup minced red onion
1 celery stalk, minced
1 garlic clove, minced
1 cup dried cranberries or dried currants
$^1/_2$ cup pecans, toasted and chopped
Freshly ground black pepper
2 tablespoons chopped fresh parsley

Combine the wild rice and 3 cups of the water in a small saucepan, and bring to a boil over high heat. Lower the heat and simmer, covered, until the rice is tender, about 45 minutes. (Most of the kernels will have burst open.) The rice should be cooked but still chewy. Drain the rice and stir in $^1/_2$ teaspoon salt.

Meanwhile, combine the remaining 1 cup water with the porcini mushrooms in a small saucepan, and bring to a boil. Remove the pan from the heat, and let the mushrooms soak for 20 minutes. Then drain the mushrooms, reserving the mushrooms and the liquid separately. Place a strainer lined with a damp paper towel over a bowl, and pour the liquid through it to catch any grit. Roughly chop the mushrooms.

Warm the olive oil in a medium skillet over medium-low heat. Add the onions and celery, and cook until the vegetables are softened, about 7 minutes. Add the reserved mushrooms, the garlic, and the cranberries, and sauté until the cranberries are heated through, about 2 minutes. Add the pecans, rice, $^1/_4$ teaspoon salt, black pepper to taste, and the mushroom soaking liquid. Cook until the liquid has been absorbed, about 2 minutes. Stir in the chopped parsley, and serve hot.

Wild Rice and Spelt Berry Salad with Grapes and Orange-Cumin Dressing

This grain salad is full of contrasting flavors and textures. Spelt, found in natural foods stores, is an ancient grain similar to wheat. Other delicious alternatives include kamut berries, wheat berries, and even barley.

SERVES 4 AS A SIDE DISH

1/2 cup wild rice, rinsed
1/2 cup spelt berries
Salt
1/2 cup finely chopped red onion
6 tablespoons hazelnuts, toasted, skinned, and chopped (see page 18)
1/4 cup chopped fresh chives
1/4 cup chopped fresh parsley
1 1/4 cups seedless red or green grapes, halved

Dressing

1 teaspoon whole cumin seeds
1 garlic clove
1/2 teaspoon salt
1/3 cup fresh orange juice
3 tablespoons fresh lime juice
2 teaspoons honey
1/3 cup extra-virgin olive oil
1/4 teaspoon freshly ground black pepper

Place the wild rice and spelt berries in a saucepan, and add water to cover by 2 inches. Cover, bring to a boil, and add a pinch of salt. Then lower the heat and simmer rapidly, partially covered, until the grains are just tender, 30 to 40 minutes. Stir in 1/2 teaspoon salt.

Drain the grains and transfer them to a medium bowl. Stir in the onions, hazelnuts, chives, parsley, and grapes.

Make the dressing: Toast the cumin seeds in a heavy-bottomed skillet over medium-low heat until fragrant, about 2 minutes. Then grind them in a spice grinder or with a mortar and pestle. Transfer the ground cumin to a small bowl.

Mince the garlic on a cutting board. Sprinkle ¼ teaspoon of the salt over the minced garlic, and mash it to a paste with the back of your knife (you can also do this with a mortar and pestle). Transfer the mashed garlic to the bowl containing the cumin, and add the orange and lime juices, honey, and remaining ¼ teaspoon salt. Whisk to blend. Then add the olive oil in a slow stream, whisking until well blended. Stir in the black pepper.

Stir the dressing into the grains, and let the salad sit for a few minutes to marry the flavors. Serve warm or at room temperature.

Cardamom and Coconut Basmati Rice

A subtle flavor of cardamom and coconut comes through in this soft, light rice. It goes with just about every Indian dish in this book.

The soaking makes the texture extra fluffy, but you don't have to soak the rice if you're in a hurry.

SERVES 4 TO 6 AS A SIDE DISH

1¼ cups white basmati rice
2½ cups water
1 teaspoon green cardamom pods
½ cup dried unsweetened coconut
½ teaspoon salt
1 teaspoon ghee or coconut oil

Wash the rice until the water runs clear, and drain it well. Transfer the rice to a small heavy-bottomed saucepan, and add the water. Let the rice soak for 30 minutes.

Stir the cardamom, coconut, salt, and ghee into the rice. Cover, and bring to a boil. Lower the heat and simmer until the rice is cooked through, about 10 minutes. Remove the pan from the heat and let it sit, covered, for 5 minutes. Fluff the rice and serve.

Variations

Cook the rice with 3 black cardamom pods and 1 teaspoon black cumin seeds. The black cardamom gives the rice a smoky flavor.

Cook the rice with 1 teaspoon green cardamom, a cassia leaf (sometimes called Indian bay leaf), or a cinnamon stick, and 2 teaspoons grated lemon zest; omit the coconut.

Moong Dhal

Sautéed spices give this creamy dhal its savory flavor but the ghee is essential. This is the first dish I turn to when I need to lighten up after a bit too much indulgence. This nourishing, savory dhal is easy to digest and makes a fitting accompaniment to other Indian dishes. Split mung beans are available in all Indian markets, but red lentils make a fine substitute.

SERVES 4 AS A SIDE DISH

1 cup moong dhal (split mung beans), washed
5 cups water
Salt
2 tablespoons ghee
1 tablespoon minced fresh ginger
1 teaspoon curry powder
Pinch of asafetida
1 teaspoon whole cumin seeds
1 teaspoon whole mustard seeds
1 teaspoon whole fennel seeds
2 teaspoons fresh lemon juice
Chopped fresh cilantro, for garnish

Combine the moong dhal and water in a medium saucepan. Cover and bring to a boil. Then lower the heat, add 1 teaspoon salt, and simmer, partially covered, until tender, 30 minutes. Check the moong dhal occasionally and add more water if necessary. Continue cooking, stirring frequently, until the dhal is creamy, another 2 to 3 minutes.

When the dhal is almost ready, warm the ghee in a medium skillet. Add the ginger, curry powder, asafetida, cumin, mustard, and fennel. Cook just until the mustard seeds begin to pop, about 2 minutes. Pour the spice mix into the dhal and stir in the lemon juice. Taste, and add another large pinch of salt if necessary. Serve hot, sprinkled with cilantro.

NOTE: *Moong dhal foams easily. Be sure to cook it with the pot partially covered to prevent spillovers.*

Tamarind Chickpeas

Serve these tangy beans with Coconut Green Beans (page 104), Cardamom and Coconut Basmati Rice (page 201), and Cucumber, Peanut, and Yogurt Raita (page 180).

SERVES 4 TO 6 AS A SIDE DISH

$1\frac{1}{2}$ **cups water**

One 1-ounce piece of tamarind (a 1-inch square of the cake)

1 teaspoon whole cumin seeds, toasted (see Note)

$\frac{1}{4}$ **cup coconut oil or ghee**

$1\frac{1}{2}$ **cups thinly sliced onions**

2 garlic cloves, minced

$\frac{1}{2}$ **teaspoon ground turmeric**

$\frac{1}{2}$ **teaspoon Indian chile powder (kashmiri) or cayenne pepper**

One 15-ounce can diced tomatoes, *or* 2 cups chopped fresh tomatoes

**Two 15-ounce cans chickpeas, drained and rinsed, *or* 3 cups
    cooked chickpeas**

Salt

**1 tablespoon natural sugar, such as maple sugar, Sucanat, or
    evaporated cane sugar**

Bring the water to a boil in a small pot. Remove it from the heat, add the tamarind, and soak for about 10 minutes. Then strain the liquid into a bowl, pushing the pulp through the mesh of the strainer. Discard the seeds. Set aside.

Grind the cumin seeds in a spice grinder or with a mortar and pestle, and set aside.

Warm the oil in a medium skillet over medium-low heat. Add the onions and cook until caramelized, about 15 minutes. Add the garlic, turmeric, and chili powder, and cook for 2 minutes. Add the strained tamarind liquid, tomatoes, cumin, chickpeas, 1 teaspoon salt, and the sugar. Cook, uncovered, until the sauce has reduced and thickened and the chickpeas are well coated, 15 to 20 minutes. Taste, and add more salt if necessary. Serve hot.

NOTE: *Dry-toast the cumin seeds in a heavy-bottomed skillet over medium-low heat until fragrant, about 2 minutes.*

Spicy Baked Beans

This dish is soothing enough to be real comfort food. It's warming, a little bit spicy, and delicious served with Quinoa-Grits Polenta (page 194).

SERVES 4 OR 5 AS A SIDE DISH

Two 15-ounce cans navy beans, drained, 1/2 cup liquid reserved,
**   *or* 3 cups cooked navy beans, 1/2 cup liquid reserved**
One 2-inch piece fresh ginger, cut into 5 thin slices
1 bay leaf
2 tablespoons Dijon mustard
1/4 cup maple syrup
3 tablespoons apple cider vinegar
Salt
1 tablespoon rum, optional
1 tablespoon extra-virgin olive oil
1 onion, cut into small dice (1 cup)
2 teaspoons ground cumin
1 teaspoon hot red pepper flakes

Preheat the oven to 350°F.

Place the beans, ginger, and bay leaf in a baking dish.

In a small bowl, mix together the mustard, maple syrup, vinegar, 1 teaspoon salt, rum (if using), and reserved bean liquid.

Warm the olive oil in a medium skillet over medium heat. Add the onions and sauté just until they begin to brown, about 7 minutes. Add the cumin and red pepper flakes, and sauté for 1 minute. Add the maple syrup mixture and stir until the liquid reaches a boil, about 1 minute. Then pour the skillet mixture over the beans and stir to combine. Cover, transfer to the oven, and bake for 30 minutes.

Remove the dish from the oven and discard the ginger and bay leaf. Let the beans rest for at least 5 minutes before serving.

Chickpeas with Charmoula Vinaigrette

Charmoula, the classic Moroccan spice mix that is so delicious on fish, makes a savory marinade for these chickpeas. The beans are tossed with seasonings and vinegar and finished with a splash of oil. They last for days in the refrigerator, improving with flavor as they sit. The chickpeas are delicious served with Quinoa-Grits Polenta (page 194) and with Roasted Red Pepper Sauce (page 174).

SERVES 6 AS A SIDE DISH

$1^{1}/_{2}$ teaspoons whole cumin seeds

6 tablespoons fresh lemon juice

4 garlic cloves, minced

$1^{1}/_{2}$ teaspoons paprika

$^{3}/_{4}$ cup fresh parsley, chopped

$^{1}/_{2}$ cup fresh cilantro, chopped

Salt

Freshly ground black pepper

3 cups cooked chickpeas *or* two 15-ounce cans chickpeas,
    drained and rinsed

3 tablespoons extra-virgin olive oil

Toast the cumin seeds in a heavy-bottomed skillet over medium-low heat until fragrant, about 2 minutes. Then grind the cumin seeds to a powder in a spice grinder or with a mortar and pestle. Transfer the cumin to a medium bowl, and add the lemon juice, garlic, paprika, parsley, cilantro, $^{1}/_{2}$ teaspoon salt, and a sprinkling of black pepper. Whisk the dressing, and then add the chickpeas. Drizzle in the olive oil, and stir to combine. Sprinkle with more black pepper. Taste, and add more salt if necessary. Serve warm or at room temperature.

Vegetarian Main Courses

Bean and Cheese Pupusas (Stuffed Tortillas)

Mujadarrah and Middle Eastern Salad

Thanksgiving Stuffing Timbales

Red Lentil Patties with Cilantro Sauce

Spring Roll Salad with Roasted Shallot Peanut Sauce
and Tamarind Dipping Sauce

Porcini-Miso Broth with Stir-fried Vegetables and
Soba Noodles

Teriyaki Tofu

Baked Tofu

Glazed Tofu

Tofu and Vegetable Stir-fry

Barbecue Spice–Rubbed Tofu

Braised Tempeh with Curried Coconut Sauce

Baked Thai Tempeh Triangles

Smokin' Drunken Chili

Sancocho Stew

Indian-Spiced Cauliflower, Chickpeas, Potatoes,
and Kale

Cauliflower, Green Bean, and Mushroom Kuku

Crispy Potato and Broccoli Kuku

Spinach Pie Kuku

These main-course

vegetarian dishes feature bean and grain ensembles, tofu, tempeh, stews, and egg dishes. ◉ There are bean and grain dishes such as the *mujadarrah* (lentils and rice with caramelized onions), as well as spicy red lentil patties and stuffed tortillas. Many of the dishes, such as the Indian cauliflower stew or the Vietnamese noodle salad with peanut and tamarind sauces, are practically meals unto themselves. They need only one dish or so to round out the flavors. The individual stuffing timbales are a lovely vegetarian main course at Thanksgiving or a hearty side for those who can never get enough stuffing. ◉ I've included three *kuku*s, fluffy, quichelike, Persian-style frittatas that form their own golden crust as they bake. They're ideal to make for a festive brunch. ◉ You will also find a number of tofu and tempeh dishes, including the Glazed Tofu, which is a great base for other dishes, such as salads and stir-fries. Tempeh becomes succulent when braised or baked in flavorful marinades, such as in Braised Tempeh with Curried Coconut Sauce. ◉ Almost all of the dishes here can be made in advance and reheated, avoiding a need for last-minute fussing. The others are quick to put together, such as the Tofu and Vegetable Stir-fry, and make perfect weeknight meals.

Bean and Cheese Pupusas (Stuffed Tortillas)

I've been enamored of *pupusas* ever since encountering them at a tiny Salvadoran restaurant on Long Island. These stuffed tortillas are delicious with black beans and cheese, but don't limit yourself; the filling opportunities are endless. The key to a light *pupusa* is to pinch off the little piece of dough that remains after you pinch the sides together. Serve them with Tomatillo Salsa (page 175) and Salvadoran Slaw (page 96) for a Central American dinner.

MAKES ABOUT 20 *pupusas;* SERVES 6

2 garlic cloves, minced
3/4 teaspoon salt
1 tablespoon extra-virgin olive oil
1/2 cup water
1/2 teaspoon ground cumin
1/2 teaspoon paprika
One 14-ounce can black beans, rinsed and drained
1 teaspoon fresh lime juice
1/4 cup minced scallions, white and green parts
Freshly ground black pepper
3 cups masa harina
2 1/2 cups warm water
2 cups grated cheese, preferably raw-milk Monterey Jack
    (from a 6-ounce piece of cheese)

Preheat the oven to 250°F.

Mash the garlic with 1/4 teaspoon of the salt in a mortar and pestle, or on a cutting board using the flat side of a knife.

Combine the olive oil and the mashed garlic in a medium skillet, and warm over medium heat. When the garlic just begins to turn golden (about 2 minutes), add the 1/2 cup water, cumin, and paprika. Simmer for 1 minute. Then add the beans and the remaining 1/2 teaspoon salt. Use a masher to mash the beans into the liquid until they are creamy. Simmer, uncovered, stirring constantly to keep the beans from sticking, until all the liquid has been absorbed, 5 to 7 minutes. The beans should be almost dry.

Stir in the lime juice, scallions, and a sprinkling of black pepper. Remove the beans from the heat and set them aside to cool to room temperature.

Combine the masa harina and the warm water in a medium bowl, and knead until the dough is soft and pliable, about 2 minutes.

Divide the dough into 18 portions. Take one portion of dough, leaving the rest in a bowl covered with plastic wrap. Form the dough into a ball, and make a depression in the center. Place the ball in the palm of your hand, and use your other hand to form a cup with walls that are ¼ inch thick. Add a spoonful of beans, covering the bottom and leaving ¾ inch on the sides. Place a tablespoon of cheese on top of the beans. Pinch the sides together so that there's an extra little piece at the top, forming a purse. Pinch off the top doughy piece and return it to the bowl. Flatten the filled dough into a pancake about ½ inch thick, trying not to let the filling ooze out. Repeat with the rest of the *pupusas*. Set the *pupusas* in a single layer on a plate. (You can layer them between pieces of parchment or wax paper.)

Heat a dry cast-iron griddle over medium-high heat. Fry the *pupusas* until brown spots appear, 1 to 2 minutes. Flip them over and cook for another minute or so. Keep the *pupusas* warm in the oven until you finish cooking them all. Serve hot.

NOTE: Pupusas *freeze very well. Lay them in a single layer on a baking sheet and freeze for a couple of hours; then stack them in a freezer bag and seal tightly. There is no need to defrost them; simply warm them in a 350°F oven for 15 minutes.*

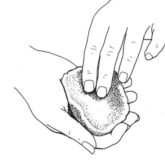

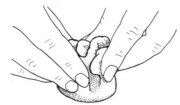

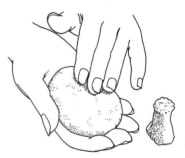

Mujadarrah and Middle Eastern Salad

Mujadarrah is one of those thoroughly satisfying dishes. The key to its flavor lies in the deeply caramelized onions. In this brown rice version, the lentils and rice cook together in the pot for the same amount of time. Although it may seem like a lot of oil, the dish makes a full six servings and the oil is key to getting the onions a rich deep brown, so please don't skimp on it. The salad is a refreshing accompaniment, and together they are delicious piled on a plate or stuffed into pita bread.

SERVES 6

Mujadarrah

1 cup lentils, preferably brown, sorted

1 cup brown basmati rice

4$\frac{1}{2}$ cups water

Salt

6 tablespoons extra-virgin olive oil

3 cups thinly sliced onions

Freshly ground black pepper

Salad

$\frac{3}{4}$ pound tomatoes, seeded and cut into small dice (about 1$\frac{1}{2}$ cups)

1 medium cucumber, peeled and cut into small dice (about 1 cup)

$\frac{1}{2}$ cup thinly sliced scallions, white and green parts

$\frac{1}{2}$ cup chopped fresh flat-leaf parsley

$\frac{1}{2}$ teaspoon salt

Freshly ground black pepper

2 tablespoons fresh lemon juice

2 tablespoons extra-virgin olive oil

Wash the lentils and rice, and drain them well. Transfer them to a medium saucepan, add the water, and bring to a boil. Then lower the heat, add 1$\frac{1}{2}$ teaspoons salt, cover, and simmer until all the liquid has been absorbed and lentils and rice are cooked through, about 40 to 45 minutes. Do not stir during the cooking time. Check occasionally to see if more water is needed. If the lentils and rice are cooked but there is still some liquid left in the pan, remove the cover and let it cook until the liquid has evaporated.

Meanwhile, warm the olive oil in a medium skillet over medium heat. Add the onions and sauté, stirring frequently, until golden brown, about 15 minutes. Remove the skillet from the heat and pour the onions into a small bowl to stop the cooking. Set aside a small amount of onions for the garnish.

When the lentils and rice are cooked, add the onions, along with any oil in the bowl, and stir to combine. Stir in a sprinkling of black pepper. Taste, and add more salt if necessary.

Make the salad: Combine the tomatoes, cucumbers, scallions, parsley, salt, black pepper to taste, lemon juice, and olive oil in a medium bowl. Stir to combine.

Top the *mujadarrah* with the reserved onions, and serve with the salad.

Thanksgiving Stuffing Timbales

Bake this hearty stuffing in ramekins. Made with wild rice, lentils, and chestnuts, this can be a hearty vegetarian main course at Thanksgiving or a sumptuous side. Once you've tasted it, you won't want to limit it to November.

SERVES 6 TO 8

1 cup French lentils

4 cups water

1 rosemary sprig, plus 1 tablespoon chopped fresh rosemary

1 sage sprig, plus 1 tablespoon chopped fresh sage

1 bay leaf

Salt

2 tablespoons extra-virgin olive oil

2 medium onions, cut into small dice

2 carrots, cut into small dice (1 cup)

2 celery stalks, cut into small dice (1 cup)

1 cup chestnuts, bottled or vacuum-packed, cut into small pieces

1 tablespoon shoyu

3/4 cup whole-wheat bread crumbs, preferably fresh (see Notes)

1/3 cup wild rice, cooked (yields 1 cup)

1/2 cup chopped fresh parsley

1/2 cup pecans, toasted and chopped

Freshly ground black pepper

Onion Glaze

2 tablespoons extra-virgin olive oil

2 medium onions, thinly sliced

2 cups thinly sliced leeks, white and light green parts

2 scallions, white and green parts, thinly sliced

3 garlic cloves, minced

Salt

1 tablespoon sherry

Freshly ground black pepper

1 teaspoon chopped fresh rosemary

Preheat the oven to 350°F. Oil 6 to 8 ramekins, and line the bottoms with rounds of parchment.

Combine the lentils, water, rosemary sprig, sage sprig, and bay leaf in a small saucepan. Cover and bring to a boil. Add 1 teaspoon salt, lower the heat, and simmer, partially covered, until the lentils are very tender, about 30 minutes. Drain the lentils, reserving the lentils and the cooking liquid separately. You should have about 1¼ cups of cooking liquid; if not, add enough water to make up the difference. Remove the rosemary, sage, and bay leaf from the lentils. Set the lentils and the liquid aside.

Warm the olive oil in a large skillet over medium heat. Add the onions, carrots, celery, and ½ teaspoon salt. Reduce the heat to medium-low, and sauté until the vegetables are softened, about 10 minutes. Add the chestnuts and shoyu, and stir to combine. Add ¼ cup of the reserved lentil cooking liquid and scrape the bottom of the skillet to loosen any brown bits. Remove the skillet from the heat, and stir in the bread crumbs and the lentils.

Stir the wild rice, parsley, pecans, chopped rosemary, and chopped sage into the lentils. Sprinkle liberally with black pepper. Taste, and add more salt if necessary. The filling should be moist.

Press the stuffing firmly into the prepared ramekins. At this point you can refrigerate the stuffing, covered, overnight.

Bake, uncovered, until the stuffing has started to brown on top, 20 to 30 minutes.

Meanwhile, make the onion glaze: Warm the olive oil in a medium skillet over medium heat. Add the onions, leeks, scallions, garlic, and ½ teaspoon salt. Sauté until the vegetables are tender, about 10 minutes. Add the sherry and the remaining 1 cup lentil cooking liquid, including the thick part that has settled to the bottom. Cook over medium heat, uncovered, until the sauce has thickened, about 10 minutes. Stir in a sprinkling of black pepper and the rosemary. Taste, and add salt if necessary.

Remove the ramekins from the oven and run a knife around the sides to loosen the stuffing. Using tongs or an oven mitt, carefully turn the stuffing out of each ramekin onto individual plates. Remove the parchment. Slather the onion glaze over the timbales, and serve.

NOTES: *The stuffing tastes the best if you use fresh bread crumbs. Just place a few slices of whole-wheat bread in a food processor or blender, and process into crumbs. Store any extra in resealable plastic bags in the freezer.*

You might find that your onion glaze absorbs the liquid if you store it overnight in the refrigerator; just add water to reconstitute it.

Red Lentil Patties with Cilantro Sauce

These little patties are scrumptious with the bright green sauce. Serve them as a vegetarian main course or as a side to fish and chicken dishes. For a whole-grain version, try using red Bhutanese rice in place of the basmati. Red Bhutanese rice, available at natural foods stores and gourmet markets, is a nutty short-grain variety with exceptional flavor. In this recipe you don't have to adjust the cooking time.

SERVES 4

1 cup white basmati rice
1/2 cup red lentils
4 cups water
1/2 teaspoon ground turmeric
3/4 teaspoon salt
2 tablespoons plus 4 teaspoons coconut oil, sesame oil, or ghee
1 teaspoon whole cumin seeds
2 cups finely diced onions
1/4 teaspoon hot red pepper flakes
1/4 cup arrowroot powder
Cilantro Sauce (recipe follows)

Wash the rice and lentils, and drain them. Place them in a medium saucepan and add the water, turmeric, and salt. Cover and bring to a boil. Then lower the heat and simmer for 10 minutes. Uncover the pan and simmer, without stirring, until the water is absorbed, 15 minutes.

Meanwhile, warm the 2 tablespoons oil in a medium skillet over medium heat. Add the cumin seeds and sauté until fragrant, 1 minute. Add the onions and cook, stirring frequently, until well browned, about 12 minutes. Stir in the red pepper flakes and remove the skillet from the heat. Add the mixture to the cooked rice and lentils. Stir to combine. Taste, and add salt if necessary. Transfer the mixture to a bowl, and let it sit until cool enough to handle, about 20 minutes.

Spread the arrowroot on a large plate. Form the lentil mixture into 8 patties. Dredge the patties in the arrowroot, and place them on a clean plate.

Heat 2 teaspoons of the oil in a medium nonstick skillet over medium-high heat. Add 4 patties and sauté until golden, about 2 minutes per side. Repeat with the remaining oil and patties. Serve warm, drizzled with the Cilantro Sauce.

Cilantro Sauce

This lively green sauce is guaranteed to invigorate your senses. If you don't like the flavor of cilantro, mint is a delicious substitute.

MAKES 1 CUP

2 tablespoons fresh lemon juice
1/4 cup unsweetened coconut milk, stirred before measuring
1 jalapeño chile, stemmed and seeded
1 garlic clove
One 1-inch piece fresh ginger
1/4 teaspoon salt
1 cup roughly chopped fresh cilantro

Combine all the ingredients in a blender and blend until smooth. The sauce will keep, covered and refrigerated, for up to 3 days.

NOTE: *The sauce will blend best if you put the liquid ingredients into the blender first.*

Spring Roll Salad with Roasted Shallot Peanut Sauce and Tamarind Dipping Sauce

This dish was inspired by Vietnamese spring rolls. To streamline the cooking, roast the shiitake mushrooms and the shallots for the sauce at the same time. Use the wide rice noodles for the tastiest and best-looking salad.

Turn this into a hearty meal by serving it with Glazed Tofu (page 223).

SERVES 8

3/4 pound fresh shiitake mushrooms

2 tablespoons extra-virgin olive oil

2 tablespoons shoyu

4 ounces (4 cups loosely packed) fettucine-style rice noodles

2 carrots, sliced into matchsticks (1 cup)

2 tablespoons chopped fresh mint

2 tablespoons chopped fresh cilantro

2 tablespoons chopped fresh chives

Roasted Shallot Peanut Sauce (recipe follows)

Tamarind Dipping Sauce (recipe follows)

1/2 cup dry-roasted peanuts, chopped, for garnish

Preheat the oven to 375°F.

Cut the stems off the shiitakes and discard them (or save them for stock). Thinly slice the caps; you should have 5 cups. Toss the shiitakes in a bowl with the olive oil and shoyu. Then spread them out on a parchment-covered baking sheet and transfer it to the oven. Roast, stirring twice, until the mushrooms are shrunken, browned, and fairly crisp, about 40 minutes. Place the mushrooms in a small bowl and set it aside.

Bring a medium pot of water to a boil. Remove the pot from the heat, add the noodles, and let them sit until softened, 3 to 4 minutes. Drain, and rinse the noodles for at least 30 seconds under cold water to prevent sticking.

Toss the noodles in a bowl with the carrots and herbs. Mound a portion of noodles on each plate, and drizzle the peanut sauce and the dipping sauce over the top. Sprinkle with the mushrooms and peanuts.

Roasted Shallot Peanut Sauce

This versatile peanut sauce is sweet with a spicy kick. It's great on a variety of dishes. Heat the sauce or serve it at room temperature.

MAKES 2 CUPS

3 medium shallots, unpeeled
1 cup unsweetened coconut milk, stirred before measuring
1/2 cup smooth peanut butter
3 tablespoons natural sugar, preferably maple sugar or evaporated cane sugar
1/2 teaspoon cayenne pepper
1 tablespoon shoyu
2 tablespoons plus 1 teaspoon fresh lime juice

Preheat the oven to 375°F.

Place the shallots on a parchment-covered baking sheet and roast until they are very tender and the juices have started to ooze out, 30 to 35 minutes. Let the shallots cool slightly, and then squeeze the pulp out of the skins. Place the shallot pulp and all the remaining ingredients in a food processor or blender, and blend until smooth.

The sauce will keep, covered and refrigerated, for up to a week. Warm before serving.

Tamarind Dipping Sauce

This tangy sauce takes only a few minutes to make and complements the sweet and spicy peanut sauce, making the noodles come alive with flavor.

MAKES 1/2 CUP

2 tablespoons natural sugar, preferably maple sugar or evaporated cane sugar
6 tablespoons water
1 tablespoon fresh lime juice
1 tablespoon tamarind concentrate
1 tablespoon shoyu
1 teaspoon chopped fresh cilantro
1 garlic clove, minced
1 teaspoon finely slivered seeded red serrano or Thai bird chile

Combine the sugar and water in a small saucepan, and warm over medium heat until the sugar dissolves. Remove the pan from the heat and mix in the lime juice, tamarind concentrate, and shoyu, stirring until smooth. Let the mixture cool slightly, and then stir in the cilantro, garlic, and chile. The sauce should be tangy and slightly sour.

The sauce will keep, covered and refrigerated, for up to 3 days.

Porcini-Miso Broth with Stir-fried Vegetables and Soba Noodles

A flavorful mound of stir-fried vegetables, soba noodles, and nori nestle in an earthy mushroom broth enriched with miso: a delicious and healthy meal. Serve this artful dish surrounded by Teriyaki Tofu (page 221) or Baked Tofu (page 222). To reduce the cooking time, soak the porcini mushrooms while you prep the vegetables. A large skillet will work just as well as a wok for stir-frying.

SERVES 4 TO 6

1/2 cup dried porcini mushrooms

3 cups hot water

2 tablespoons dark miso, such as barley or hatcho miso

2 tablespoons sesame oil

1 tablespoon minced fresh ginger

3 garlic cloves, minced

1 jalapeño pepper, stemmed, seeded, and minced

1/2 pound fresh shiitake mushrooms, stemmed and sliced (3 cups)

2 tablespoons shoyu

6 ounces soba noodles

4 cups shredded Napa cabbage or bok choy

1/4 pound (1 cup) sugar snap or snow peas

Salt

1/4 cup thinly sliced scallions, white and green parts, for garnish

1 sheet nori, cut into thin 2-inch-long strips, for garnish

Combine the porcini and the hot water in a bowl, and let sit for 20 minutes. Drain, reserving the soaking liquid. Strain the mushroom liquid through a strainer lined with cheesecloth or a damp paper towel. Chop the mushrooms and set them aside.

In a small bowl, combine the miso with 1/2 cup of the hot porcini liquid. Set it aside. Bring a medium saucepan of salted water to a boil.

While the water is heating, warm the oil in a large skillet or wok over high heat until a haze forms, about 3 minutes. Add the ginger, garlic, and jalapeño, and stir-fry for 1 minute. Add the shiitakes, reserved porcini, and shoyu, and cook, stirring, until the mushrooms have released their juices and shrunk, about 2 minutes.

Meanwhile, add the soba noodles to the boiling water and cook for 4 minutes.

When the mushrooms are cooked, add the cabbage, snap peas, and 2 cups of the porcini liquid to the skillet. Cover, and cook until the vegetables are bright green and the cabbage is wilted, 2 minutes. Stir in the miso broth. Remove the skillet from the heat. Taste, and add a sprinkling of salt if necessary.

Drain the soba noodles and divide them among four pasta plates or shallow soup plates. Spoon the broth over the noodles, and arrange the vegetables over each portion. Sprinkle with the scallions, and stack a few nori strips in the middle.

NOTE: *Cut the nori with a scissors to get thin, even strips. The even pieces make a graceful stack.*

Tempeh and Tofu

Originating in Indonesia, tempeh is a high-protein soybean cake made by splitting, cooking, and fermenting soybeans and injecting them with a tempeh culture called a rhizopus mold. The fermentation binds the soybeans into a compact white cake and makes it, along with miso and shoyu, one of the most digestible forms of soy. The acceptable mold that is found on tempeh is white, black, or gray. Any other color is not desirable and probably will be accompanied by an unpleasant aroma. Tempeh often comes with a variety of ingredients that are fermented with the beans: rice, wild rice, arame, and other vegetables.

To avoid an unpleasant experience, refrain from eating tempeh straight from the package. Tempeh needs some added fat—either in the baking marinade or when sautéed—and it needs liquid to make it succulent and tasty. Steam tempeh before baking it to open up the "pores" and help it absorb the marinade. On the stovetop, sauté and then braise the tempeh in a flavorful liquid, or braise and then sauté it, to let the liquid infuse it. Tempeh's nutty, mushroomlike flavor can handle assertive flavors well.

Tempeh's block shape is less than appealing. Cut into various geometric shapes, however, tempeh not only is more appetizing but also offers a good flat surface, suitable for sautéing.

Tofu is made from soymilk coagulated with nigari or calcium sulfate and then pressed into blocks. While it does not have much personality on its own, tofu absorbs the juices and flavors of ingredients it's cooked with, and marinated and manipulated in inventive ways, it affords countless varieties of satisfying tastes and textures. Uncooked, it has the consistency of a firm custard. Tofu is available in firm, extra-firm, soft, and silken forms, depending on the coagulant and the percentage of water it contains. Because firmer tofu holds its shape better, it is ideal for stir-frying, grilling, and baking. Soft or silken tofu is better suited to dips and cream toppings. The boxed silken tofu found on the shelf is useful only when you need a smooth cream base with no pronounced soy flavor.

The best tofu is found in the refrigerator section of natural foods markets or grocery stores. Once the package is opened, store the tofu, covered with water, in a container in the refrigerator. Change the water daily, and the tofu will last up to a week.

Pressing tofu removes excess water, firms the texture, and allows it to absorb other flavors. A simple way to press tofu is to sandwich it between two plates with a weight on top. Let it sit for 30 minutes, and then drain. Another method is to wrap the tofu in a towel or bamboo mat and set it on a cutting board, plate, or tray near the sink. Raise one end a few inches and put a 2- to 4-pound weight on top. The water will drain into the towel or into the sink. You can also place the tofu in a colander over a bowl. Place a plate over the tofu and a weight on top of that. Let the tofu sit for at least 30 minutes.

Teriyaki Tofu

This stovetop teriyaki is sweetened with rice syrup, which makes a delicious glaze. The tofu is browned and then simmered as the sauce turns a rich mahogany color. It's a natural with Porcini-Miso Broth with Stir-fried Vegetables and Soba Noodles (page 218), and fabulous with Asian Slaw (page 95). If you'd like some teriyaki vegetables to go with the tofu, cut up carrots, daikon, and burdock and simmer them along with the tofu.

SERVES 4

1 pound firm tofu, drained and rinsed
1/3 cup brown rice syrup
1/4 cup shoyu
1/4 cup sake or mirin
1/4 cup apple juice or cider
1 tablespoon toasted sesame oil
1 tablespoon sesame oil or canola oil

Place the tofu on a pie plate and set a second plate on top. Weight the plate with a heavy can and press the tofu for at least 15 minutes. Drain.

Place the tofu cake on its side and cut it into thirds. Cut the 3 squares in half, forming triangles. Cut triangles down the middle to make 12 smaller triangles

Whisk the brown rice syrup, shoyu, sake, apple juice, and toasted sesame oil together in a small bowl. Set it aside.

Pat the tofu triangles dry. Warm the oil in a large nonstick skillet over medium-high heat, and sauté the tofu until golden, about 2 minutes per side. This can be done in two batches if necessary. Add the marinade and cook, uncovered, stirring occasionally, until the liquid has reduced to a syrupy consistency and the tofu is coated, about 15 minutes. Serve warm, drizzled with the glaze.

Baked Tofu

Baking tofu is one of the most convenient ways to infuse it with great flavor and texture. The marinade is a savory basic which is also luscious on tempeh. Serve this with Porcini-Miso Broth with Stir-fried Vegetables and Soba Noodles (page 218).

SERVES 4

1 pound firm or extra-firm tofu

3 tablespoons sesame oil

2 tablespoons brown rice vinegar

2 tablespoons apple juice or cider

2 tablespoons mirin

1 tablespoon shoyu

1 teaspoon toasted sesame oil

Place the tofu on a pie plate and set a second plate on top. Weight the plate with a heavy can and press the tofu for at least 30 minutes. Drain.

Make the marinade by whisking together the sesame oil, vinegar, apple juice, mirin, shoyu, and toasted sesame oil.

Place the tofu cake on its side and cut it into 3 thin slices. Turn the cake flat again, and cut diagonally through all 3 layers to make 6 triangles. Cut the triangles down the middle to form smaller triangles. Arrange the triangles in a single layer in an 8 by 8-inch baking dish, fitting the pieces together like a mosaic. Pour the marinade over the tofu. Let it sit for at least 30 minutes, turning once.

Meanwhile, preheat the oven to 375°F.

Bake the tofu in its marinade until it is golden brown and the marinade has been absorbed, about 40 minutes. Store, covered and refrigerated, for up to 2 days.

Glazed Tofu

A few minutes of simmering in a luscious glaze flavors this firm tofu. The cubes hold their shape in stir-fries and salads. Use it in place of the chicken in Asian Chicken Salad with Crispy Wonton Strips (page 268) and in the Tofu and Vegetable Stir-fry (page 224).

SERVES 4

1 pound firm or extra-firm tofu

2 tablespoons shoyu

3 tablespoons maple syrup

3 tablespoons mirin

1 tablespoon sesame oil or coconut oil

Place the tofu on a pie plate and set a second plate on top. Weight the plate with a heavy can, and press the tofu for 15 minutes. Drain.

Mix the shoyu, maple syrup, and mirin together in a bowl and set aside.

Pat the tofu dry. Cut the tofu into ¾-inch cubes. Heat the oil in a medium non-stick skillet over medium-high heat. Add the tofu and fry, flipping the cubes every 3 minutes, until golden, about 10 minutes. (You don't need to brown all six sides.) Add the shoyu mixture and simmer, flipping the tofu occasionally, until the sauce coats the tofu with a syrupy glaze, 3 to 4 minutes.

Remove from the skillet and use for stir-fries or salads. This can be prepared up to 2 days ahead.

Tofu and Vegetable Stir-fry

This wonderfully simple dish is easy to prepare after a hard day at work. The bright colors and fresh flavors make it as lovely to look at as it is delicious to eat. If you haven't already made the Glazed Tofu, prep the vegetables while you press the tofu; then glaze the tofu. Add some soba noodles and you have an entire meal in under half an hour.

SERVES 4

2 tablespoons plus 1 teaspoon sesame oil or canola oil
$\frac{1}{2}$ pound fresh shiitake mushrooms, stemmed and cut into $\frac{1}{4}$-inch pieces
1 pound broccoli, cut into florets
2 red bell peppers, cut into 1-inch cubes
3 garlic cloves, minced
1 tablespoon minced fresh ginger
$\frac{1}{2}$ teaspoon hot red pepper flakes
2 tablespoons water
1 recipe Glazed Tofu (page 223)
2 tablespoons fresh lemon juice
2 tablespoons shoyu
2 tablespoons mirin
1 tablespoon arrowroot powder
Salt

Warm the 2 tablespoons oil in a large skillet over medium-high heat until shimmering. Add the mushrooms, broccoli, and peppers, and cook for about 2 minutes, stirring constantly.

Clear a small space in the center of the skillet and add the remaining 1 teaspoon oil along with the garlic, ginger, and red pepper flakes. Cook until golden, about 1 minute. Add the water and scrape up any brown bits that have stuck to the skillet. Stir in the tofu, mix thoroughly, and cover. Cook until the vegetables are tender, about 2 minutes.

Stir the lemon juice, shoyu, mirin, and arrowroot together in a small bowl. Add this to the vegetables and stir, tossing until the vegetables are coated. Sprinkle with salt, and serve hot.

Barbecue Spice–Rubbed Tofu

This is a variation on the Butterflied Barbecue Spice–Rubbed Chicken (page 265). It makes a great sandwich with barbecue sauce and grilled vegetables, and is delicious chopped up in a grilled vegetable salad. If you don't want to grill it, you can sauté the tofu in a nonstick skillet.

Serves 4

1 pound firm or extra-firm tofu
2 tablespoons Barbecue Spice Rub (page 266)
2 tablespoons extra-virgin olive oil, plus more for grilling
1 recipe Barbecue Sauce (page 267)

Place the tofu on a pie plate and set a second plate on top. Weight the plate with a heavy can, and press the tofu for about 30 minutes.

Lay the tofu on its side and cut it into 4 lengthwise slices. Mix the spice rub with the olive oil in a small bowl, and using a brush, brush the rub on the tofu. Place the slabs back together in a block, and wrap it in plastic wrap. Chill the tofu in the refrigerator for at least 1 hour and up to 24 hours to absorb the spices.

Heat a grill or grill pan to medium-hot. Brush one side of the tofu with olive oil. Grill the tofu, oiled side down, for 2 to 3 minutes, rotating the tofu halfway through to get crosshatched grill marks. Oil the second side, flip the tofu over, and repeat. Serve topped or accompanied by the barbecue sauce.

Braised Tempeh with Curried Coconut Sauce

In this Indian fusion dish, protein-packed tempeh, simmered and sautéed, is slathered with a luscious coconut sauce. Serve it with Green Leaf, Date, and Cashew Salad (page 87) and Cardamom and Coconut Basmati Rice (page 201) for a vegetarian Indian feast.

SERVES 6

1 pound tempeh (two 8-ounce packages)
1½ cups water
¼ cup apple juice or mirin
¼ cup shoyu
One 2-inch piece fresh ginger, unpeeled, cut into 6 pieces
2 teaspoons curry powder
1 teaspoon paprika

Curried Coconut Sauce

1 tablespoon coconut oil or extra-virgin olive oil
½ cup minced onion
2 garlic cloves, minced
One 14-ounce can unsweetened light coconut milk
1 tablespoon maple sugar or evaporated cane sugar
2 teaspoons curry powder, preferably a spicy blend
¼ teaspoon garam masala
½ teaspoon salt
1 teaspoon fresh lemon juice

1 tablespoon coconut oil or extra-virgin olive oil
½ cup dried unsweetened coconut, toasted, for garnish (see Note)

Cut each ½-pound piece of tempeh into 12 triangles (see illustration, page 228). Place the tempeh in a large skillet and add the water, apple juice, shoyu, ginger, curry powder, and paprika. Cover, and bring to a boil. Then lower the heat and simmer for 15 minutes. Remove the tempeh from the skillet and set it aside.

Meanwhile, make the sauce: Warm the oil in a medium skillet over medium-low heat. Add the onions and garlic, and sauté until golden, about 5 minutes. Then add the coconut milk, sugar, curry powder, garam masala, and salt. Bring to a boil, reduce the heat, and simmer, uncovered, until the sauce has thickened, about 5 minutes. Stir in the lemon juice and set aside.

Warm the oil in a nonstick skillet over medium-high heat. Add the tempeh and sauté, turning once, until golden, about 4 minutes. Serve hot with the coconut sauce, and garnish with the toasted coconut.

NOTE: *To toast coconut: Dry-toast coconut in a heavy-bottomed skillet, stirring constantly until lightly golden, 2 to 3 minutes. Or spread on a baking sheet and place in a 350°F oven until lightly golden, 3 to 4 minutes.*

Baked Thai Tempeh Triangles

Turn these flavorful triangles into a dazzling dish by serving them with Yellow Pepper–Coconut Milk Sauce (page 173), Spinach-Basil Sauce (page 172), and rice. A quick steam before baking with the marinade helps the tempeh absorb the maximum amount of flavor.

SERVES 6

1 pound tempeh (two 8-ounce packages)
¼ cup apple juice or cider
½ cup water
2 tablespoons maple syrup
¼ cup shoyu
2 tablespoons fresh lemon juice
¼ cup canola oil
1 tablespoon red or green Thai curry paste
½ cup roughly chopped fresh cilantro
3 garlic cloves

Preheat the oven to 350°F.

Cut each 1⁄2-pound package of tempeh into 12 triangles. Place the tempeh in a steamer basket and steam over a pot of simmering water for 5 minutes.

Meanwhile, make the marinade: Whisk the apple juice, water, maple syrup, shoyu, lemon juice, and oil in a medium bowl until thoroughly blended. Stir in the curry paste, cilantro, and garlic cloves.

Place the tempeh in a single layer in a 9 by 11-inch baking dish, and pour the marinade over it. Bake the tempeh, turning it once, until it is golden brown and most of the marinade has been absorbed, 40 to 45 minutes. Serve hot.

NOTE: *Thai curry paste comes in a jar; both red and green versions are readily available.*

Smokin' Drunken Chili

This festive vegetarian chili, which tastes as if it has been cooking all day, is long on flavor but short on cooking time. It's especially delicious when prepared with a mix of kidney and black beans. Chipotle chiles are smoky and hot, so adjust the quantity to suit your preference.

SERVES 4

1 tablespoon extra-virgin olive oil
2 onions, cut into small dice (2 cups)
1/2 medium green bell pepper, cut into small dice
Salt
1 or 2 chipotle chiles in adobo sauce, minced
3 garlic cloves, minced
2 teaspoons ground cumin
1 teaspoon dried oregano
1/2 pound seitan
2 tablespoons tomato paste
One 14-ounce can diced tomatoes, preferably fire-roasted
Two 15-ounce cans kidney beans, black beans, pinto beans, or a
      combination, drained and rinsed, *or* 3 cups cooked beans
1 cup beer or water
1 tablespoon fresh lime juice
1/4 cup chopped fresh cilantro, for garnish
1/2 avocado, cut into wedges, for garnish

Warm the olive oil in a medium skillet over medium-low heat. Add the onions, bell peppers, and 1 teaspoon salt. Cook until the onions are translucent, about 10 minutes. Then add the chiles, garlic, cumin, and oregano, and cook for 3 minutes.

Meanwhile, place the seitan in a food processor and process until ground.

Add the ground seitan, tomato paste, and diced tomatoes to the skillet and cook, stirring constantly, for 5 minutes.

Pour the contents of the skillet into a medium pot, and add the beans and beer. Cover and simmer, stirring occasionally to prevent the chili from sticking, for 15 to 20 minutes. Stir in the lime juice, and add salt if needed. Sprinkle each serving with cilantro and garnish with a wedge of avocado.

Sancocho Stew

Sancocho is a favorite dish in Colombia and throughout the Spanish-speaking Caribbean. (The Spanish word *sancocho* means "stew.") Its singular flavor comes from a combination of Latin American root vegetables that meld together beautifully. Feel free to substitute other root vegetables for the ones listed here.

SERVES 4 TO 6

2 tablespoons extra-virgin olive oil

1 onion, cut into small dice (1 cup)

1 celery stalk, cut into ¾-inch-thick slices

Salt

1 green plantain, peeled, halved, and cut into ¾-inch chunks (see Notes)

½ pound yuca, cut into ¾-inch chunks (1 cup) (see Notes)

One 14-ounce can diced tomatoes, preferably fire-roasted

1 teaspoon ground cumin

Pinch of saffron threads

¼ cup dry white wine

2½ cups water, vegetable stock, or chicken stock

One 14-ounce can unsweetened light coconut milk

½ pound thin-skinned potatoes, such as Red Bliss, cut into 1-inch chunks (about 1 cup)

¼ pound green beans, halved, ends trimmed (about 1 cup)

2 ears corn, husked and cut into 1-inch-thick wheels

1 tablespoon fresh lime juice

Cayenne pepper

2 tablespoons thinly sliced scallions, white and green parts

2 tablespoons chopped fresh cilantro

Warm the oil in a medium saucepan over medium-low heat. Add the onions and celery, and sauté until beginning to soften, about 7 minutes. Add 1½ teaspoons salt, the plantains, and the yuca, and cook for 5 minutes.

Add the tomatoes, cumin, saffron, and wine. Raise the heat and simmer, uncovered, until reduced by half, about 10 minutes.

Add the water, coconut milk, and potatoes. Cover and bring to a boil. Reduce the heat and simmer until the potatoes are tender, about 20 minutes. Add the green beans and corn wheels and cook, partially covered, for 5 minutes.

Remove from the heat and stir in the lime juice and a pinch of cayenne. Let the mixture sit for at least 15 minutes. Taste, and add a sprinkling of salt if necessary. Stir in the scallions and cilantro, and serve hot.

NOTES: *Plantains, or* platanos, *resemble large bananas. They are eaten at every stage of ripeness, from green to yellow, but are inedible in their raw state. Use the green ones here, as the ripe ones are too sweet. To peel a green plantain, cut off the ends and make three or four slits down the length of the plantain, cutting just through the skin. Use a paring knife to peel off the skin.*

Yuca is a starchy tuber with white flesh and barklike dark brown skin. It ranges dramatically in length, from 4 inches to 2 feet, and it has a fibrous core that needs to be removed. I find it easiest to cut the root into 2-inch-thick cylinders. Stand the yuca upright on one end. Using downward strokes of a knife, peel off the skin. Quarter the white flesh. Cut out the core on each quarter. The cored quarters are ready for chopping or grating.

To cut corn wheels: Lodge a knife crosswise in the corn, and whack the knife with the palm of your hand to cut through the cob.

Indian-Spiced Cauliflower, Chickpeas, Potatoes, and Kale

This fragrant stew, with its tasty blend of Indian spices, was inspired by one of cookbook author Julie Sahni's recipes. Although kale is not traditionally Indian, it rounds out the dish beautifully, making it a meal in a pot.

Be sure to prep and measure the vegetables and spices before you begin cooking, because the dish comes together quickly. Serve it with the Cucumber, Peanut, and Yogurt Raita (page 180) and Cardamom and Coconut Basmati Rice (page 201).

SERVES 4 TO 6

1/4 cup ghee or coconut oil

2 teaspoons whole cumin seeds

1 teaspoon ground cumin

2 tablespoons ground coriander

1 teaspoon ground turmeric

1/2 teaspoon ground Indian chile powder *or* 1/4 to 1/2 teaspoon cayenne pepper (see Note)

1 small head (1 to 1 1/4 pounds) cauliflower, cut into 1 1/2-inch florets

2 medium (1/2 pound) thin-skinned potatoes, cut into 1-inch pieces

One 15-ounce can chickpeas, drained and rinsed, *or* 1 1/2 cups cooked chickpeas

One 15-ounce can crushed tomatoes, preferably fire-roasted

1 cup water

4 cups shredded kale

Salt

1/4 cup finely chopped fresh cilantro

Heat the ghee in a large heavy-bottomed pot over medium-high heat. Add the cumin seeds and fry until they turn brown, about 20 seconds. Add the ground cumin, coriander, turmeric, and chile powder. Stir for a moment, and immediately add the cauliflower and potatoes. Stir constantly for 5 minutes.

Add the chickpeas and crushed tomatoes. Scrape up any brown bits on the bottom of the pot, and continue cooking until the purée thickens, about 3 minutes. Then add the water, kale, and 2 teaspoons salt. Reduce the heat and simmer, covered, until the vegetables are tender and cooked through, about 15 minutes. Remove the pot from the heat. Taste, and add a bit more salt if necessary. Serve hot, sprinkled with the cilantro.

This dish reheats beautifully with the addition of a little water.

NOTE: *Indian chile powder is ground red chile. It is available in Indian stores and comes in various degrees of spiciness. Cayenne pepper makes a fine substitute, but you may want to use a smaller amount.*

Kukus

A *kuku*, or Persian-style frittata, is a light quichelike dish made with a lot of vegetables and just enough eggs to bind them. It's unlike a frittata or a quiche in that it doesn't have a distinctive egg flavor, yet has a light texture. Best of all, *kukus* make their own golden crust as they bake, so they are, in essence, a crustless pie. You can make them with or without dairy and with any vegetables you like, as long as you cook the vegetables thoroughly before adding them to the eggs. There is no last-minute fussing with these dishes, making them ideal for company. For a large crowd, I get the filling ready the day before. An hour before serving, I mix the eggs, baking powder, and flour into the filling and place the *kukus* in the oven to bake. *Kukus* are tasty at room temperature and also make great leftovers. Use a glass pie plate for the best results.

Cauliflower, Green Bean, and Mushroom Kuku

The cauliflower is light and fluffy—no need for cheese here. To round out the meal, serve the *kuku* with Shredded Romaine Salad with Dill and Scallions (page 81) and *Mujadarrah* (page 210). For a stylish brunch, start with Orange Walnut Crêpes (page 286) with Citrus Compote Supreme (page 284).

SERVES 4

1 small head cauliflower or half a large head, broken into
    medium florets (4 cups)
$1/4$ pound green beans, ends trimmed, cut into $1/4$-inch pieces (1 cup)
4 tablespoons butter, ghee, or coconut oil
1 medium onion, thinly sliced (1 cup)
2 cups sliced cremini mushrooms
2 garlic cloves, minced
$1^{1}/4$ teaspoons salt
4 eggs
Freshly ground black pepper
$1/2$ teaspoon baking powder
1 tablespoon unbleached white flour
$1/2$ cup chopped mixed fresh herbs (a combination of parsley,
    chives, and dill is delicious)

Set a steamer basket over a pot of simmering water. Add the cauliflower and steam until it is very tender, 10 minutes. Remove the cauliflower from the steamer and use a fork to mash it into small pieces. Set it aside in a large bowl.

Steam the green beans until very soft, about 5 minutes. Add the beans to the cauliflower.

Warm 1 tablespoon of the butter in a medium skillet over medium-low heat. Add the onions, mushrooms, and garlic, and sauté until the onions are browned, about 10 minutes. Add this mixture to the cauliflower and beans, and stir in $3/4$ teaspoon of the salt.

Preheat the oven to 350°F.

Break the eggs into a medium bowl. Add the remaining $1/2$ teaspoon salt, a generous sprinkling of black pepper, the baking powder, and the flour. Whisk together thoroughly; there will probably be a few lumps.

Mix the egg batter and the herbs into the vegetables, stirring to combine thoroughly.

Place 2 tablespoons of the butter in a 9-inch ovenproof pie plate, and place it in the oven. Heat the butter for a couple of minutes, until hot. Remove the pie plate, swirl the butter around to coat the bottom, and pour in the egg mixture, evening it out with a spatula. Return the pie plate to the oven and bake, uncovered, for 30 minutes.

Remove the *kuku* from the oven and gently scatter little pieces of the remaining 1 tablespoon butter over the top (if you are using oil, drizzle it). Place the dish back in the oven and bake until golden brown, 20 to 30 minutes.

Unmold the *kuku* by loosening the edges with a knife. Slide it onto a serving platter, and serve hot or at room temperature.

Crispy Potato and Broccoli Kuku

This falls somewhere between a broccoli-stuffed baked potato and a Spanish potato frittata, known as a *tortilla*. It can be served hot or at room temperature, with bread and salad.

SERVES 4 TO 6

1 pound (2 medium-large) russet potatoes

2 tablespoons extra-virgin olive oil

1 teaspoon salt

1 large head broccoli, broken into florets (about 4 cups)

1 onion, thinly sliced (1 cup)

1 large bunch (1/2 pound) arugula, washed, thick stems removed,
  and finely chopped (11/2 cups)

4 large eggs

Freshly ground black pepper

1 tablespoon unbleached white flour

1/2 teaspoon baking powder

2 tablespoons butter, ghee, or coconut oil

Preheat the oven to 375°F.

Peel the potatoes and cut them into small dice; you should have about 1½ cups. Toss the potatoes in a bowl with 1 tablespoon of the olive oil and ½ teaspoon of the salt. Spread the potatoes out on a parchment-covered baking sheet, and roast, stirring every 10 minutes, until tender and browned, 30 to 40 minutes. Transfer the potatoes to a medium bowl. Lower the oven heat to 350°F.

Set a steamer basket over a pot of simmering water. Add the broccoli and steam until it is very tender, 10 minutes. Remove it from the heat, use a fork to mash it into small pieces, and stir it into the potatoes.

Warm the remaining 1 tablespoon olive oil in a medium skillet over medium heat. Add the onions and sauté until golden, 8 to 10 minutes. Add the onions to the broccoli and potatoes. Stir the arugula into the broccoli-potato mixture.

Break the eggs into a medium bowl. Sprinkle with the remaining ½ teaspoon salt, black pepper to taste, the flour, and the baking powder. Whisk together until well combined; don't worry if there are a few lumps. Mix the egg mixture into the vegetable mixture, stirring to combine.

Place 1 tablespoon of the butter in a 9-inch ovenproof pie plate, and place it in the oven. Heat the butter for a couple of minutes, until hot. Remove the pie plate, swirl the butter around to coat the bottom, and pour in the egg mixture, evening it out with a spatula. Return the pie plate to the oven and bake, uncovered, for 30 minutes.

Remove the *kuku* and gently scatter little pieces of the remaining 1 tablespoon butter over the top (if you are using oil, drizzle it). Place the dish back in the oven and bake until golden brown, 15 to 20 minutes.

Unmold the *kuku* by loosening the edges with a knife. Slide it onto a serving platter, and serve hot or at room temperature.

You can make this up to a day in advance and reheat it.

Spinach Pie Kuku

With the addition of ricotta, Gruyère, and eggs, the Italian vegetable classic of sautéed spinach with pine nuts and raisins is transformed into a main course worthy of Cosimo di Medici.

SERVES 4 TO 6

1/4 cup raisins

1/4 cup rum or water

2 pounds fresh spinach, stemmed and washed, *or* 1 1/2 pounds
    baby spinach, washed

2 tablespoons extra-virgin olive oil

1/2 cup finely diced red onion

1/4 cup pine nuts

2 garlic cloves, minced

1 teaspoon salt

Freshly ground black pepper

Freshly grated nutmeg

1 cup ricotta cheese, preferably fresh

1 cup grated Gruyère cheese, preferably raw-milk Gruyère

4 eggs, lightly beaten

1 tablespoon unbleached white flour

1/2 teaspoon baking powder

2 tablespoons butter, ghee, or coconut oil

Preheat the oven to 350°F.

Combine the raisins and the rum in a small pot. Bring to a boil and simmer until all of the liquid is absorbed and the raisins are plumped, about 3 minutes. Set aside.

Place the spinach in a large skillet. Cook over medium heat, stirring frequently or tossing with tongs to push the uncooked leaves to the bottom of the skillet, just until the leaves have wilted, about 3 to 4 minutes. (You don't have to add water to the skillet; the water clinging to the wet leaves is enough to cook them.) Remove the spinach and place it in a strainer. Squeeze it against the strainer to remove any excess water. Place the spinach on a cutting board, and chop it into small pieces.

Warm the oil in a large skillet over medium heat. Add the onions and pine nuts, and cook until the onions are softened and the pine nuts are lightly golden, about 6 minutes. Stir in the garlic, spinach, raisins, 1/2 teaspoon of the salt, and a sprinkling of black pepper. Stir thoroughly until heated through. Remove the skillet from the heat and sprinkle nutmeg to taste over the mixture. Transfer the mixture to a large bowl, and stir in the ricotta, Gruyère, eggs, flour, baking powder, remaining ½ teaspoon salt, and a sprinkling of black pepper.

Place 1 tablespoon of the butter in a 9-inch ovenproof pie plate, and place it in the oven. Heat the butter for a couple of minutes, until hot. Remove the pie plate, swirl the butter around to coat the bottom, and pour in the egg mixture, using a spatula to even it out. Return the pie plate to the oven and bake, uncovered, for 30 minutes.

Remove the *kuku* from the oven and gently scatter the remaining 1 tablespoon butter over the top (if you are using oil, drizzle it). Place the dish back in the oven and bake until golden brown, 15 to 20 minutes.

Unmold the *kuku* by loosening the edges with a knife. Slide it onto a serving platter, and serve hot or at room temperature.

Fish and Chicken

Orange-Glazed Flounder with Watercress

   Orange-Glazed Tofu with Watercress

Red Snapper Provençale

Black Bass in Leek-Saffron-Tomato Broth

Salmon Medallions with Lime-Mustard Teriyaki

Turkish Stuffed Trout in Parchment

Seared Sesame-Crusted Tuna

Broiled Miso Black Cod

Fish in Charmoula

Pecan-Crusted Trout with Lemon-Sage Butter

Fish Tacos with Designer Guacamole and Cabbage Slaw

Salt Cod and Potato Cakes

Porcini Mushroom Ragout with Chicken

   Porcini Mushroom Ragout with Tempeh

Roast Chicken with Maple Glaze

Butterflied Barbecue Spice–Rubbed Chicken

Asian Chicken Salad with Crispy Wonton Strips

Seven-Vegetable Moroccan Stew

Sautéed Chicken with Mango and Red Onion Chutney

Some of these fish

and chicken recipes are classics with a fresh twist; others involve creative uses of ethnic flavor combinations, with inspiration ranging from Turkey to Japan and from Provence to Morocco. The techniques have been streamlined for minimum fuss and maximum flavor. The dishes include everything from quick weeknight meals to gorgeous presentations worthy of an impressive dinner party. They are simple enough for a novice cook, and interesting enough for those with more experience. The recipes that require more preparation, such as the miso-marinated Broiled Miso Black Cod or the Salt Cod and Potato Cakes, are low on actual labor. A number of the recipes include rubs and pastes. They are quick to make and easy to store; rubs store in the pantry for months, and the pastes keep in the refrigerator for weeks. Once you have these on hand, the dish is quickly assembled. ◎ Even if you're a strict vegetarian, don't skip this chapter. A few of the recipes offer vegetarian options that are just as delicious as their fish and chicken counterparts. The Seven-Vegetable Moroccan Stew, for example, has a vegetarian version using chickpeas. The barbecue rub on the chicken is excellent on tofu as well. The Porcini Mushroom Ragout is wonderful on chicken and scrumptious over braised tempeh. Flexitarians should try the vegetarian alternatives for variety. ◎ These days it is prudent to exercise caution when it comes to animal products. With fish, there are three main concerns: the toxicity level; whether the fish is wild or farm-raised; and if the particular species is overfished. The very largest fish in the sea—including swordfish, king mackerel, shark, marlin, and tilefish—contain the highest level of mercury. For the same reason, the Environmental Protection Agency recommends eating fresh tuna only once a month and no more than 6 ounces of canned albacore tuna a week. If you're going to have tuna only occasionally, make it a fabulous dish to remember: You'll find seared tuna with sesame seeds here, and tuna burgers in the "Burgers" chapter. ◎ Farm-raised fish are lower in the beneficial omega-3 fatty acids than are wild fish because they do not consume small fish rich in epa (eicosapentaenoic acid) and dha (docosahexaenoic acid). The fish are cooped up in tight pens, often in polluted water. Salmon, for instance, are fed antibiotics along with additives to make their flesh pink—the color that occurs naturally in the wild. All Atlantic salmon is farm-raised, so it's a better bet to eat salmon from the Pacific. In addition, wild salmon tastes much better. I've included a number of recipes with fish that have especially high amounts of omega-3 fatty acids, such as anchovies and salmon. ◉ Buy your seafood from a reliable store where the fish are displayed on a lot of ice or in a proper cooler. Whole fish should have glistening skins and brilliant eyes. Fillets and steaks should look translucent, with unblemished flesh and no traces of bruises or spots. The flesh should look firm, not flaking or falling apart. If the fish you had in mind does not look good, pick another type. If you purchase packaged fish, first smell the package; a bad odor will penetrate even several layers of packaging. Once at home, fish should not be stored uncooked for more than a day. ◉ The best chicken to buy is organic, cage-free chicken. Organic chickens that are fed with high amounts of omega-3s, such as flax seed, produce eggs that contain higher amounts of omega-3s. The term "organic" means that the chicken feed is organic rather than genetically engineered soy or corn. It also means the animals were given no antibiotics or artificial growth hormones and were not debeaked. Luckily, organic poultry is in greater demand nowadays, and it is becoming easier and easier to find places that carry it. It is worth seeking out for these reasons and also because of its superior flavor. The term "free range" by itself does not mean much; the FDA allows farmers to label their chickens "free range" when they open the coop doors for only five minutes a day. ◉ When it comes to animal products, it is a good idea to investigate your sources. Once you're knowledgeable about the conditions in which animals are raised, you're more likely to seek out those purveyors that treat their animals humanely. ◉ Organic chickens and wild fish are pricier than their conventional counterparts. The extra expense is worth it for your health, the well-being of the environment, and the delight of your palate. Furthermore, buying organic means voting with your dollars. It's an important step toward increasing humane farming practices. The more interest there is in organic, the more available these products become.

Orange-Glazed Flounder with Watercress

Cook up a pot of basmati rice, prep your watercress, have everything at your finger-tips, and within minutes you'll have a sizzling meal in a pan. Although my favorite fish for this is fluke because of its firm flesh, you can use any other thin fish fillet, with equally delicious results. Tofu works well here too; see the variation at the end of the recipe.

SERVES 4

1 cup fresh orange juice
¼ cup shoyu
¼ cup water
¼ cup sake, mirin, or dry sherry
1 scallion, white and green parts, thinly sliced
Four 5-ounce pieces flounder, fluke, sole, or tilapia fillet
Salt
Freshly ground black pepper
¼ cup unbleached white flour
2 tablespoons plus 1 teaspoon coconut or canola oil
2 garlic cloves, thinly sliced
2 bunches watercress, washed, thick stems removed
1 tablespoon sesame seeds
Few drops of toasted sesame oil
½ lemon, cut into wedges

Pour the orange juice into a medium skillet, bring it to a boil, and lower the heat. Simmer rapidly, uncovered, until the juice is reduced to ¼ cup, about 10 minutes. Transfer the orange juice to a small bowl and add the shoyu, water, and sake. Stir in the scallions, and set aside.

Season the fish with salt and black pepper to taste. Spread the flour on a plate and lightly press each fillet into it, making sure both sides are completely dusted.

Heat 2 tablespoons of the oil in a large, heavy-bottomed skillet over high heat. Immediately add the fish. Reduce the heat to medium and sauté until both sides are lightly golden, 2 to 3 minutes on each side. Divide the fish among four warmed plates.

Add the remaining 1 teaspoon oil and the garlic to the skillet and sauté until lightly browned, about 30 seconds. Carefully add the orange juice marinade to the skillet, and cook until thickened, about 1 minute. Pour the marinade over the fish.

(CONTINUED NEXT PAGE)

Add the watercress to the skillet and cook until just wilted, about 30 seconds. Remove the skillet from the heat, and stir in the sesame seeds and a sprinkling of salt and black pepper. Drizzle a few drops of sesame oil over the watercress.

Mound some watercress next to the fish on each plate. Squeeze a lemon wedge over each fillet, and serve.

Orange-Glazed Tofu with Watercress (SERVES 4)

1 pound firm tofu

Drain and rinse the tofu. Lay the tofu block on its side and cut it into 4 equal slices. Cut through the block diagonally to make 8 triangles. Keeping the block intact, place the tofu on a pie plate. Set another plate on top, and weight it with a heavy can. Press for 15 minutes. Drain. Pat the tofu dry.

Follow the recipe above, substituting the tofu for the flounder.

Red Snapper Provençale

This is one of my favorite standbys. It's a variation on puttanesca sauce, with fennel adding a distinctive touch. Like that notorious sauce, you can make this in a hurry. For a delicious and colorful dinner, serve the snapper with Quinoa Primavera (page 195) and roasted asparagus (page 166). Niçoise olives are especially tasty, but they're not pitted. Just warn everyone at the table to watch for pits.

SERVES 4

2 tablespoons extra-virgin olive oil

1 fennel bulb, trimmed and thinly sliced (2 cups) (see Note)

One 14.5-ounce can diced tomatoes

3 garlic cloves, minced

1/2 teaspoon hot red pepper flakes

1/2 cup niçoise olives (24 olives) *or* 1/2 cup halved pitted
    kalamata olives

4 teaspoons capers, drained and rinsed

4 anchovy fillets, finely chopped

Four 5-ounce thick white fish fillets, such as red snapper,
    black or striped bass, or grouper

Salt

Freshly ground black pepper

1/4 cup chopped fresh parsley

1 tablespoon grated lemon zest

Warm the olive oil in a large skillet over medium-low heat. Add the fennel and sauté until it is softened, about 10 minutes. Add the tomatoes, garlic, red pepper flakes, olives, capers, and anchovies. Simmer until the tomatoes are reduced by half, 5 to 7 minutes. (You can make the sauce to this point up to a day in advance. Cover, refrigerate, and reheat before continuing. You may have to add 1/4 cup water to the skillet if all of the liquid has been absorbed.)

Add the fillets to the sauce, and sprinkle salt and black pepper over each fillet. Cover the skillet and cook until the fish is opaque, 5 to 10 minutes, depending on the thickness of the fillets. Check after 5 minutes to see if there is enough liquid in the pan. If not, stir in 1/4 cup water. If there is too much liquid (for instance, if you added too much because you thought you didn't have enough), just uncover the pan and cook until the liquid evaporates, about 1 minute.

Spoon the sauce over the fish, and sprinkle with the parsley and lemon zest. Divide the fish among four plates, and divide any extra sauce among the fish.

NOTE: *To trim fennel, cut off any protruding tops. Shave any discolored or bruised parts off the bulb. Cut the fennel bulb in half, and remove the hard core with a paring knife. Slice the fennel lengthwise into very thin slices.*

Black Bass in Leek-Saffron-Tomato Broth

This easy and elegant stovetop braise bursts with Mediterranean flavors. It is great for a weeknight dinner, simple enough for a novice cook. When you want to impress your guests, serve it with Frisée, Endive, and Celery Salad (page 90) and Easy Polenta (page 192).

SERVES 4

2 tablespoons extra-virgin olive oil

2 cups diced leeks, white and light green parts

One 14-ounce can diced tomatoes,
    preferably fire-roasted

2 garlic cloves, minced

1/2 teaspoon saffron threads

1/4 teaspoon hot red pepper flakes

1 bay leaf

1/4 cup white wine, preferably dry

Four 5-ounce fillets of striped or black bass,
    or halibut or grouper

Salt and freshly ground black pepper

1/4 cup chopped fresh parsley

1 tablespoon grated orange zest

Warm the olive oil in a large skillet over medium-low heat. Add the leeks and cook until softened, about 4 minutes. Add the tomatoes, garlic, saffron, red pepper flakes, bay leaf, and wine. Simmer until the tomatoes have reduced by half, 5 to 7 minutes. (You can make the sauce to this point up to a day in advance. Cover, refrigerate, and reheat before continuing. You may have to add 1/4 cup water to the skillet if all of the liquid has been absorbed.)

Add the fish to the sauce, and season it with a sprinkling of salt and black pepper. Cover the skillet and cook until the fish is opaque, 5 to 10 minutes, depending on the thickness of the fillets. Check after 5 minutes to see if there is enough liquid in the skillet. If not, stir in 1/4 cup water. If there is too much liquid when the fish is cooked, uncover the skillet and cook for a minute to thicken the juices.

Spoon some of the tomato mixture over the fish, and sprinkle with the parsley and lemon zest. Divide the fish among four plates, and divide any extra sauce among the fish.

NOTES: *Muir Glen organic fire-roasted tomatoes, available in natural foods stores and gourmet markets, are delicious and add good flavor to the recipe.*

Make sure to buy saffron threads; the powder is sometimes adulterated. Although saffron is hand-harvested and quite pricey, you need to use only very small amounts to take advantage of its distinctive flavor.

Salmon Medallions with Lime-Mustard Teriyaki

The salmon takes a quick dip in a lime marinade while you make a luxurious mahogany glaze. If you prefer, you can use salmon fillets. The salmon may be either grilled or baked.

SERVES 4

Two 12- to 16-ounce salmon steaks

Marinade

¼ cup extra-virgin olive oil
2 tablespoons fresh lime juice
2 tablespoons shoyu

Glaze

¼ cup maple syrup
¼ cup shoyu
2 tablespoons fresh lime juice
1 tablespoon balsamic vinegar
1 tablespoon Dijon mustard
2 tablespoons water

Rinse the salmon steaks and pat them dry with a clean towel. Cut out and remove the center bone. Divide each steak in half, and coil the flaps inward to form a circle with the skin side toward the center. Secure it with white cotton twine tied around the out-

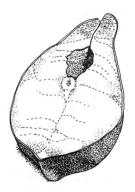
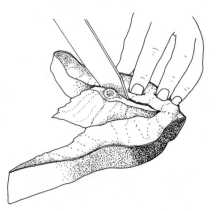

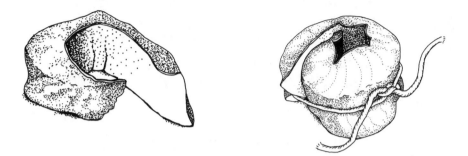

side. Brush your finger over the salmon to see if there are any bones left, and if there are, remove them with your fingers, tweezers, or pliers.

Make the marinade: In a small bowl, mix together the olive oil, lime juice, and shoyu.

Lay the salmon in a baking dish and pour the marinade over it. Leave the salmon in the marinade for 5 minutes. Then turn it over and marinate for up to 30 minutes.

Meanwhile, prepare the glaze: Whisk the maple syrup, shoyu, lime juice, balsamic vinegar, mustard, and water together in a small saucepan. Bring to a boil, reduce the heat, and simmer until the mixture thickens to a glaze consistency, 5 to 6 minutes.

To grill the salmon: Preheat an outdoor or indoor grill. Remove the salmon from the marinade and pat it dry. Grill the salmon until it is just cooked and slightly pink in the middle, 3 to 5 minutes on each side. Remove the string. Serve with 1 tablespoon warm glaze spooned over each serving.

To bake the salmon: Preheat the oven to 400°F. Remove the salmon from the marinade and place it in a shallow baking dish or on a parchment-covered rimmed baking sheet. Cook just until the salmon is lightly pink in the middle, 8 to 10 minutes, depending on the thickness of the fish. Remove the string. Serve with 1 tablespoon warm glaze spooned over each serving.

NOTE: *Don't be afraid to cook the glaze until it is syrupy; you will know it's done when it starts to bubble furiously.*

Turkish Stuffed Trout in Parchment

These neat heart-shaped parchment packages conceal a whole trout stuffed with an exotic blend of herbs and onions, almonds, dates, and cinnamon. For an Istanbul extravaganza, serve the trout with Dolma Pilaf (page 196), Shredded Romaine Salad with Dill and Scallions (page 81), and Zucchini Latkes (page 118).

SERVES 4 TO 6

2 tablespoons plus 4 teaspoons extra-virgin olive oil
1 cup finely chopped onion
1 cup fresh bread crumbs
1/2 cup sliced almonds, toasted
1/4 cup chopped dates
1/4 cup chopped fresh parsley
1/4 cup chopped fresh dill
1/4 teaspoon ground cinnamon
Salt
Freshly ground black pepper
1 tablespoon fresh lemon juice
Four whole 12- to 16-ounce trout, gutted and cleaned,
    backbone, head, and tail removed
1 large egg white

Preheat the oven to 400°F.

Warm the 2 tablespoons olive oil in a medium skillet over medium-low heat. Add the onions and cook until they are softened, about 7 minutes. Add the bread crumbs and almonds, and stir for a few seconds. Then stir in the dates, parsley, dill, cinnamon, and 1/4 teaspoon salt. Add a generous sprinkling of black pepper and the lemon juice. Set aside.

Cut 4 pieces of parchment paper to measure 20 by 15 inches. Fold each one in half, short end to short end. Draw half a heart shape on the paper, beginning at the fold and going out to the edge. Use scissors to cut out the shape, and unfold the parchment.

Sprinkle the trout lightly with salt, inside and out. Open each trout like a book, and spread 1/2 cup of the filling evenly over the whole trout. If the trout are different sizes, give the smaller ones a little less filling and the larger ones a little more. Fold the trout closed over the filling.

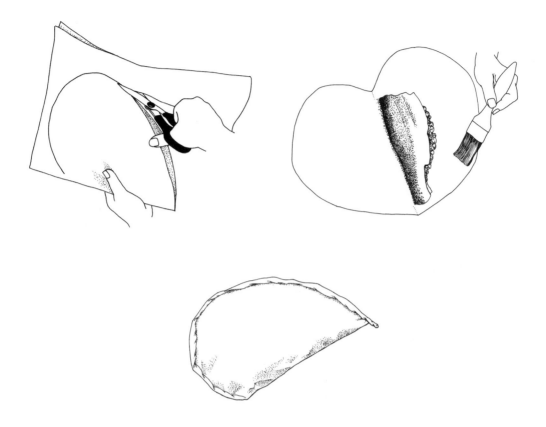

Place each trout on one side of a parchment heart, and drizzle 1 teaspoon olive oil over each fish. Brush the beaten egg white along the edges of the parchment. Fold the paper over the fish and crimp the edges together. Fold the edges over twice, ending with a twist at the bottom of the heart.

Place the parchment packages on a baking sheet and bake until the paper is puffed and browned, about 15 minutes. Transfer the packages to a platter, and use sharp scissors to cut them open. Slide the contents of each package onto a plate, and serve.

NOTE: *If you wish to serve half a trout, it's easiest to cut through the fish after it's baked.*

Seared Sesame-Crusted Tuna

This is a decadent way to eat tuna; the thick marinade adds a layer of flavor and secures the sesame seeds. You don't have to use black sesame seeds if you can't find them, but the mixture of black and white is striking.

Have your fishmonger cut thick steaks, at least $1\frac{1}{2}$ inches thick. If you don't see what you want, ask for it. They almost always stash a loin of tuna in the back.

SERVES 4

$\frac{1}{4}$ cup minced shallots

$1\frac{1}{2}$ teaspoons shoyu

1 teaspoon toasted sesame oil

1 tablespoon Dijon mustard

$1\frac{1}{2}$ teaspoons dry sherry, mirin, or sake

1 tablespoon natural brown sugar, such as Sucanat or maple sugar

1 to $1\frac{1}{4}$ pounds tuna, cut at least $1\frac{1}{2}$ inches thick

Dipping sauce

2 tablespoons shoyu

2 tablespoons water

1 tablespoon mirin

1 tablespoon brown rice vinegar

1 teaspoon toasted sesame oil

1 cup sesame seeds (preferably $\frac{1}{2}$ cup white sesame seeds
    and $\frac{1}{2}$ cup black)

2 tablespoons sesame oil, olive oil, or coconut oil

Prepare the fish: Combine the shallots, shoyu, toasted sesame oil, mustard, sherry, and sugar in a bowl. Cut the fish into 4 pieces. Slather the fish with the mixture and marinate for at least 30 minutes and up to 24 hours, making sure all the pieces are coated; if marinating for more than 30 minutes, cover and refrigerate.

Prepare the dipping sauce: Combine the sauce ingredients in a small bowl, and mix well. Divide the sauce among four small dishes.

Mix the sesame seeds together if you are using two colors, and spread them out on a plate. Dredge all sides of the fish in the seeds.

Warm the oil in a medium nonstick or cast-iron skillet over medium-high heat. Add the fish and sear it for 2 minutes on all sides, or until the white sesame seeds are golden brown.

Transfer the fish to a cutting board. If you want it to be a bit more cooked on the inside, let it rest for a few minutes before cutting it; the residual heat will cook the fish a little more. Cut the fish into ½-inch-thick slices and fan them out on each plate. Serve with the dipping sauce.

Broiled Miso Black Cod

This is a dish that you rarely see outside of fine Japanese restaurants, and it's guaranteed to elicit moans of appreciation at the table. The fish is marinated in a blend of miso, sake, and mirin for a sweet and savory combination. Black cod (sablefish) has a smooth, buttery texture and a sweet, rich flavor. Chilean sea bass is also delicious, but I avoid it because it is so overfished. Pollack makes a good substitute for the black cod, and in a pinch, salmon works well too.

SERVES 4

1/2 cup mellow or sweet white miso

1/2 cup sake

1/2 cup mirin or dry sherry

1 tablespoon natural brown sugar, such as maple sugar
    or Sucanat

2 tablespoons shoyu

1 tablespoon minced fresh ginger

1 tablespoon brown rice vinegar

1 1/2 pounds black cod, skin on

1/4 cup snipped fresh chives or thinly sliced scallions,
    white and green parts

Mix the miso, sake, mirin, sugar, shoyu, ginger, and vinegar together in a medium bowl. Remove and reserve 1/3 cup of the marinade.

Arrange the fish in a 2-inch-deep baking dish that is just large enough to hold it in one layer. Pour the remaining marinade over the fish, and turn the fish over to coat it well. Cover the dish, place it in the refrigerator, and let it marinate for at least 2 hours and up to overnight.

Preheat the broiler.

Remove the fish from the marinade, letting any excess liquid drip off. Place the fish on a broiler pan and broil, 10 to 15 minutes, depending on the thickness of the fish. If your fillet is thick, and is sufficiently browned on top after broiling but not thoroughly cooked, cover and finish by baking in a 400°F oven until cooked through, about 5 minutes.

Transfer the fish to a platter and drizzle the reserved marinade over it. Serve hot, sprinkled with the chives.

Fish in Charmoula

Here's a dish that lends itself to easy entertaining: *Charmoula,* the classic Moroccan herb and spice vinaigrette, is poured over fish that is then baked on a bed of onions, sun-dried tomatoes, and olives. Gaeta olives, if you can find them, are especially tasty. Serve the fish with Potato Salad with Caramelized Onions (page 115) and a side of roasted asparagus (page 166).

SERVES 4

1/4 cup plus 1 tablespoon extra-virgin olive oil

1 onion, thinly sliced (1 cup)

1/4 cup sun-dried tomatoes, soaked in warm water until softened,
    drained, and cut into thin strips

1/2 cup olives, preferably Gaeta or kalamata

3 garlic cloves, minced

1/4 cup chopped fresh parsley

1/4 chopped fresh cilantro

1 teaspoon paprika

1 teaspoon ground cumin

1/4 cup fresh lemon juice

Salt

Four 5-ounce pieces striped bass, red snapper, or thick
    white fish fillets, skinned

Freshly ground black pepper

Preheat the oven to 400°F.

Warm 1 tablespoon of the olive oil in a medium skillet over medium-low heat. Add the onions and sauté until softened, about 10 minutes. Add the sun-dried tomatoes and the olives, and sauté to heat through. Pour the mixture into a baking dish that is large enough to hold the fish in a single layer.

Prepare the *charmoula:* Stir the garlic, parsley, cilantro, paprika, cumin, lemon juice, remaining 1/4 cup olive oil, and 1/4 teaspoon salt together in a small bowl.

Sprinkle the fish with salt and pepper, and place it on top of the onion mixture. Cover the fish with the *charmoula.* Bake until the fish is cooked through, about 20 minutes. Serve hot.

Pecan-Crusted Trout with Lemon-Sage Butter

In this delicious recipe, whole folded trout is pan-fried on the skin side, so the crusted skin is crisp and wonderful; the fish is succulent and not at all greasy. Each trout serves 1 to 2 people, depending on their appetite and what else you're serving. I usually find 4 fish is the perfect amount for 6 people. The pecan crust is great on boneless chicken, too. For a delicious harvest-time meal, serve this with Indonesian Corn Chowder (page 47) and Gazpacho Salad (page 98).

SERVES 4 TO 6

1 cup pecans

**7 slices whole-grain bread, preferably dense seven-grain
    or spelt, crusts removed**

1/2 cup thinly sliced fresh sage

4 whole trout, backbones and heads removed

Salt and freshly ground black pepper

Dijon mustard

Lemon-Sage Butter

1/4 cup (1/2 stick) butter

10 fresh sage leaves

1 teaspoon grated lemon zest

1 tablespoon fresh lemon juice

Coconut oil or canola oil, for frying

Place the pecans and the bread in a food processor and process until they form coarse crumbs; you should have 4 cups. Stir in the sage. Spread the crumbs on a flat plate or baking pan.

Rinse each trout and pat it dry. Sprinkle salt and pepper over the inside cavity and outer skin of the fish. Fold each trout closed like a book, so that the skin is on the outside. Spread a thin layer of mustard over the skin on both sides of each trout. Dredge the trout in the crumb mixture, pressing firmly to adhere the mixture on both sides. Use your hands to fill in any blank spots and press on a thick coat.

Make the Lemon-Sage Butter: Combine the butter, sage leaves, and lemon zest in a small saucepan and place over medium heat. Cook until the butter begins to brown, 3 to 4 minutes. Then stir in the lemon juice and remove the pan from the heat. Set it aside.

Pour oil to a depth of about ⅛ inch in two large skillets (the skillets should be large enough to fit the length of the fish). Heat over medium heat until a hand held 4 inches from the pan feels really hot. Gently add 2 trout to each skillet—you should hear a good sizzle when they touch the pan—and cook until golden brown, 3 to 4 minutes. Using two spatulas, gently turn the trout over. Cook until golden, 3 minutes. Serve the trout drizzled with the Lemon-Sage Butter.

NOTE: *Ask your fishmonger to butterfly the trout, removing the heads and backbones.*

Fish Tacos with Designer Guacamole and Cabbage Slaw

I used to frequent one Mexican restaurant just for their fish taco. When they took it off the menu I devised my own so that I could indulge any time I want. For a beautiful presentation, serve this open-faced taco as one gorgeous stack: a corn tortilla, a layer of guacamole, the fish, and a mound of slaw on top. You can make the slaw well in advance, but don't stir in the watercress until a few hours before serving. The guacamole is best served fresh and lasts 2 days, refrigerated.

SERVES 4

Cabbage Slaw

4 cups thinly sliced green cabbage
1 teaspoon salt
1 cup grated jicama
4 red radishes, cut into thin rounds
1 bunch watercress, thick stems removed
2 jalapeño peppers, stemmed, seeded, and minced
1/4 cup fresh lime juice
1 teaspoon honey
Freshly ground black pepper

Spice rub

1 tablespoon dried oregano, preferably Mexican
2 tablespoons ground cumin
1 tablespoon paprika
1 tablespoon chile powder
1 tablespoon freshly ground black pepper

Four 5- to 6-ounce mahi-mahi fillets, skinned
Salt
2 tablespoons extra-virgin olive oil
1 tablespoon fresh lime juice
4 corn tortillas
1 recipe Designer Guacamole (page 176)

Make the slaw: Mix the cabbage and salt together in a medium bowl. Place a bowl or plate on top of the cabbage, and set a weight on top of the plate (a heavy can will do). Let the cabbage sit for 30 minutes.

Stir the jicama, radishes, watercress, and jalapeños into the cabbage. In a small bowl, mix the lime juice, honey, and a sprinkling of black pepper together. Stir this into the cabbage mixture and let it sit for at least 30 minutes.

Prepare the spice rub: Mix the oregano, cumin, paprika, chile powder, and black pepper together in a small bowl. Set it aside.

Preheat an indoor or outdoor grill, or preheat the oven to 400°F.

Sprinkle both sides of the fish with salt, then with the spice rub, and then with the olive oil.

To grill the fish: Cook the fish for about 3 minutes on the grill. Then turn it 90 degrees without turning it over, to create a crosshatch effect. Cook for another 2 minutes. Turn the fish over and repeat.

To bake the fish: Place the fish on a parchment-covered rimmed baking sheet and bake until cooked through, 8 to 10 minutes.

Remove the fish from the heat and sprinkle each piece with the lime juice.

Heat a heavy-bottomed skillet, such as cast iron, over medium-high heat, and place the tortillas in the skillet one at a time until warmed and softened, about 30 seconds per side. You can also warm the tortillas directly over a gas burner for a couple of seconds per side.

Layer the tortillas with guacamole, fish, and cabbage slaw, and serve.

NOTES: *Mahi-mahi, also known as dolphinfish (not to be confused with dolphins), has a thick skin that should be removed before cooking. It is most widely available in the summer months. It is a firm-fleshed fish that is best suited to broiling, grilling, or baking. You can also use black bass, red snapper, cod, haddock, or grouper for these tacos. Grilled or baked halibut, monkfish, and tuna are other delicious options.*

You won't need all of the rub for 4 fillets. Save the remainder in a covered jar at room temperature, and you'll be ready to make the fish tacos again at a moment's notice.

Salt Cod and Potato Cakes

Salt cod, known as baccalà, is a comfort food in many parts of the world. The cod has been preserved with salt, so you need to soak it overnight in water to reconstitute it and remove the salt. For a tropical feast, serve these tasty cakes with Watercress and Hearts of Palm Salad with Plantain Chips (page 86).

MAKES 7 CAKES; SERVES 4 TO 6

1 pound salt cod (baccalà)
3/4 pound (1 large) russet potato, cut into 1-inch chunks (2 cups)
Salt
4 tablespoons extra-virgin olive oil
1 red bell pepper, cut into small dice
1/4 cup thinly sliced scallions, white and green parts
Freshly ground black pepper
2 teaspoons fresh lime juice

Soak the salt cod in cold water to cover in the refrigerator overnight or for up to 24 hours; change the water at least once during this time.

Drain and rinse the cod. Place the cod in a medium pot, cover with fresh water, and bring to a boil. Drain the water and cover with fresh water. Lower the heat and simmer the cod until cooked through, 5 to 10 minutes. Drain the cod, flake it with a fork into chunky pieces, and set it aside in a medium bowl. You should have about 2 cups.

Place the potatoes in a medium saucepan, cover with water, and add 1/2 teaspoon salt. Bring to a boil. Then reduce the heat and simmer, uncovered, until the potatoes are tender, 10 to 15 minutes. Drain the potatoes, reserving 1/4 cup of the cooking liquid.

Place the potatoes, the reserved cooking liquid, and 1 tablespoon of the olive oil in a bowl, and mash the potatoes. Stir in 1/4 teaspoon salt.

Warm 1 tablespoon of the oil in a medium skillet over medium heat. Add the bell peppers and cook until they are softened, about 5 minutes. Stir in the scallions and cook for another minute. Add the pepper-scallion mixture to the cod, and stir in the mashed potatoes. Add a generous sprinkling of black pepper and the lime juice, and stir to combine thoroughly. Taste, and add a pinch of salt if necessary.

Form the mixture into seven 1-inch-thick cakes, handling them as little as possible. Place them on a plate and refrigerate for at least 30 minutes.

Warm 1 tablespoon of the oil in a medium nonstick skillet over medium-high heat. Add 4 fish cakes and sauté until golden, about 3 minutes per side. Repeat with the remaining 1 tablespoon oil and 3 fish cakes. Serve hot.

NOTES: *You can purchase baccalà in most fish markets. It can often be found in 1-pound packages in the refrigerator section.*

Remember to change the water while the cod soaks to remove the excess salt. If you forget, you can bring water to a boil and discard it two times before cooking the baccalà.

Porcini Mushroom Ragout with Chicken

I developed this recipe when I catered a meal for a dinner party where the guest of honor was vegetarian and the rest of the group insisted upon chicken. Because both tempeh and chicken entrées were topped with the same sauce, the two dishes looked alike and the guest of honor did not feel like the odd man out. Best of all, preparing the two dishes required very little extra work from me. The ragout is equally delicious over polenta.

SERVES 4

1/2 cup (1/2 ounce) dried porcini mushrooms
3 cups water
1/4 cup shoyu
1/4 cup dry sherry
2 tablespoons red wine vinegar
Salt and freshly ground black pepper
One 2 1/2- to 3-pound chicken, cut into parts (each breast cut into 2 pieces),
    rinsed and thoroughly dried
2 tablespoons coconut oil or extra-virgin olive oil

Ragout

2 tablespoons extra-virgin olive oil
1 cup thinly sliced onions
Salt
3 garlic cloves, minced
6 ounces cremini mushrooms, sliced (3 cups)
1 tablespoon shoyu
1 tablespoon unbleached white flour
2 tablespoons dry sherry
Freshly ground black pepper
1/4 cup chopped fresh parsley, preferably flat-leaf
1 teaspoon fresh thyme
1 teaspoon fresh lemon juice

Combine the porcini mushrooms and the water in a saucepan and bring to a boil. Remove the pan from the heat and let sit for 20 minutes. Then drain, reserving the mushrooms and liquid separately. Pour the liquid into a bowl through a strainer lined with a damp paper towel (to catch any grit). Chop the mushrooms and set them aside.

Make the marinade: Pour 1 cup of the porcini soaking liquid into a medium bowl and add the shoyu, sherry, and vinegar. Set it aside.

Salt and pepper the chicken. Warm the oil in a large heavy-bottomed skillet over medium-high heat until it is shimmering. Add the chicken pieces and cook until browned on both sides, about 4 minutes per side. Remove the chicken from the skillet and discard the excess fat, leaving only a thin film on the bottom of the skillet. Return the chicken to the skillet and add the marinade. Cover and simmer, turning occasionally, until the pieces are tender, 20 to 25 minutes.

Meanwhile, make the ragout: Warm the oil in a medium skillet over medium heat. Add the onions and a pinch of salt, and cook until they are softened, about 7 minutes. Add the garlic, the cremini and reserved porcini mushrooms, and the shoyu, and cook until dry, about 10 minutes. Add the flour and stir to coat the mushrooms. Add the sherry and 1½ cups of the porcini soating liquid, and simmer gently until thickened, 7 to 10 minutes. Add ¼ teaspoon salt and a sprinkling of black pepper. Stir in the parsley, thyme, and lemon juice. Taste, and add a pinch more salt if necessary.

Serve the chicken with the ragout ladled over it.

Porcini Mushroom Ragout with Tempeh (SERVES 4 TO 5)

Substitute two 8-ounce packages of tempeh for the chicken. Slice the tempeh diagonally (see page 228) into 12 pieces. Sauté the tempeh in the coconut oil until brown, and then simmer it in the marinade, covered, until most of the marinade has been absorbed, 10 minutes. Serve slathered with the ragout.

NOTES: *Dried porcini mushrooms come in different sizes, from small to large. If they are very small, there's no need to chop them any further.*

Buy a whole chicken and have the butcher cut it up as follows: 2 drumsticks, 2 thighs, 4 breast pieces, 2 wings, and the back. Save the wings, back, and neck for stock. When I have accumulated backbones, necks, and wings from 3 chickens, I make Roasted Chicken Stock (page 45).

Wash the cremini mushrooms by swishing them around in a bowl of water right before slicing. Rub the mushrooms with your hands to dislodge the dirt, and lift the mushrooms out of the water.

Roast Chicken with Maple Glaze

This super-moist chicken with its shiny lacquered glaze is one of the easiest dinners you can make. It's ready to go into the oven in under 10 minutes. The chicken is delicious with Sautéed Broccoli Rabe with Garlic and Red Pepper Flakes (page 145) and Lacquered Carrots with Coriander (page 108).

SERVES 4

One 3- to 4-pound chicken, rinsed and patted dry
Salt
Freshly ground black pepper
1/3 cup maple syrup
1/3 cup fresh orange juice
2 tablespoons Dijon mustard
2 tablespoons extra-virgin olive oil
1 tablespoon chopped fresh thyme
1/4 teaspoon cayenne pepper

Preheat the oven to 400°F.

Set the chicken on a cutting board, breast side down. Using kitchen shears, cut along both sides of the backbone and remove it (see illustration, page 265). (Freeze the backbone to make chicken stock later.) Flip the chicken over and press down on the breast to flatten it a little.

Rub 1 teaspoon salt all over the chicken, including under the skin, and set it, breast side up, in an 8 by 11½-inch baking dish. Sprinkle it generously with black pepper.

In a small saucepan, combine the maple syrup, orange juice, mustard, olive oil, thyme, cayenne, and 1 teaspoon salt. Whisk to blend. Place the pan on the heat and simmer, uncovered, until thickened, 5 minutes. Pour the mixture evenly over the chicken.

Roast the chicken, basting or brushing it every 15 minutes with the pan juices, until an instant-read thermometer inserted in the deepest part of the thigh registers 170° to 175°F, about 50 minutes. Keep an eye on the pan juices; if they seem to be burning, add a couple tablespoons of water to the pan.

Let the chicken rest for a few minutes. Then cut it into pieces, drizzle it generously with the pan juices, and serve.

Butterflied Barbecue Spice-Rubbed Chicken

Serve this chicken with the tangy barbecue sauce and you'll always get rave reviews. Although you can make this with chicken parts, it's tastier with a whole chicken. Removing the backbone and opening the chicken cuts down on the roasting time. I recommend using poultry shears to do this.

SERVES 4

One 3- to 4-pound chicken
¼ cup extra-virgin olive oil
¼ cup Barbecue Spice Rub (recipe follows)
1 teaspoon salt
Barbecue Sauce (recipe follows)

Wash the chicken and pat it dry. Turn the chicken back side up and place it on a cutting board. Using kitchen shears, cut through the rib bones on both sides of the backbone, and remove it in one piece.

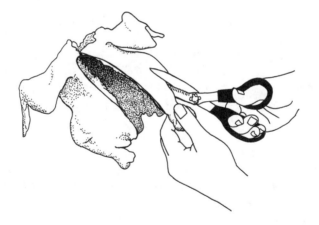

In a small bowl, mix the olive oil and spice rub together. Set it aside.

Preheat the oven to 450°F.

Place the chicken breast side up and spread it open. Press firmly on the breastbone to crack it and flatten the chicken. Trim off all excess fat. Rub 1 teaspoon salt all over the chicken, including under the skin. Brush the spice paste liberally over both sides of the chicken. Loosen the skin with your fingers, and slip some of the spice paste under the skin.

Place the chicken, breast side up, on a rack in a roasting pan. Bake until the skin is crisp and browned and the juices run clear, 55 to 65 minutes. (You can test for doneness by inserting an instant-read thermometer in the thickest part of the thigh. It should register 165°F). Let the chicken rest for 10 minutes.

Cut the chicken into serving-size pieces and serve it hot, slathered with the barbecue sauce.

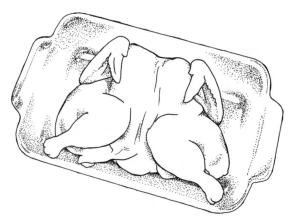

Barbecue Spice Rub

This super-quick spice rub tastes as delicious on tofu as it does on chicken; it gives the food a beautiful deep red color. The recipe makes enough rub for 4 pounds of tofu or 2 whole chickens. For the freshest and tastiest spice rub, start with whole cumin seeds and black peppercorns and grind them in a spice grinder or with a mortar and pestle.

MAKES ½ CUP

- **1 tablespoon salt**
- **2 tablespoons natural brown sugar, preferably maple sugar, Sucanat, or evaporated cane sugar**
- **1 tablespoon ground cumin**
- **1 tablespoon chile powder**
- **1 tablespoon freshly ground black pepper**
- **½ teaspoon cayenne pepper**
- **2 tablespoons paprika**

Mix all the ingredients together in a bowl. Store in a tightly covered container at room temperature for up to 4 months. Do not refrigerate.

Barbecue Sauce

Send heavenly aromas wafting through your kitchen with this hickory-laced sauce, which nicely complements the spicy barbecue rub. I'm partial to New Mexican chile powder, but when I want to crank up the heat I use chipotle chile powder. The sauce keeps for at least a month in the refrigerator. I like to have some around to slather over just about everything.

MAKES 2½ CUPS

2 tablespoons extra-virgin olive oil
1 onion, diced (1 cup)
2 garlic cloves, minced
½ teaspoon hot red pepper flakes
¾ teaspoon chile powder, preferably New Mexican
One 28-ounce can crushed tomatoes, preferably fire-roasted
¼ cup apple cider vinegar
3 tablespoons honey
3 tablespoons molasses
1 teaspoon liquid smoke
1 tablespoon Dijon mustard
1 teaspoon salt
Freshly ground black pepper

Warm the oil in a medium saucepan over medium heat. Add the onions and cook until they are translucent, about 7 minutes. Add the garlic, red pepper flakes, and chile powder, and sauté for 3 minutes. Add the tomatoes, vinegar, honey, molasses, liquid smoke, mustard, and salt. Bring to a boil. Then reduce the heat and simmer, partially covered, for 20 to 30 minutes.

Sprinkle the sauce with freshly ground black pepper. Transfer it to a blender or use an immersion blender to blend the sauce until smooth. Add up to ¼ cup water to thin it to the desired consistency. Taste, and add more salt if necessary. Serve hot.

NOTE: *Liquid smoke is simply mesquite smoke mixed with water. It is readily available at gourmet stores and upscale supermarkets. Although this recipe calls for only 1 teaspoon liquid smoke, it is essential in getting that authentic barbecue flavor.*

Asian Chicken Salad with Crispy Wonton Strips

This salad is showy and scrumptious whether you make it with the chicken or with tofu. I roast the chicken to make the chicken salad especially flavorful, and I use glazed tofu to give the vegetarian version extra flavor. If you're a true flexitarian, you'll want to try both versions.

SERVES 6

4 bone-in chicken breasts, *or* **1 whole chicken, cut into 8 to 10 pieces,**
    or **1 recipe Glazed Tofu (page 241)**
Salt and freshly ground black pepper
$1/2$ cup diced celery
$1/4$ cup thinly sliced scallions, white and green parts
$1/4$ cup chopped fresh cilantro
$1/2$ cup chopped unsalted cashews
3 tablespoons coconut oil or canola oil
10 wonton wrappers, cut into strips

Dressing

$1/4$ cup brown rice vinegar
2 tablespoons shoyu
$1/4$ cup mirin
2 teaspoons toasted sesame oil
2 teaspoons sesame oil or canola oil
$1/2$ teaspoon salt
Freshly ground black pepper
2 teaspoons minced garlic
2 teaspoons minced fresh ginger

2 bunches watercress, thick stems removed

If you are using the chicken: Preheat the oven to 400°F. Salt and pepper the chicken and place it on a rack in a roasting pan. Roast for 35 to 40 minutes, or until the chicken is tender and the thickest part of the breast registers 160°F on an instant-read thermometer. Let the chicken cool for 10 minutes before handling.

Remove the skin, and cut the meat into small pieces; you should have 4 cups.

(Save the bones to make chicken stock.) Place the chicken in a medium bowl and add the celery, scallions, cilantro, and cashews.

If you are using the tofu: Combine it with the celery, scallions, cilantro, and cashews in a medium bowl.

Prepare the wontons: Line a plate with paper towels and place it near the stove. Heat the oil in a medium skillet over medium-high heat. Test the heat by dropping a wonton strip in the oil; it should crisp within a few seconds. When the oil is hot enough, add the wonton strips and fry, turning once (tongs are especially useful here), until light golden brown, about 30 seconds. Place the fried wontons on the paper towels to drain, and set them aside.

Make the dressing: In a small bowl, combine the rice vinegar, shoyu, mirin, toasted and sesame oils, salt, and black pepper to taste. Stir in the garlic and ginger.

Toss the chicken or tofu mixture with the dressing, and arrange the salad on a bed of watercress. Garnish with the crispy wontons.

Seven-Vegetable Moroccan Stew

This meal-in-a-pot will be on your table in under an hour. You can make it with chicken, or for a vegetarian version, omit the chicken and include the chickpeas. Make it with or without the classic harissa spice paste, whichever you prefer. The key to getting golden crispy chicken is hot oil and dry chicken.

SERVES 4 TO 6

2 tablespoons extra-virgin olive oil
1 chicken, cut into pieces
2 onions, diced (2 cups)
3 garlic cloves, minced
1 green bell pepper, cut into $1/2$-inch-wide lengthwise strips
2 celery stalks, cut into 2-inch pieces
One 28-ounce can tomatoes, drained and coarsely chopped
$2 1/2$ cups water or chicken or vegetable stock
1 bay leaf
Large pinch of saffron threads
2 small ($1/2$ pound) turnips, quartered
2 carrots, halved crosswise and quartered lengthwise
One 15-ounce can chickpeas, rinsed and drained, optional
Salt
Freshly ground black pepper
$3/4$ cup peas, fresh or frozen
1 small zucchini, cut into quarters lengthwise, then cut in half
$1/2$ cup raisins
$1/2$ cup fresh cilantro, chopped
Harissa (recipe follows), optional
4 to 6 lemon wedges, for garnish

Heat the olive oil in a large heavy-bottomed soup pot over medium-high heat until shimmering. Add the chicken pieces and cook until browned on both sides, about 4 minutes per side. Remove the chicken and set it aside. Pour out the excess fat, leaving only a thin film on the bottom of the pot.

Add the onions, garlic, and bell peppers to the pot, and sauté over medium-low heat until the onions soften, about 10 minutes. Add the celery, tomatoes, water, bay leaf, and saffron. Add the reserved chicken, cover, and bring to a boil. Then reduce the heat and simmer for about 25 minutes.

Add the turnips, carrots, chickpeas (if using), 1 teaspoon salt, and a sprinkling of black pepper to the pot. Simmer, partially covered, until the vegetables and chicken are tender, 20 minutes. At this point you can set the stew aside for a few hours or refrigerate it overnight; bring the stew back to a simmer before continuing with the recipe.

Add the peas, zucchini, and raisins to the stew. Simmer until the zucchini and peas are cooked through but still bright, 5 to 10 minutes. Stir in the cilantro.

Stir up to 1 tablespoon of the harissa into the pot of stew; pass more harissa at the table for people to add to their servings.

Serve the stew in individual bowls, with lemon wedges alongside.

For a traditional Moroccan presentation, remove the vegetables and chicken from the stew (with a slotted spoon) and serve them on a platter around a big mound of couscous. Stir some harissa into the broth and pass the spiced broth around the table for people to add to their individual servings.

NOTE: *For a beautiful cut, place the celery on its side and cut it into diagonal pieces. They will resemble fish tails.*

Harissa

Harissa is a potent deep orange Moroccan spice paste. It is traditionally stirred into stews, but it's a great pepper blend to have on hand to add pizzazz to any dish. If you are using very small chiles, such as cayenne peppers, there is no need to seed them.

MAKES ABOUT ½ CUP

¾ cup (¾ ounce) dried hot red chile peppers, such as Indian chiles, whole cayenne pepper, or chile de árbol
¼ cup sun-dried tomatoes
1 teaspoon whole caraway seeds
1 teaspoon whole cumin seeds
1 teaspoon whole coriander seeds
1 tablespoon water
¼ cup olive oil
1 garlic clove
¼ teaspoon salt

Remove the seeds and stems from the chiles, unless they are small. Place the chiles and the sun-dried tomatoes in a small saucepan and add water to cover. Bring to a boil, remove from the heat, and let the mixture sit until softened, about 20 minutes.

(CONTINUED NEXT PAGE)

Meanwhile, grind the caraway, cumin, and coriander seeds together in a spice mill or with a mortar and pestle.

Drain the peppers and sun-dried tomatoes, and transfer them to a food processor. Add the water, olive oil, garlic, salt, and ground spices, and process until the mixture forms a thick paste. Transfer it to a glass jar, cover tightly, and refrigerate. The harissa will keep for months in the refrigerator.

Sautéed Chicken with Mango and Red Onion Chutney

This is a seriously tasty dish, and one that is both easy *and* fancy. Adjust the amount of red pepper flakes according to how hot your curry powder is. For the best results, make sure the mangoes are not overly ripe or mushy. Have all the ingredients ready before you start cooking, because this dish cooks before you know it. It reheats well, too.

SERVES 3 OR 4

3 boneless, skinless chicken breasts
Salt
Freshly ground black pepper
2 tablespoons coconut oil or extra-virgin olive oil
1 red onion, cut into 1/2-inch dice (1 cup)
1/2 red bell pepper, cut into 1/4-inch dice (1/2 cup)
2 tablespoons minced fresh ginger
2 mangoes, peeled and cut into 3/4-inch cubes (2 cups)
1/2 cup unsweetened pineapple juice
2 tablespoons apple cider vinegar
1/4 cup natural sugar, preferably maple sugar or evaporated cane sugar
1 tablespoon curry powder
1/4 teaspoon hot red pepper flakes

Remove the tenderloin, the little piece that is attached under the breast, from each chicken breast and set it aside. Slice the rest of the chicken on an angle into 3/4-inch-wide pieces. Season with salt and pepper.

Warm the oil in a large skillet over medium-high heat until it is shimmering.

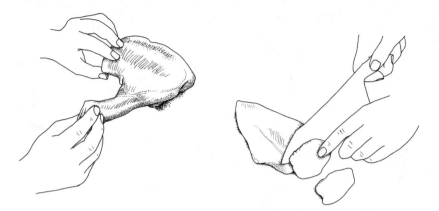

Add half of the chicken pieces (including the tenderloins) and cook, flipping once, until lightly browned and just barely cooked through, 1 to 2 minutes per side. Transfer the chicken to a plate. Repeat with the remaining chicken.

Return the skillet to medium heat. Add the onions and bell peppers, and scrape up any brown bits that have stuck to the pan. Sauté until softened, about 4 minutes. Add the ginger and sauté until fragrant, 20 to 30 seconds.

Stir in the mangoes, pineapple juice, vinegar, sugar, curry powder, red pepper flakes, and ¼ teaspoon salt. Simmer, uncovered, stirring occasionally, until thickened, 3 to 4 minutes. Stir in the chicken, along with any juices that have collected in the plate. Cover, and cook for 1 minute to heat through. Taste, and add a sprinkling of salt if necessary.

Sweet Snacks and Desserts

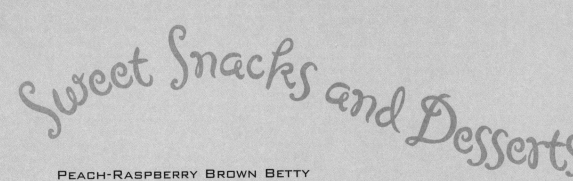

Peach-Raspberry Brown Betty

Citrus Compote Supreme

Orange Walnut Crêpes

Roasted Peaches with Caramel Sauce

Strawberry Soup

Mango Soup

Spiced Plum Soup

Ginger Coconut Ice Cream

A Trio of Fruit Sorbets

    Blackberry Sorbet

    Raspberry Sorbet

    Peach Sorbet

Light-as-a-Feather Chocolate Mousse

    Very Berry Sauce

A Pair of Luscious Puddings

    Chocolate Coconut Pudding

    Lemon Pudding

Phyllo Cups

Chocolate Phyllo Cigars

Baklava

Butter Crust

Coconut Oil Crust

Cranberry Apple Crumb Pie

Pomegranate-Pear Cornmeal Tart

Naked Carrot Cake

"Pumpkin" Pie

Browned Butter Berry Galette

Indian Pudding Cake

Coconut Whipped Cream

Triple Gingerbread

Granola Bars

Caramel Popcorn with Peanuts

Chocolate Lovers' Brownies

Pecan Lace Tuiles

Chocolate Chip Cookies

Peanut Butter Cookies

Semolina Cookies

Sesame Biscotti

Chai

There are those who think the only way to

be healthy is to give up on sugar and eschew all desserts. A hedonist revels in a sweet treat now and again, and wouldn't dream of renouncing all sweets. Desserts make a gathering celebratory and festive. Of course the healthy hedonist—who wants to feel good after eating as well as before—should make intelligent choices about which desserts to choose. The right amount of sweetness can round out the meal and leave one with a sated, happy feeling. ◉ The road of moderation—modest portions of desserts made with good-quality ingredients—is the key. And of course the sweets have to be delectable, or there's no point in making them! In this chapter, I've included a wide variety of sweet snacks and desserts, ranging from the fairly decadent to the modest daily variety. You'll find desserts that are suitable for an elegant gathering as well as energy boosters that are good to grab in a hurry. Certain recipes are sure to appeal to the child in you—such as a sinfully delicious and healthy version of caramel popcorn. ◉ The overdose of refined sugar in many typical desserts can send you on a blood-sugar roller-coaster ride, but you can feast on the sweets in this book and feel fantastic afterward. These are pleasures that have some real food value. The emphasis here is on light desserts that won't leave you weighted down, so many of them incorporate fresh fruit. Even the desserts made with dough are light. Most of the brownies and the cakes are made with oat flour, which is the lightest whole-grain flour available. The dairy-free chocolate mousse is cloudlike in texture. ◉ I have included vegan desserts as well as those that use eggs and butter. Many of the desserts can be made with dairy or dairy-free ingredients. A small amount of coconut milk provides just the right rich texture needed in certain puddings, crêpes, and toppings. ◉ The recipes are straightforward, and most of them go together quickly. It is the combination of the ingredients and the technique that makes the desserts shine. Once you learn how to use a few ingredients such as agar and arrowroot, and a few techniques such as making pie dough, the rest is easy. ◉ So celebrate life with scrumptious sweets. Be the person who brings a tray of luscious cookies to a celebratory event. Rejoice in the fact that you can nourish yourself and others with high-quality fun food. It's okay to make something mouthwatering, and it's good to know when to exercise restraint. Remember, there's always more where that came from, especially if you can make it yourself. Consume just enough to make you feel fabulous. Nurture yourself and your loved ones with sweet pleasures.

Ingredients

FATS AND MILKS

For fats, I use either butter or coconut oil, and occasionally extra-virgin olive oil. Food manufacturers have long known that saturated fats make baked goods last a long time on the shelf. Butter and coconut oil produce the best baked goods. Coconut oil is one of the few oils that can take the heat necessary to deodorize it without destabilizing the oil. Purchase unsalted cultured organic butter. ◉ Coconut oil can be used as an alternative to butter in all the recipes in the book. You may notice that there is a little more butter in the measurement than oil. That is because butter is about 20 percent water, while coconut oil contains no water. ◉ Do not use virgin coconut oil for baking unless you want coconut flavor. The virgin oil is expensive, so it's best treated as a condiment. Omega Nutrition, a company that produces superior oils, makes an amazing coconut oil that is suitable for baking and cooking. If this brand is not available in your natural foods store, speak to the manager about ordering it, or order it directly from the company (see Resources). Coconut oil can be used in many forms: melted, semisolid when creaming oil and sugar together, and firm for pie crusts. Coconut oil melts at around 76°F, so at room temperature it is usually in a semisolid state, perfect for creaming. If your kitchen gets hot, it will turn to liquid. For a pie crust, measure out an approximate amount of the oil and refrigerate it until it is firm; then chop the solid oil and measure what you need. If you need melted oil, melt it first and then measure. ◉ If melted coconut oil is mixed with cold liquid ingredients, it tends to harden. Either make sure your ingredients are at room temperature or put them in a saucepan to heat them. A whir in a blender will smooth out any problems with the wet ingredients. ◉ When I want a creamy, rich texture without using cow's milk, I turn to coconut milk. Coconut milk is a product to which few people are allergic. It has a rich texture and body, and either adds delicious flavor or stays unobtrusively in the background, depending on the recipe. Full-fat soy milk also works in the recipes, but I believe coconut milk is a superior product.

FLOURS AND LEAVENERS

For pastry dough, I use unbleached white flour mixed with whole-wheat pastry flour, which has a lower gluten content than regular whole-wheat flour. Gluten is what gives structure to breads and pizza doughs, something you want to avoid in pie crusts and cookies. ◉ I also use oat flour in the brownies and the cake recipes. With oat flour, you can make a completely whole-grain baked good with a light texture, since oats are more absorbent than wheat. Oat flour yields a sweet cakelike crumb, and oat baked products retain their freshness longer than wheat because oats contain a natural antioxidant. ◉ I use chickpea flour, a high-protein flour made from roasted chickpeas, in the peanut butter cookies, making them a high-protein snack. ◉ I use organic eggs, baking powder, and baking soda as the leaveners. Aluminum-free baking powder, available in natural foods stores, is the healthiest variety. Baking soda requires the presence of something acidic, which is why some of the recipes with baking soda have a small amount of vinegar in them.

SWEETENERS

There are some luscious alternatives to refined white sugar and artificial sweeteners. Maple syrup, made by reducing sap tapped from a maple tree, is a good all-purpose sweetener. The quality varies dramatically, however. Some cheaper brands contain chemical antifoamers and mold inhibitors, as well as residue from the formaldehyde pellets used to keep the tap holes from healing. The Canadian government, the state of Vermont, and organic certification codes prohibit the use of these pellets. Grade A is the more delicately flavored syrup, and Grade B the more robust. They both are delicious in any of the recipes in this book. Stay away from anything labeled "pancake syrup." ◉ Maple sugar is crystallized maple syrup, and a wonderful all-purpose sweetener. It is my favorite granulated sweetener. Unfortunately, it is quite pricey. I've included Web sources for ordering (see Resources), since these tend to be more economical than purchasing it from a store. Of all the dry sugars, maple sugar is the mildest tasting and usually the most finely granulated. ◉ Rapadura is a natural sweetener made from dried granulated cane juice. Only the water and fiber are removed, so the mineral salts and vitamins naturally present are retained. It is moist, with a slight taste of molasses and a coarse granular texture. It's the same sugar as *jaggery* in India and *panela* in Spanish-speaking countries. *Jaggery* and *panela* come in molded forms, so they have to be grated or melted before they are used. Sucanat, a word coined from "sugar cane natural," is the same thing in an un-refined form. Be sure to check the label, because sometimes what is called Sucanat is simply granulated refined cane juice with the molasses mixed back in. Sucanat is good in desserts that have other strong flavors, such as chocolate or peanut butter. Barley malt syrup, made from sprouted barley, is a fairly mild sweetener with a strong, distinctive flavor and a consistency and color similar to molasses. I usually use it in combination with other sweeteners. It's a must in the Caramel Popcorn with Peanuts. ◉ Brown rice syrup is a very mild sweetener with a subtle butterscotch flavor, making it a great choice for savory food as well as desserts. Baked goods made with rice syrup tend to be crisp, so it is good for lace cookies, or tuiles. For desserts, it is best used in tandem with other sweeteners. It is another essential ingredient in the Caramel Popcorn with Peanuts. ◉ Molasses is a by-product of the sugar-refining process. Thick, dark, and sweet, it retains vitamins and minerals lost in refining. Always use unsulfured molasses, since the sulfured variety tastes of residues of sulfur dioxide. Because molasses has a strong flavor, I use small quantities as an accent in desserts such as the gingerbread and the Indian Pudding Cake. ◉ Honey is best when it has not been heated to temperatures over 105°F and is minimally filtered. I use honey in small amounts, as an accent—stirred into chai, in yogurt, in citrus salad—but rarely for baking. It is sweeter than sugar, so a little goes a long way. Darker honeys are more mineral-rich and stronger in flavor than the lighter ones.

Granulated cane juice, milled cane sugar, raw cane juice, dehydrated cane juice, turbinado sugar, evaporated cane sugar, and Florida crystals are all names for sugar. They are all similar to white sugar, but they have not gone through quite as much processing, and they often are organic. When the flavor of a less refined sugar is too overpowering, these varieties serve an important function. I almost always opt for maple sugar, but all of these will work in any of the recipes. Any pesticides and chemicals used on the cane will be concentrated during processing, so it is wise to purchase organic sugar. Used respectfully, these have a place, and they all taste a lot better than white sugar. You can also combine these with maple sugar with good results.

CHOCOLATE

While not necessarily something to indulge in with total abandon, chocolate is a heavenly healthy hedonist ingredient. Chocolate transports those who love it to enraptured states. Chocolate is rich in phenylethylamine, which is what the brain manufactures when stimulated by the emotion of love. Chocolate starts out in pods from the cocoa tree. The cocoa pods are harvested and roasted, and the shells are removed. The seeds are ground into an oily paste called chocolate liquor. Cocoa powder is pure chocolate liquor with most of the cocoa butter pressed out of it. The remaining dry cake, which is pulverized, becomes cocoa powder. The term "dutched" or "Dutch process" means that the powder is treated with a mild alkali to mellow the flavor and make it more soluble. Chocolate is the chocolate liquor with the addition of sugar, vanilla, and extra cocoa butter. The flavor depends on where the beans were grown, what they were blended with, and how they were processed. Whether it is bittersweet or semisweet depends on how much chocolate liquor and sugar is in the product. Bitter (unsweetened) chocolate consists of 95 percent chocolate liquor with 5 percent added cocoa butter. It is used as an ingredient. There are more wonderful chocolate varieties in the marketplace today than ever before, including organic chocolate sweetened with grain syrup, Rapadura, or Sucanat. I recommend experimenting with different chocolates until you find a couple that you really like. My favorite unsweetened chocolate is made by Scharffen Berger, and my favorite chips are the Tropical Source brand, which come in semisweet and espresso-flavored. These chocolate chips feel velvety smooth in the mouth and have an intense chocolate flavor. For mocha flavor, I use instant espresso granules.

VANILLA

Vanilla beans are an ambrosial ingredient in compotes and sweets. Open up the pod and release the little beans, and the scent and flavor infuse whatever you are cooking. Unfortunately, the price of vanilla beans fluctuates wildly, mostly depending on the political and climatic conditions in Madagascar, which grows 60 percent of the world's vanilla crop. Cyclones that hit Madagascar a few years back destroyed a lot of the inventory that was ready for shipping. The market has not yet recovered, and political instability and fear of civil wars has made vanilla farmers harvest their beans early, which affects the quality of the beans. Vanilla has been pricey for a number of years, although things are starting to improve, so treat your vanilla beans with care: Store them in a cool place, away from direct sunlight, but not in the refrigerator or freezer. Consider using them more than once, as long as they maintain their natural moisture. You can test a bean by wrapping it around your finger: If it doesn't crack or break, it's still good. Vanilla beans remain moist for about a year. Buy pure vanilla extract that is suspended in alchohol, which is vastly superior to a glycerin base. Vanillin is not real vanilla but is chemically synthesized from the lignin in wood wastes.

OTHER INGREDIENTS

It's also good to have a supply of nuts on hand. If you have space, store them in the freezer to keep them fresh. I keep a few liquors for flavoring, such as Grand Marnier, framboise, brandy, and rum, and vodka for the sorbets. I also keep a supply of thickeners on hand, such as arrowroot, kudzu, and agar. Almond extract, apple cider vinegar, and finely ground sea salt round out the healthy hedonist dessert pantry. Don't forget to keep a stash of organic eggs in the refrigerator.

Equipment

Making dessert is infinitely more pleasurable if you have the basic tools. I recommend investing in a stand mixer. Although you can use a hand-held mixer for the recipes here, nothing beats a stand mixer for stirring cookie batter, mixing bread dough, and whipping egg whites. You'll also need some baking sheets. I recommend aluminum, since it conducts heat wonderfully. However, because it's not a good idea to have aluminum touch the food directly, make sure to have a roll of parchment paper on hand to line the baking sheet. Silicone mats can be used over and over again to line baking sheets; Silpat is the most common brand. These are wonderful and are used in all professional kitchens. I'm assuming you have some basic bakeware such as muffin tins, cake pans, and a 9-inch pie plate. I recommend a springform pan and a 9-inch tart pan with a removable bottom as well. What you may not have but are sure to find useful are a citrus reamer, a dough scraper, and a pastry wheel that creates a fluted edge. A set of 3-inch ramekins is also lovely when you wish to make individual desserts. I also highly recommend owning an ice cream maker, just for the sheer pleasure of it. There's a variety for everyone, ranging from a $65 hand-cranked model to a $1,000 stainless steel maker that weighs 66 pounds and has an internal refrigerator.

Peach-Raspberry Brown Betty

Here's a dessert that sings of summer. Add a scoop of ice cream for a light yet decadent bowl of comfort. The bread cubes absorb the juices as the dish bakes, making this a light, fruity bread pudding.

SERVES 6

2 pounds (about 10 small) peaches or nectarines
1 cup raspberries
2 cups sourdough or country-style bread cubes, crusts removed (1-inch pieces)
$1/2$ cup maple syrup
2 teaspoons vanilla extract
1 teaspoon grated lemon zest
Salt

Topping

$1/2$ cup pecans, chopped into small pieces
1 cup fresh bread crumbs
$1/4$ cup natural sugar, such as maple sugar or evaporated cane sugar
$1/4$ teaspoon ground cinnamon
3 tablespoons melted coconut oil or melted unsalted butter

Preheat the oven to 400°F.

Bring a saucepan of water to a boil, and blanch the peaches in the water for about 1 minute to loosen the skins. Remove the peaches from the water with a slotted spoon, and let them cool for a couple of minutes. Then slip the skins off, cut the peaches in half, and remove the pits. Cut each half into $1/2$-inch slices.

Combine the peaches, raspberries, bread cubes, maple syrup, vanilla, lemon zest, and a pinch of salt in a medium bowl. Toss to mix. Spoon the filling into an 8 by 8-inch baking dish.

Make the topping: Mix the pecans, crumbs, sugar, and cinnamon in a bowl. Drizzle in the oil, tossing the mixture with a spoon or with your fingers until evenly coated. The topping should be fairly moist.

Spread the topping evenly over the fruit. Bake for 15 minutes. Then reduce the oven temperature to 350°F, and bake until the topping is browned and the fruit is bubbling, 15 minutes. Serve warm or at room temperature.

Citrus Compote Supreme

This dish is an homage to one of my favorite childhood treats, broiled grapefruit with cinnamon and honey. In this more sophisticated rendition, orange, blood orange, grapefruit, and tangerine segments are tossed with a citrus reduction, a bit of honey, a sprinkling of cinnamon, and a drizzle of orange-blossom water. The orange-blossom water, readily available in most gourmet markets and Middle Eastern stores, lends a mysterious quality. Serve the compote over the Orange Walnut Crêpes (page 306) for a great starter at a brunch gathering. You can make the compote a day in advance, but wait to stir in the mint until just before you serve the dish.

SERVES 4 TO 6

2 pink grapefruits
2 blood oranges
2 navel oranges
2 tangerines
1 tablespoon honey
1/2 teaspoon orange-blossom water
1/2 teaspoon ground cinnamon
2 tablespoons chopped fresh mint

Supreme all the citrus fruits, holding them over a bowl to catch the juices. (See illustrations). You should have about 3 cups of segments. Place the fruit in a strainer over the bowl, and let it sit for 30 minutes. You should have about 3/4 cup of juice. Place the fruit in a serving bowl.

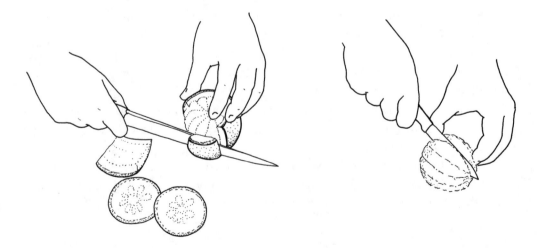

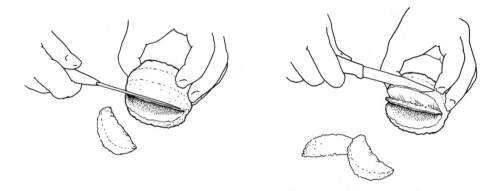

Pour the juice into a medium skillet, and place it over high heat. Boil the juice, uncovered, until it is reduced to 2 tablespoons, about 10 minutes. Stir in the honey and orange-blossom water. Stir this syrup into the fruit, and sprinkle the cinnamon over it.

Right before serving, add the mint and stir to combine. Serve chilled or at room temperature.

Orange Walnut Crêpes

These dessert crêpes, flecked with orange zest and walnuts, are as beautiful as they are tasty. For an elegant brunch, pair the crêpes with Citrus Compote Supreme (page 284). Make the crêpes the day before (or earlier than that if you wish to freeze them) and just pop them in the oven to warm them up. You can't tell the difference in flavor at all between the dairy and the nondairy versions, so the choice is yours.

MAKES TEN TO TWELVE 7-INCH CRÊPES

3/4 cup milk or coconut milk

3/4 cup water

2 eggs

2 tablespoons melted coconut oil or melted unsalted butter,
    plus more for oiling the skillet

1/2 teaspoon salt

2 tablespoons natural sugar, preferably maple sugar or
    evaporated cane sugar

1/2 cup whole-wheat pastry flour

1/2 cup unbleached white flour

1/4 cup walnuts, toasted and chopped into small pieces

1 teaspoon grated orange zest

Blend the milk, water, eggs, coconut oil, salt, sugar, and both flours in a stand mixer until smooth. Stir in the walnuts and the orange zest. Let the batter rest, unrefrigerated, for at least 20 minutes or as long as 2 hours. It should have the consistency of heavy cream.

Rub a 7-inch nonstick skillet over medium-high heat with oil and heat. Pour a scant 1/4 cup crêpe batter into the skillet, tilting the skillet quickly to coat the bottom. Cook until the top of the crêpe appears dry and the bottom is golden, about 30 seconds. Loosen the crêpe with a spatula, turn it over, and cook until brown spots appear on the bottom, about 20 seconds. Slide the crêpe out onto a plate. Re-oil the pan between crêpes. Repeat with the remaining batter, stacking the crêpes on the plate.

For a vegan version, omit the eggs and add 2 tablespoons arrowroot. Use 2 cups original-flavor full-fat soy milk in place of the water and coconut milk.

NOTE: *Make crêpes in advance and refrigerate for several days or freeze for up to a month. Store with parchment paper separating them. Wrap the parchment-layered bundle in aluminum foil, and place in a 350°F oven to warm, about 15 minutes.*

Roasted Peaches with Caramel Sauce

Here peaches bake in a vanilla-infused syrup, which reduces to a luscious dairy-free caramel sauce. Serve the peaches topped with your favorite frozen dessert, and ladle some caramel sauce over the top. The caramel sauce will keep in the refrigerator for weeks. Enjoy the sauce cold, warm, or at room temperature.

SERVES 6 TO 8

2 pounds (4 to 8) peaches
1/2 cup maple syrup
1/2 cup brown rice syrup
1/3 cup water
1 cinnamon stick
Pinch of salt
1 vanilla bean
1 cup original-flavor soy milk or coconut milk
1 teaspoon fresh lemon juice
Ginger Coconut Ice Cream (page 291) or vanilla ice cream

Preheat the oven to 400°F.

Bring a medium pot of water to a boil. Add the peaches and blanch them for about 1 minute. Then remove the peaches with a slotted spoon and let them cool briefly. Slip off the skins. Halve the peaches and remove the pits.

Combine the maple syrup, rice syrup, water, cinnamon stick, and salt in an 8 by 11-inch baking dish, and whisk to combine.

Cut the vanilla bean in half lengthwise. Open the bean, cut side up, and flatten it. Scrape out the seeds with the tip of a knife (a butter knife works best for this). Add the seeds and the pod to the baking dish.

Arrange the peaches, cut side up, in the baking dish. Bake, turning the peaches over after 10 minutes, until they are tender, 15 to 20 minutes.

Remove the baking dish from the oven. Using a slotted spoon, remove the peaches from the syrup and set them aside. Discard the cinnamon stick and the vanilla bean pod. Pour the pan syrup into a large skillet, and add the soy milk and lemon juice. Bring the mixture to a boil, lower the heat, and simmer rapidly, uncovered, until thickened and reduced to 1 cup, about 15 minutes.

Serve the peaches warm, topped with ice cream and drizzled with the caramel sauce.

About Fruit Soups

On the hottest, stickiest days of summer my romantic fantasies get the best of me, and I envision intimate candlelit parties on the patio under the stars. For times like this, a pastry dessert often feels too heavy. I want something refreshing that will satisfy my sweet tooth without leaving me feeling bogged down—a feeling I don't appreciate when I'm wearing a swimsuit. Fruit soups are the perfect answer. Restaurants have long understood that these sweet elixirs make you feel light and energetic after eating a big meal. There's no need to limit fruit soups to a restaurant experience, however; they are the perfect tonics to make at home. Requiring the minimum of ingredients and time at the stove, these soups are easily transportable in a thermos or cooler, which makes them ideal for picnics. Set a scoop of sorbet afloat in the middle, and you have a luscious dessert worthy of an elegant summer soirée.

Strawberry Soup

Port wine gives this soup its deep, rich flavor, although you can substitute another sweet dessert wine such as Madeira or Marsala with good results. Simmering it for 10 minutes cooks out much of the alcohol, leaving only the flavor. A very fine mesh strainer, such as a chinois, is best for removing the tiny strawberry seeds. You can dress this up by adding a scoop of lemon or lime sorbet.

SERVES 4

1 cup water
1 cup port
1 tablespoon grated orange zest
1/2 cup evaporated cane sugar
3 cups strawberries, washed and hulled
1 cup blueberries
1 cup raspberries
1 cup blackberries, halved crosswise

Combine the water, port, orange zest, and sugar in a medium saucepan, and bring to a boil. Lower the heat and simmer until the liquid is reduced to 1¾ cups, about 10 minutes.

Place the strawberries in a heatproof bowl. Pour the hot liquid over the strawberries, and let sit for 5 minutes. Then blend the strawberries with the liquid in a blender until creamy. Strain the strawberry purée through a very fine mesh strainer into a medium bowl. Stir the blueberries, raspberries, and blackberries into the soup, and chill in the refrigerator before serving. Make up to a day ahead.

NOTE: *You can also make this soup very successfully with frozen organic strawberries. Simply pour the hot liquid over the frozen berries; there is no need to defrost them. Then blend, strain, and add the other ingredients. This makes an instant chilled soup.*

Mango Soup

This satiny soup has a subtle hint of coconut flavor. Serve it with a scoop of Ginger Coconut Ice Cream (page 291) floating in the middle of the bowl.

SERVES 4

One 14-ounce can unsweetened light coconut milk
1 cup water
½ cup evaporated cane sugar
1 tablespoon rum
Pinch of salt
2 large ripe mangoes, peeled and sliced (about 3 cups)
2 tablespoons fresh lime juice
1 tablespoon grated lime zest
1 kiwi, peeled and cut into small pieces, for garnish
4 strawberries, sliced, for garnish

Combine the coconut milk, water, sugar, rum, and salt in a saucepan over medium heat, and cook until the liquid comes to a boil and the sugar dissolves, about 5 minutes.

Put half of the mango slices in a blender, pour in half of the hot liquid, and blend until smooth. Repeat with the remaining mangoes and liquid.

Strain the mixture through a fine-mesh strainer into a container. Stir in the lime juice and zest. Refrigerate the soup until well chilled.

Serve cold, garnished with pieces of kiwi and strawberry.

Spiced Plum Soup

A richly colored soup with heady spices, this is a cooling luxury. Toasting the whole spices first adds significantly to the flavor. Use purple-skinned, dark-fleshed plums for the most appetizing results. You can also make this soup with apricots, peaches, or nectarines—whatever stone fruit looks most luscious at the market.

SERVES 4

2 whole star anise
1 cinnamon stick
1 teaspoon green cardamom pods
One 3-inch piece fresh ginger, unpeeled, cut into thin rounds
4 cups water
½ cup evaporated cane sugar
1 vanilla bean
2 pounds (about 6) red-fleshed plums, plus 1 extra plum, sliced, for garnish
1 teaspoon ginger juice (see Note), optional

In a heavy-bottomed skillet over medium heat, dry-toast the star anise, cinnamon stick, and cardamom pods until fragrant and lightly browned, about 1 minute. Transfer the spices to a cutting board or a mortar and pestle, and lightly crush them.

Place the crushed spices, ginger, water, and sugar in a medium saucepan. Cut the vanilla bean in half lengthwise, scrape out the seeds with the tip of a knife, and add

the seeds and the pod to the liquid. Bring to a boil over medium heat. Then lower the heat and simmer until the liquid is reduced to 3 cups, about 10 minutes.

Meanwhile, cut each plum in half and remove the pit.

Add the plums to the reduced liquid and simmer until they are softened and the skins are starting to slip off, about 10 minutes. Transfer the plums to a bowl with a slotted spoon, and slip off the skins. Strain the poaching liquid over the plums and discard the spices.

In two batches, blend the plums and the poaching liquid in a blender until smooth. Strain the soup through a fine-mesh strainer into a bowl. Stir in the ginger juice (if using). Refrigerate the soup until chilled.

Garnish each bowl of soup with a few pieces of sliced plum.

NOTE: *To make ginger juice, grate a 1-inch piece of unpeeled fresh ginger. Squeeze the pulp to extract 1 teaspoon of juice.*

Ginger Coconut Ice Cream

This ice cream is delicious on the Indian Pudding Cake (page 318). There is no need to peel the ginger—just grate it on the large holes of a box grater. The flavor of the ginger comes through after the ice cream has been in the freezer for several hours.

MAKES 1 QUART

Two 14-ounce cans unsweetened coconut milk
1/2 cup natural sugar, preferably maple sugar or
    evaporated cane sugar
1/2 cup grated unpeeled fresh ginger

Combine the coconut milk, sugar, and ginger in a medium saucepan, cover, and bring to a boil over medium heat. Lower the heat, uncover, and simmer gently for 5 minutes to concentrate the ginger flavor.

Strain the liquid into a bowl, and let it cool to room temperature (discard the ginger). Then refrigerate it for an hour or so, until chilled.

Freeze according to your ice cream maker's instructions. Let the ice cream sit in the freezer for a couple of hours before serving.

A Trio of Fruit Sorbets

These vibrant, flavorful sorbets make a refreshing and light finale to any meal. Each one is a tasty summer cooler; served together they are dazzling. The only special equipment required here is an ice cream maker. The little bit of vodka included in each recipe keeps the texture smooth and the sorbet from becoming too icy.

Blackberry Sorbet (MAKES 5 CUPS)

4 cups fresh blackberries
3/4 cup apple-raspberry cider or raspberry-apple juice
3/4 cup maple syrup
2 tablespoons fresh lime juice
Pinch of salt
Grated zest of 1 lime
1 tablespoon vodka

Blend the blackberries with the cider in a blender. Strain the mixture through a fine-mesh strainer into a bowl, to remove the seeds. Stir in the maple syrup, lime juice, salt, lime zest, and vodka.

Freeze according to your ice cream maker's instructions. Let the sorbet sit in the freezer for a couple of hours before serving.

Raspberry Sorbet (MAKES 5 CUPS)

4 cups raspberries
3/4 cup apple-raspberry cider or raspberry-apple juice
3/4 cup maple syrup
1/4 cup fresh orange juice
Pinch of salt
Grated zest of 1 orange
1 tablespoon framboise or vodka

Blend the raspberries with the cider in a blender. Strain the mixture through a fine-mesh strainer into a bowl, to remove the seeds. Stir in the maple syrup, orange juice, salt, orange zest, and framboise.

Freeze according to your ice cream maker's instructions. Let the sorbet sit in the freezer for a couple of hours before serving.

Peach Sorbet (MAKES 5 CUPS)

2 cups peach nectar or juice
One 2-inch piece fresh ginger, unpeeled, cut into 3 slices
2 tablespoons fresh lemon juice
1/2 cup maple sugar or evaporated cane sugar
Pinch of salt
2 pounds peaches, halved and pitted
1 tablespoon vodka

Combine the nectar, ginger, lemon juice, maple sugar, salt, and peaches in a medium saucepan. Cover and bring to a boil. Then lower the heat and cook until the peaches are completely tender, about 2 minutes. Remove the peaches with a slotted spoon, and slip off the skins.

Place the peaches in a blender. Discard the ginger slices, and pour the liquid into the blender. Add the vodka, and blend until smooth. Pour the mixture into a shallow container and chill thoroughly.

Freeze according to your ice cream maker's instructions. Let the sorbet sit in the freezer for a couple of hours before serving.

Light-as-a-Feather Chocolate Mousse

This dairy-free mousse whips up extra-light and fluffy. It's also extra-easy: no need to separate the eggs or to melt the chocolate in a double boiler. A generous dash of cocoa makes it extra-chocolatey. It has a sophisticated flavor; if you like it a little sweeter, start with semisweet chocolate. For a beautiful presentation, top the mousse with Very Berry Sauce or layer it with Coconut Whipped Cream (page 319).

SERVES 8

6 ounces semisweet or bittersweet chocolate,
    coarsely chopped
3/4 cup unsweetened coconut milk
2 tablespoons unsweetened cocoa powder
2 tablespoons brandy or other liqueur
4 large eggs
1/4 cup natural sugar, preferably maple sugar,
    evaporated cane sugar, or Sucanat
Very Berry Sauce (recipe follows), optional

Combine the chocolate, coconut milk, and cocoa powder in a small heavy-bottomed saucepan over medium-low heat, and stir until the chocolate begins to melt. Remove the pan from the heat and stir until the chocolate is completely melted. Stir in the brandy.

Combine the eggs and sugar in the bowl of a stand mixer and whisk them together by hand. (This way you won't have to change bowls.) Set the bowl over a pot of simmering water and stir gently and thoroughly, scraping the bottom frequently, until the liquid is hot to the touch (about 160°F on an instant-read thermometer). Remove the bowl from the heat and attach it to the mixer. Beat with the whisk attachment at high speed until the mixture has the consistency of whipped cream, about 5 minutes.

Pour the chocolate mixture into a medium bowl. Stir one fourth of the egg mixture into the chocolate. Then fold in the remaining egg mixture, one third at a time, until no streaks remain. Pour the mousse into eight 1/2-cup bowls or a single large bowl. Refrigerate until chilled and set, at least 2 hours, or up to overnight.

Top each serving with Very Berry Sauce if desired.

Very Berry Sauce

This delicious all-purpose sauce is loaded with berries. Prepared with fresh or frozen berries, it's wonderful to have on hand. Serve it with the Light-as-a-Feather Chocolate Mousse over waffles or French toast, or with Peach Sorbet (page 293).

MAKES ABOUT 3 CUPS

1 cup blueberries
1 cup raspberries
1 cup blackberries
2 cups strawberries, hulled and quartered
1 tablespoon maple syrup
1/2 teaspoon fresh lemon juice

Mix the berries together in a medium bowl. Transfer 1½ cups of the mixed berries to a blender or food processor, and blend until smooth. Strain the puréed berries through a fine-mesh strainer to remove the seeds; you should have about 1 cup strained juice. Stir the maple syrup and lemon juice into the strained berry juice. Then stir the liquid into the remaining berries in the bowl. Serve chilled or at room temperature. Make up to 3 days ahead.

About Agar, Arrowroot, and Kudzu

Agar, also called agar-agar, is a vegetarian form of gelatin, made from a red seaweed that is processed into flakes, bars, or powder.

The flakes are the most useful, most commonly available, and the type I use the most. They are found in natural foods stores, in the section with the other sea vegetables or macrobiotic ingredients. One-quarter cup of flakes will gel 1 quart of liquid. Sometimes I add a higher proportion of agar when I know I'm going to blend or process the dish I'm making.

To use the flakes, place them in a saucepan with cold liquid. Soak them in the liquid for 5 minutes or so before you turn on the heat. The liquid must be brought to a boil slowly; stir every once in a while to make sure nothing has stuck to the pot. Once the liquid reaches a boil, immediately lower the heat and allow the liquid to simmer softly until all of the agar has thoroughly dissolved; this takes about 10 minutes. Make sure that you see gentle bubbles moving, or the agar won't dissolve. If you can't tell whether the agar has dissolved, pour a spoonful onto a plate; you will be able to see if any bits remain. Once the agar has dissolved, you are ready to proceed with the next step of the recipe or to remove the pot from the heat.

One bar of agar is equivalent to about $\frac{1}{4}$ cup agar flakes. Agar bars have to be soaked in cold water for a few minutes until they soften, then squeezed to remove excess liquid. Rip the bar apart a bit before adding it to the pot of cold liquid, to make dissolving easier.

Agar powder dissolves quite easily. It has a bit of a sea taste that the other versions do not, so I use it only when there is a strong sweetener that will overpower that flavor. The powder is five times as strong as the flakes, so 1 tablespoon of powder is equivalent to 5 tablespoons of flakes. Because of its concentrated form, a little powder goes a long way; it dissolves in a small amount of liquid. You can also bake with agar powder, which you cannot do with the other forms. You can order agar powder by mail (see Resources); it lasts indefinitely, as do the other types of agar-agar.

Agar dissolves slowly in certain liquids, especially thick ones; so when using coconut milk, first dissolve the agar quickly in a measurement of water and then add the thicker milk. It does not set in acidic liquids, such as pineapple juice, pomegranate juice, cranberry juice, or wine.

Kudzu and arrowroot are both healthful substitutes for cornstarch; they are pretty much interchangeable. Agar works once the liquid has chilled; kudzu and arrowroot when the liquid is hot. Agar gelatinizes; kudzu and arrowroot thicken. Together they give a custardlike texture to a dish. Arrowroot and kudzu must be dissolved in a cold liquid before you add them to the pot—this is called a slurry—or else you'll end up with a lumpy mess. If it has visible lumps when you pour it in, you'll have a lumpy end product.

For most cooking purposes, I prefer arrowroot to kudzu. Arrowroot works well in puddings, and it's a good pie thickener. I use it as a binder in place of eggs in the vegan version of the crêpes, and it binds the pecan-lace tuiles as well. It also dissolves more readily than kudzu.

Kudzu, which comes in big white chunks, is imported from Japan, even though the plant itself is a ground cover that grows wild all over the southern United States. It is quite expensive, so I use it mostly for its medicinal value as a stomach soother.

After you add your dissolved arrowroot mixture to the hot simmering liquid, stand at the stove and stir, stir, stir. Stir continuously, stopping for a moment occasionally to see what's happening, and then continue to stir until the mixture has gone from cloudy to clear and you feel it thicken slightly. This takes only a matter of minutes. When you see a few bubbles, you know the liquid is about to boil and it's time to remove it from the stove. Don't let the liquid boil away after you've added the arrowroot; it could break and lose its strength. Kudzu is a lot stronger in this regard. You can reheat anything thickened with kudzu without harming its integrity.

A Pair of Luscious Puddings

Here are two voluptuous vegan puddings: chocolate coconut and lemon. Coconut milk gives each one a subtle flavor and velvety texture. They taste great with Very Berry Sauce (page 295) and are lovely with Coconut Whipped Cream (page 319).

If you don't have a lot of experience cooking with agar, read "About Agar, Arrowroot, and Kudzu" (page 296) and you'll be all set.

Chocolate Coconut Pudding

For a gorgeous presentation, serve this in Phyllo Cups (page 301) garnished with Coconut Whipped Cream (page 319) and a Chocolate Phyllo Cigar (page 302).

SERVES 6

1 1/2 cups water

1 cup maple syrup

4 tablespoons agar flakes

One 14-ounce can unsweetened coconut milk

2 tablespoons arrowroot powder or kudzu

1/4 cup unsweetened cocoa powder

1/4 teaspoon salt

1/2 cup (2 ounces) semisweet shaved chocolate or chocolate chips

2 teaspoons vanilla extract

Combine the water, maple syrup, and agar flakes in a medium saucepan, and let sit for 5 minutes to soften the agar. Then slowly bring the liquid to a boil. Lower the heat, and simmer gently for 5 to 10 minutes to thoroughly dissolve the agar. Stir frequently to make sure the agar is not sticking to the bottom.

Stir the coconut milk well, and transfer 1/4 cup to a small bowl. Mix it with the arrowroot to make a slurry, and set aside.

Add the remainder of the coconut milk, the cocoa powder, and the salt to the pot on the stove. As soon as the liquid reaches a boil, stir in the arrowroot mixture. Stir constantly until bubbles appear and the mixture thickens a bit, about 1 minute.

Immediately remove the pot from the heat and stir in the chocolate and the vanilla. Let the chocolate sit for a few minutes, and then whisk it in until it is thoroughly melted. Pour the pudding into a shallow pan. When the pudding has cooled enough to stop steaming, chill it in the refrigerator until set, about 45 minutes. Then transfer the pudding to a food processor and process until smooth. Chill again after processing. Pudding keeps, covered and refrigerated, for up to 4 days.

Lemon Pudding

This makes a delicious accompaniment to the Triple Gingerbread (page 320).

Serves 6

1 1/2 cups water
1/4 cup agar flakes
1/4 teaspoon ground turmeric
Pinch of salt
One 14-ounce can unsweetened coconut milk
2 tablespoons arrowroot powder or kudzu
1/2 cup maple syrup
1/2 cup brown rice syrup
3/4 cup fresh lemon juice
2 teaspoons grated lemon zest
2 teaspoons vanilla extract

Combine the water, agar flakes, turmeric, and salt in a small saucepan and let sit for 5 minutes. Then slowly bring the liquid to a boil. Lower the heat and simmer gently until the agar has dissolved, about 10 minutes. Stir occasionally to make sure none of the flakes stick to the sides of the pot.

Meanwhile, stir the coconut milk well, and transfer 1/4 cup to a small bowl. Mix it with the arrowroot to make a slurry, and set aside.

Add the remainder of the coconut milk, the maple syrup, rice syrup, and lemon juice to the agar mixture and raise the heat to medium. As soon as the mixture reaches a boil, add the slurry, stirring continuously. Keep stirring, raising your spoon occasionally to see if bubbles have formed, until the liquid changes from cloudy to clear, thickens slightly, and is just starting to bubble, about 1 minute. Immediately remove the pan from the heat and stir in the lemon zest and the vanilla.

Pour the pudding into a shallow pan and let it rest until it stops steaming, about 30 minutes. Refrigerate the pudding until it is chilled and completely firm, 45 minutes or so.

Transfer the pudding to a food processor, and process until smooth. Place it in a bowl or other container, and refrigerate until thickened, about 1 hour. The pudding thickens considerably once it is refrigerated.

NOTE: *If your slurry has been sitting around for a while, make sure to whisk it before adding it to the pot. If you're using kudzu, make sure it's really dissolved well before adding it in.*

About Phyllo

Phyllo is made from flour and water, rolled to make the thinnest possible dough. It is widely available frozen, in 1-pound packages. Even though some phyllo projects take a bit of work, they are worth the effort because they can be made well in advance and then taken straight from the freezer to the oven. I use phyllo quite a bit in entertaining, for small soirées and for large parties.

There are a few traditional Greek bakeries in the United States that make their own phyllo. If you are in New York, I heartily recommend a visit to Poseidon Bakery (see Resources). Their phyllo puts any of the commercial variety to shame. If you arrive at noon and request it, they'll let you in the back to watch them stretch the dough into paper-thin sheets.

A few points to remember when using phyllo:

- Keep the phyllo covered at all times. Open the package, lay the unrolled sheets on a sheet of parchment or wax paper, and cover them with a kitchen towel. Place a damp towel on top of the dry one to keep the moisture in. After you pull out a sheet, cover the stack right away. Phyllo dries out quickly.

- The dough defrosts quickly at room temperature, but it defrosts best in the refrigerator. Once defrosted, it keeps for about a week in the refrigerator. You can roll up and refreeze unused phyllo if it has not been exposed to air.

- Phyllo is forgiving. Even if it tears or crinkles, chances are that by the time you fold it or layer it, you won't even notice any flaws.

- Be sure to brush oil or melted butter between all the layers. The fat is what pushes the layer of dough up, making the phyllo flaky. It doesn't matter what kind of fat you use, as long as you use something. My favorites for desserts are coconut oil, melted butter, and melted ghee. For savory dishes I use those as well, along with extra-virgin olive oil on occasion. Brush a thin film over each layer of phyllo. If you fold it, remember to brush the folded-over surface. Always spread a layer of oil or butter over the completed piece or the phyllo will be too dry. Use a pastry brush to apply the fat, and don't douse the dough—a thin film is best.

All filled phyllo pastries can be frozen before baking. Spread the pastries in a single layer on a baking sheet and freeze for about 2 hours. When they are frozen solid, you can stack them however you like (I usually use resealable freezer bags). When you are ready to bake them, spread the pastries out on a baking sheet without defrosting. You'll need only a few extra minutes of baking time.

Phyllo that is not filled, like the cups, or phyllo pastries that have a dry filling, like the cigars, can be baked up to a week in advance and kept in a covered container at room temperature.

Phyllo Cups

These flowerlike cups come in handy for a party. For a gorgeous presentation, fill the cups with Light-as-a-Feather Chocolate Mousse (page 294) or Chocolate Coconut Pudding (page 298), top them with a dollop of Coconut Whipped Cream (page 319), and stand a Chocolate Phyllo Cigar (page 302) upright in the center. The unfilled cups keep very well for up to a week when stored in a covered container at room temperature.

MAKES 12 PHYLLO CUPS

8 sheets phyllo dough, defrosted
Melted coconut oil or melted unsalted butter

Preheat the oven to 375°F.

Unroll the phyllo dough, making sure to cover the dough that isn't being used. Place a sheet of phyllo on a clean surface and lightly brush a layer of oil over it, making sure to cover the entire exposed surface. Do this with a light touch. Add another layer of phyllo on top of the first, and brush it with oil. Do this until you have 4 layers.

Cut the phyllo stack in half lengthwise, and cut each half into thirds. You should have 6 squares. If necessary, trim the squares with a knife to even them out.

Press each square into a muffin cup, folding and ruffling the phyllo until you get a desirable flowerlike shape. Every cup will have its own character, depending on how you ruffle and fold the edges. Repeat, spacing the phyllo cups in every other muffin cup. (Using a muffin pan with 12 muffin cups, you will fit 6 phyllo cups.) Poke holes in the bottom of each cup with a fork or a paring knife (to keep the phyllo from puffing up during baking).

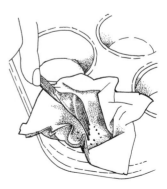

Bake the phyllo cups until golden brown, 8 to 10 minutes. Remove, and repeat with the remaining phyllo. Store in a covered container at room temperature for up to 1 week.

Chocolate Phyllo Cigars

Crisp and chocolatey, these cookielike confections are just the right accompaniment to a creamy dessert, such as Light-as-a-Feather Chocolate Mousse (page 294) or the Chocolate Coconut Pudding (page 298). For best results, roll the cigars as thin as possible. The cigars will keep for up to a week, stored in a covered container at room temperature.

MAKES ABOUT 30 CIGARS

½ **pound phyllo dough, defrosted**
½ **cup melted unsalted butter or coconut oil**
¼ **cup sugar, preferably maple sugar**
½ **cup dried unsweetened coconut**
1 **cup (4 ounces) shaved semisweet chocolate**

Preheat the oven to 375°F.

Cut the sheets of phyllo in half lengthwise, and cut each half into thirds; you should have 6 squares from each sheet. Stack the squares into a pile. Keep the phyllo well covered—under a dry towel with a damp towel over that—to prevent it from drying out. Be sure to cover the phyllo each time you pull off a layer.

Lay 1 sheet of phyllo flat on a clean work surface. Lightly brush butter over the phyllo, working from the edges to the center. Sprinkle it lightly with sugar and co-

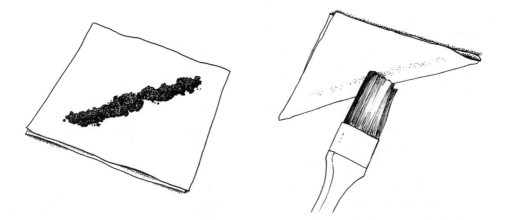

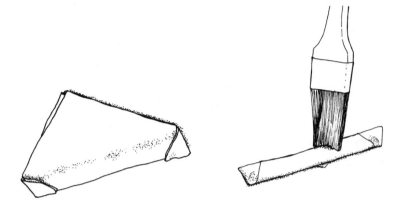

conut. Lay a second sheet on top of the first, and brush it with butter. Sprinkle about 1 teaspoon of the shaved chocolate in a thin diagonal line across the center (which will become the crease), leaving 1 inch bare at each corner. Fold the phyllo in half, forming a triangle and sandwiching the chocolate in the middle. Brush the crease with butter. Fold in the corners and roll the phyllo into a cigar shape. (See illustrations.) Repeat with the remaining phyllo squares. Place the cigars on a parchment-covered baking sheet, and brush them lightly with butter or oil. Sprinkle with sugar.

Bake the phyllo cigars until they are crisp and golden, 7 to 9 minutes.

Baklava

Here layers of phyllo and pistachio bake into a classic delicacy. I find that most traditional baklavas are too sweet; this version, laced with rose water, is just sweet enough. The flavor improves as it sits, so if possible, prepare it a day ahead so that the dough can absorb the syrup. Rose water is available in gourmet markets, natural foods stores, and any store selling Middle Eastern products.

MAKES 36 PIECES

2½ cups unsalted shelled pistachios
⅓ cup maple sugar or unrefined cane sugar
1 teaspoon ground cinnamon
⅛ teaspoon ground cloves
1 pound phyllo dough, defrosted
½ cup melted unsalted butter, coconut oil, or ghee

Syrup

1 cup maple sugar or unrefined cane sugar
1 cup water
1 cup rice syrup
One 3-inch strip lemon zest
1 cinnamon stick
1 teaspoon rose water

Preheat the oven to 350°F. Brush an 8 by 11½-inch baking pan with butter or oil.

Chop the pistachios by hand into very small pieces. (You can use a food processor, but it turns the nuts into powder.) Mix the nuts, maple sugar, cinnamon, and cloves together in a medium bowl.

Unfold the phyllo and cut it to size, allowing for it to measure twice the width of the baking pan (see illustration, opposite). Keep the phyllo well covered—under a dry towel with a damp towel over that one—to prevent it from drying out. Be sure to cover the phyllo each time you pull off a layer.

Place 1 sheet of phyllo in the baking pan, letting the extra width hang over the side. Brush the dough in the pan lightly with melted butter. Fold the extending half over, and brush it with butter. Continue layering, folding, and brushing the pastry with butter until one third of the phyllo has been used.

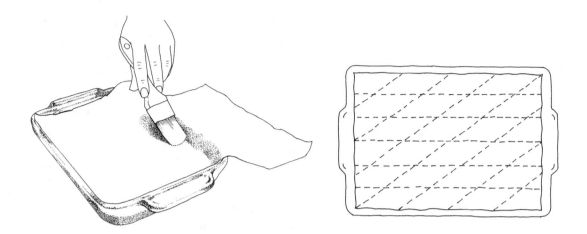

Spread the nut mixture over the pastry. Then layer the remaining pastry sheets as before, brushing each layer with melted butter.

Brush the final layer with butter. Cut the pastry with a sharp knife, forming 36 small diamond-shaped pieces. Make sure you cut through all the layers.

Bake the baklava until golden, 35 to 40 minutes.

Meanwhile, make the syrup: Combine the maple sugar, water, rice syrup, lemon zest, and cinnamon stick in a small saucepan and bring to a boil. Reduce the heat and simmer gently until the liquid has the consistency of thick maple syrup, about 20 minutes. Remove the pan from the heat and remove the cinnamon stick and lemon zest. Stir in the rose water.

As soon as the baklava comes out of the oven, pour the syrup over it. Recut the pieces, and allow the baklava to stand for several hours, so that the syrup is absorbed into the pastry.

Serve at room temperature. Store the baklava, covered, at room temperature for up to 1 week.

Butter Crust

This is a great all-purpose pie crust, with just enough whole-grain flour to take on an earthy quality. Making your own pie crust is no big deal; it takes just seconds in a food processor.

MAKES 1 CRUST

3/4 cup unbleached white flour, chilled
1/2 cup whole-wheat pastry flour, chilled
1/2 teaspoon baking powder
1/4 teaspoon salt
2 tablespoons maple sugar, Sucanat, or evaporated cane sugar
1/2 cup (1 stick) chilled unsalted butter, cut into small pieces
1 teaspoon apple cider vinegar
3 tablespoons ice water

Place the two flours, baking powder, salt, and sugar in a food processor, and process for a couple of seconds to combine. Add the butter and pulse until the mixture resemble crumbs, 7 to 10 pulses. The crumbs should be uneven in size.

Stir the vinegar into the ice water, and add this to the flour mixture. Pulse for a couple of seconds, just to combine. Do not process so long that the dough becomes a ball.

Remove the dough from the processor and gather it into a ball. With the heel of your hand, press the dough onto the work surface to bind the ball together. Form the dough into one flattened disk. Wrap the disk in plastic wrap and chill in the refrigerator for at least 1 hour.

You can make the dough up to 2 days in advance and keep it in the refrigerator, and you can freeze the dough for up to 1 month. After you refrigerate the dough, depending on the time of year or how cold it is, you may have to give it a couple of whacks with a rolling pin to soften it enough for rolling.

Coconut Oil Crust

Coconut oil produces a tender, flaky, flavorful crust. Although the oil is solid at room temperature, the warmth of a kitchen melts it quite quickly. Measure out a little more oil than you think you'll need and keep that portion in the refrigerator. When the oil is hard, just chop it up and measure it again in a dry measure. The oil expands in the cold, so it is important to measure it in the form you need it. Any extra oil can go back in the jar.

A coconut oil crust can be made by hand or in a food processor. I prefer to use the food processor and finish the crust by hand.

To make the rolling easy, simply refrigerate the crust for about 5 minutes (no longer!) before rolling it out.

MAKES 1 CRUST

3/4 cup unbleached white flour, chilled
1/2 cup whole-wheat pastry flour, chilled
1/2 teaspoon baking powder
2 tablespoons maple sugar, Sucanat, or evaporated cane sugar
1/4 teaspoon salt
6 tablespoons (1/4 cup plus 2 tablespoons) thoroughly chilled coconut oil
1 teaspoon apple cider vinegar
5 to 6 tablespoons ice water

Place the two flours, baking powder, sugar, and salt in a food processor, and process for a couple of seconds to combine. Add the solid coconut oil and pulse for about 15 seconds, or until the oil is coated and the mixture resembles wet sand. Pour the mixture into a mixing bowl.

Stir the vinegar into the ice water, and drizzle it over the dough, a spoonful at a time, tossing lightly as you go, until the dough holds together when squeezed. Do not add any more water than is absolutely necessary.

Gather the dough into a ball. Wrap in plastic wrap, and refrigerate for about 5 minutes before rolling it out.

NOTE: *To form the dough by hand, work the oil into the dry ingredients with your fingers or a pastry cutter, making sure there are no pieces larger than a small pebble.*

Cranberry Apple Crumb Pie

This is an exciting variation on a classic. You may find that it is even more popular than traditional apple pie at Thanksgiving. Use wonderful autumn apples available such as Ida Red, Winesap, Cortland, Mutsu, Jonagold, Northern Spy, or Rome, or reliable standbys, equal parts Granny Smith and Golden Delicious. The cranberries are given a quick cook, so that they bake and melt into the apples, giving the fruit a rosy hue. The streusel topping is irresistible.

SERVES 8 TO 10

1 cup cranberries, fresh or frozen
1/4 cup maple syrup
4 pounds (8 medium) apples
1/4 cup (1/2 stick) unsalted butter *or* 3 tablespoons coconut oil
1 cup maple sugar, Sucanat, or date sugar
Pinch of salt
2 teaspoons ground cinnamon
3/4 teaspoon ground allspice
2 teaspoons grated lemon zest
1 tablespoon fresh lemon juice
3 tablespoons unbleached white flour
1 recipe Butter Crust or Coconut Oil Crust dough (pages 306, 307)

Crumb Topping

3/4 cup whole-wheat pastry flour
1/2 cup pecans, toasted and chopped into small pieces
1/2 cup maple sugar
1/2 teaspoon baking powder
1 teaspoon ground cinnamon
1/2 teaspoon salt
4 to 5 tablespoons melted coconut oil or melted unsalted butter

Combine the cranberries and the maple syrup in a small saucepan and cook over medium heat until the cranberries burst and thicken, 5 to 10 minutes. Set aside.

Peel, core, and quarter half of the apples. Cut each quarter into 4 lengthwise slices.

Melt the butter in a large skillet over medium heat. Add the apple slices and ½ cup of the maple sugar and cook, stirring frequently, until the apples are caramelized and tender, 6 to 7 minutes. Remove from the heat.

Peel, core, and quarter the remaining apples. Cut each quarter into thin slices, no thicker than ¼ inch. Toss them with the cooked apples. Add the reserved cranberries, the remaining ½ cup sugar, and the cinnamon, allspice, lemon zest, and lemon juice. Stir in the flour. Set the mixture aside.

Make the topping: In a medium bowl, toss the flour, pecans, maple sugar, baking powder, cinnamon, and salt together. Slowly drizzle in the oil, 1 tablespoon at a time, tossing with your fingers until the mixture is moistened. The mixture should be like damp sand with pebbles of various sizes, ranging in size from crumbs to large pebbles. Use the last tablespoon of oil only if the topping seems dry.

Assemble the pie: Have a 9-inch pie plate ready. Roll the dough out on a lightly floured board or between two pieces of parchment paper. Start from the center and move outward, rolling the dough until it is as thin as possible (about ¹⁄₁₆ inch). Transfer the dough to the pie plate, lightly pushing it to meet the contours of the plate. Trim the overhang to extend ½ inch past the rim of the plate. Then fold the overhang under and tuck it in so that it's flush with the edge of the plate. Make a decorative edge by pressing the dough between the forefinger of one hand and the thumb and forefinger of the other. Repeat this motion to make a handsome border around the entire pie.

Pour the filling into the crust and smooth it down evenly. Sprinkle the crumb topping over the fruit, distributing it to cover all of the fruit. Place the pie in the refrigerator for at least 45 minutes or up to overnight to chill.

Preheat the oven to 350°F.

Loosely tent the pie with aluminum foil. Place it on the middle rack in the oven, and bake for 30 minutes. Remove the foil and bake until the crust is golden brown and the juices are starting to bubble, 20 to 30 minutes.

Remove the pie from the oven and let it cool to room temperature before slicing.

Pomegranate-Pear Cornmeal Tart

This is an impressive-looking dessert to serve with all your holiday meals. The crimson hue of the pomegranate syrup looks beautiful over the fanned-out pears. With its three layers, this may appear to be an elaborate dessert, but it is in fact quite simple to make.

SERVES 8 TO 10

Poached pears

3 semi-firm pears, preferably Anjou

3 cups pomegranate juice

1 cup port

1 cinnamon stick

6 whole star anise

Crust

1/2 cup sliced almonds, lightly toasted

1/2 cup unbleached white flour

1/4 cup cornmeal

1/4 cup melted unsalted butter or melted coconut oil

3 tablespoons maple syrup

1/2 teaspoon almond extract

Pinch of salt

Cake

1/2 cup sliced almonds, lightly toasted

1/2 cup unbleached white flour

1/2 cup cornmeal

1/2 teaspoon baking powder

1/4 cup melted unsalted butter or melted coconut oil

6 tablespoons maple syrup

1 egg

1 egg yolk

1 teaspoon vanilla extract

1/2 teaspoon almond extract

1/4 teaspoon salt

Garnish

¼ cup sliced almonds, toasted

Poach the pears: Peel the pears, cut them in half, and remove the cores. Place the pears in a medium saucepan and add the pomegranate juice, port, cinnamon stick, and star anise. Place a round of parchment, with a small steam vent cut in the middle, on top to keep the pears submerged (see illustration). Bring the liquid to a boil, reduce the heat, and simmer until pears are tender-firm, about 20 minutes. Remove the pears from the liquid with a slotted spoon, and place them in a dish in a single layer to cool. Strain the cooking liquid into a medium skillet, and discard the cinnamon stick and star anise.

Place the skillet over high heat and reduce the poaching liquid until the juices have thickened and formed a glaze, about 30 minutes. You will probably have only about ½ inch of glaze in the pot, about ½ cup of liquid. Be careful not to reduce the

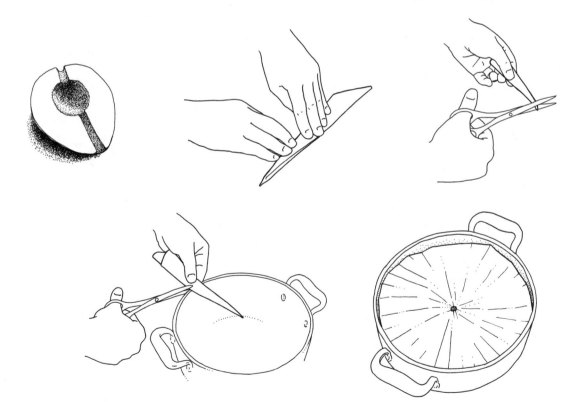

(CONTINUED NEXT PAGE)

liquid down to the point where it burns. If you are unsure, remove the skillet from the heat and let the liquid sit until you can measure it. If you reduced it too far and it has turned into a gelatinous glob but not burned, you can reconstitute it with a little water. It needs to be thick enough to brush on as a glaze when the tart is baked and cooled. Set the glaze aside.

Meanwhile, when the pears are cool enough to handle, pat them dry. Use a paring knife to cut the thick end of each pear into very thin slices (about 12 slices), keeping the thin end intact so that the slices are connected and you can fan them out.

Make the crust: Preheat the oven to 350°F and oil a 9-inch tart pan that has a removable bottom.

Combine the almonds, flour, and cornmeal in a food processor and process until the nuts are finely ground into the flour. Transfer to a medium bowl. In a small bowl, whisk the melted butter, maple syrup, almond extract, and salt together. Pour this into the flour-nut mixture and mix with a wooden spoon or rubber spatula until the dry ingredients are thoroughly moistened.

Press the crust mixture evenly onto the bottom of the oiled tart pan. You may wish to use a piece of plastic wrap between your fingers and the nut mixture to make it easier to smooth. Do not press the crust mixture up the sides of the pan. Bake until the crust is lightly browned, 10 to 15 minutes. Remove the crust from the oven.

Make the cake: Combine the almonds, flour, and cornmeal in a food processor and process until finely ground. Transfer to a medium bowl. Whisk in the baking powder.

In another medium bowl, whisk the melted butter, maple syrup, egg, yolk, vanilla extract, almond extract, and salt until thoroughly combined. Pour the wet ingredients into the dry, and stir just until the dry ingredients are thoroughly moistened.

Spread the batter evenly over the crust in the tart pan. (A small offset spatula is great for this.) Arrange the fanned-out pear halves attractively on top of the batter. You will probably be able to fit only 5 halves in the 9-inch tart pan. Strew the 1/4 cup of almonds over the surface between the pears.

Bake until a toothpick inserted in the center comes clean, 20 to 30 minutes. Let the tart cool for 15 to 20 minutes. Then use a pastry brush to lightly dab the glaze over the entire surface of the tart, including the pears and almonds. Unmold the tart, and serve.

Naked Carrot Cake

This light version of an old favorite has some unusual touches. It doesn't need a frosting.

If you can't find oat flour, you can make it by grinding rolled oats in a spice grinder or food processor. Make sure to add an extra ¼ cup of oats; then measure after they are ground to get the right amount of flour.

SERVES 10 TO 12

2½ cups oat flour
2 teaspoons baking soda
1 teaspoon salt
1 teaspoon ground cinnamon
¼ teaspoon ground nutmeg
¼ teaspoon ground allspice
¼ teaspoon ground cloves
1½ cups natural sugar, preferably maple sugar or evaporated cane sugar
4 eggs
1 cup extra-virgin olive oil
4 cups grated carrots
½ cup dried currants
¾ cup walnuts, toasted and chopped into small pieces
½ cup dried unsweetened coconut, optional

Preheat the oven to 350°F. Oil a 9-inch springform pan.

Whisk the oat flour, baking soda, salt, cinnamon, nutmeg, allspice, and cloves together in a bowl. Whisk in the sugar.

In another bowl, whisk together the eggs and the oil. Stir the wet ingredients into the dry, mixing with a wooden spoon or a rubber spatula just until the dry ingredients are moistened. Then stir in the carrots, currants, walnuts, and coconut (if using). Pour the batter into the prepared pan and bake until a toothpick inserted in the center comes out dry, 60 to 70 minutes. Check after 45 minutes; if the cake starts to look browned, lay a piece of aluminum foil over the top and continue to bake until cooked through.

Cool for 10 minutes in the pan. Unmold and finish cooling on a rack. Serve at room temperature. Store at room temperature, covered, for up to 4 days.

"Pumpkin" Pie

This glossy dairy-free pie has just the right combination of sweet spices for your holiday celebrations. Coconut milk adds a satiny quality to the texture of the filling. Roasting your own squash is no big deal, and once you've tried it, you'll never go back to canned. For a luscious combination, serve this with Coconut Whipped Cream (page 319).

Serves 8 to 10

One 2- to 2½-pound butternut squash
½ cup maple syrup
½ cup unsweetened coconut milk
¾ teaspoon ground cinnamon
¾ teaspoon ground ginger
¼ teaspoon freshly grated nutmeg
½ teaspoon salt
1 tablespoon light rum
1 egg
2 egg yolks
1 recipe Butter Crust or Coconut Oil Crust dough (pages 306, 307)
¼ cup gingersnap crumbs

Preheat the oven to 350°F.

Cut the squash lengthwise down the middle. Do not remove the seeds. Place the squash face down on a parchment-covered baking sheet, and bake until it is completely tender and the juices are starting to bubble, about 45 minutes.

Remove the squash from the oven and set it aside until it is cool enough to handle. Discard the seeds. Scoop out the flesh and put it in a colander or strainer over a bowl. Let it sit for about 10 minutes to drain off any excess liquid. Then transfer the squash to a food processor and process until smooth. Measure out 2 cups of the purée for the pie. Reserve any extra for another use.

Return the 2 cups squash purée to the food processor, and add the maple syrup, coconut milk, cinnamon, ginger, nutmeg, salt, and rum. Process until smooth. Taste, and adjust the sweetness by adding up to ¼ cup extra sweetener if necessary (not all winter squashes are equally sweet). Add the egg and egg yolks, and process to mix them in completely. Set the filling aside.

Have a 9-inch pie plate ready. Roll out the dough on a lightly floured board or between two pieces of parchment paper. Start from the center and move outward, rolling the dough until it is as thin as possible (about $1/16$ inch). Transfer the dough to the pie plate, lightly pushing it to meet the contours of the plate. Trim the overhang to extend $1/2$ inch beyond the rim of the plate. Then fold the overhang under and tuck it in so that it is flush with the edge of the plate. Make a decorative edge by pressing the dough between the forefinger of one hand and the thumb and forefinger of the other. Repeat this motion to make a decorative border around the edge of the entire pie.

Press the gingersnap crumbs over the bottom of the crust and halfway up the sides. Chill the pie crust in the refrigerator for 30 minutes.

Place a piece of parchment in the pie shell and weight the parchment with dry beans or pie weights. Bake the pie shell for 10 minutes, just enough to firm the crust but not enough to color it. Remove the pie weights and the parchment.

Pour the filling into the pie shell and bake, uncovered, until the crust is golden brown, about 40 minutes. Then place a foil collar around the crust (see Note) and bake until a knife inserted in the middle comes out clean, 25 to 40 minutes. Remove the pie from the oven and let it cool to room temperature (at least 2 hours) before cutting it.

NOTE: *To make a collar for the crust, take a piece of aluminum foil that is larger than the pie plate. Fold the piece into quarters. Using the center-fold corner as the center, cut out a quarter-round the size of a quarter of the pie plate. Open up the foil; you should have a circle of foil. Trim off the excess foil at the corners to form a ring. Shape the ring so it will curve over the rim of the pie crust, leaving the filling exposed and the crust covered.*

Browned Butter Berry Galette

A small amount of browned butter lends a toasted nutty quality to this free-form tart and makes for a sublime experience. Serve the galette warm, topped with ice cream, if you like to send your guests into seventh heaven.

SERVES 6

Pastry

3/4 **cup unbleached white flour**
3/4 **cup whole-wheat pastry flour**
1/4 **teaspoon salt**
2 **teaspoons evaporated cane sugar or maple sugar**
1/2 **cup (1 stick) chilled unsalted butter, cut into small pieces**
1/4 **cup very cold water**

Filling

1/4 **cup (**1/2 **stick) unsalted butter**
3 **to 4 cups mixed fresh berries (blueberries, blackberries,**
     raspberries, and a few strawberries)
2 **tablespoons plus 2 teaspoons maple sugar or**
     evaporated cane sugar
2 **tablespoons honey**

Place the flours, salt, and sugar in a food processor and process for 2 seconds. Add the butter and pulse until the mixture becomes crumbs, 6 or 7 pulses. The crumbs should be uneven, with some mere crumbs and some the size of small pebbles. Add the cold water and pulse for a couple of seconds just to combine. Do not process so long that the dough becomes a ball.

Remove the dough from the bowl and gather it into a ball. With the heel of your hand, press the dough into the work surface board to bind the ball together. Form it into 1 flattened disk for a 12-inch galette or 6 small disks for individual galettes. Wrap the disk(s) in plastic wrap and refrigerate for at least 1 hour and up to 2 days.

Heat the 1/4 cup butter in a small saucepan over medium-low heat until it is browned and nutty, 4 to 5 minutes. Watch the butter carefully so that it does not burn. Remove the pan from the heat, pour the browned butter into a small bowl, and set it aside.

Preheat the oven to 375°F. Remove the dough from the refrigerator. On a lightly floured surface, working from the center outward, roll the large disk into a large round about ⅛ inch thick; roll individual disks into small rounds. Pile the berries in the center of the pastry round(s), leaving a 1½-inch border around the edges. Sprinkle 2 tablespoons of the maple sugar over the berries, and drizzle the honey over them. Drizzle the browned butter over the fruit. Fold the edges of the dough over the berries to create a free-form tart. The dough makes a border around the fruit but does not cover it completely. Brush the pastry border with water, and sprinkle the remaining 2 teaspoons sugar over it. Bake until the pastry is golden and crisp, 20 to 30 minutes. Remove the galette(s) from the oven and let cool for about 10 minutes. Serve warm or at room temperature.

Indian Pudding Cake

This version of the classic New England cornmeal and molasses-based pudding is a sliceable cake with a pudding-like texture, flavored with traditional sweet spices. Serve it with Coconut Whipped Cream (page 319) or Ginger Coconut Ice Cream (page 291).

SERVES 8 TO 10

2 1/2 cups milk *or* one 14-ounce can unsweetened
    coconut milk plus 1 cup water
3/4 cup polenta or cornmeal
1/4 cup molasses
1/4 cup maple syrup
3/4 cup natural sugar, preferably maple sugar or
    evaporated cane sugar
1/2 teaspoon salt
1 1/2 teaspoons ground cinnamon
1/4 teaspoon ground nutmeg
3/4 teaspoon ground ginger
1 tablespoon grated orange zest
1 teaspoon vanilla extract
4 eggs, separated

Whisk the milk, polenta, molasses, maple syrup, 1/4 cup of the sugar, and the salt in a medium metal bowl.

Fill a 4-quart saucepan two-thirds with water and bring it to a simmer. Cover the metal bowl with foil, set it over the simmering water, and cook until the polenta is thick and stiff, 40 minutes. Stir the polenta three or four times as it cooks, and add water to the saucepan below if necessary. (You can also cook it in a double boiler.) When the polenta is done, a spoon should be able to stand up in it.

Meanwhile, preheat the oven to 350°F. Oil or butter a 9-inch springform pan.

When the polenta is cooked, remove the bowl from the simmering water and stir in the cinnamon, nutmeg, ginger, orange zest, vanilla, and egg yolks.

In a large bowl, or in the bowl of a stand mixer, whip the egg whites until frothy. Slowly add the remaining 1/2 cup sugar and continue beating until the whites are stiff and glossy. Fold a quarter of the egg whites into the polenta to lighten the batter. Then fold in the remaining whites, one fourth at a time, until well combined.

Pour the batter into the prepared pan and bake until a knife inserted in the cake comes out clean, about 45 minutes. Cool the cake on a rack for 15 minutes. Then release the sides of the pan and set the cake on a plate. Serve it warm or at room temperature, with your favorite topping. It will keep, at room temperature, for up to 3 days.

Coconut Whipped Cream

This tasty cream with its subtle hint of coconut is delicious on "Pumpkin" Pie (page 314) or layered with the Light-as-a-Feather Chocolate Mousse (page 294).

MAKES 1½ CUPS

1 cup heavy whipping cream, preferably organic
¼ cup unsweetened coconut milk
½ teaspoon vanilla extract
¼ cup natural sugar, such as evaporated cane sugar

Pour the cream, coconut milk, vanilla, and sugar into the bowl of a stand mixer fitted with the whip. Whip on high speed until soft peaks form, about 5 minutes. Transfer the whipped cream to a bowl and refrigerate for up to 3 days.

Vegan version

You can whip the cream from a can of coconut milk into a delicious nondairy whipped topping: Place the can of coconut milk in the freezer in order to separate the cream from the water. Open the can, scoop out the cream, and place it in a food processor. Add ½ teaspoon vanilla extract and ¼ cup sugar, and process until whipped and light. Keep refrigerated for up to 4 days.

This technique works best when the cream has separated from the water. If the can has been shaken or the contents have not separated, the coconut cream will not be thick enough to whip properly.

Triple Gingerbread

This moist gingerbread perfumes your kitchen as it bakes. It contains three types of ginger for great flavor—ground, fresh, and crystallized—and is studded with raisins. Bake the gingerbread in a square pan or in muffin cups. For a hedonistic touch, top it with Lemon Pudding (page 299) or Coconut Whipped Cream (page 319).

SERVES 10 TO 12

2 cups oat flour
1/2 teaspoon baking soda
1/2 teaspoon salt
1 tablespoon ground ginger
1/2 teaspoon ground cloves
1/4 teaspoon ground cinnamon
1/2 cup melted coconut oil
1 cup maple syrup
1/2 cup molasses
2/3 cup light coconut milk
2 eggs, lightly beaten
1 tablespoon apple cider vinegar
2 tablespoons vanilla extract
1 tablespoon finely chopped fresh ginger
1 tablespoon chopped crystallized ginger
1/2 cup raisins

Preheat the oven to 350°F. Oil an 8 by 8-inch baking dish or line a 12-cup muffin tin with paper liners.

Sift the flour, baking soda, salt, ground ginger, cloves, and cinnamon into a medium bowl. Whisk to combine. Combine the oil, maple syrup, molasses, coconut milk, eggs, vinegar, and vanilla in a blender, blend until smooth.

Pour the liquid ingredients into the dry, whisking them together just until all the liquid is absorbed. The batter will be quite wet. Stir in the fresh and crystallized ginger and the raisins.

Pour the batter into the prepared baking dish or muffin tin, and place it on the middle rack in the oven. Bake until the gingerbread is springy to the touch and a toothpick inserted in the center comes out clean, 45 to 50 minutes for the cake, 25 minutes for the muffins. Let the cake cool in the pan cool and then cut it into squares; or remove the muffins from the tin and let them cool on a wire rack. Serve the gingerbread warm or at room temperature. It will keep for up to 3 days.

NOTE: *You can whisk the wet ingredients by hand if you like. Make sure to have the maple syrup and molasses warm or at room temperature so the coconut oil doesn't get clumpy. If that does happen, a whir in the blender will smooth the wet ingredients right out.*

Granola Bars

These bars are perfect for a breakfast-on-the-run or a healthy snack. They will keep at room temperature, covered, for up to a week; you can also freeze them. Vary the bars by substituting your favorite nuts or dried fruits for the ones suggested here, or by using other nut butters or fruit purées for the almond butter.

MAKES 8 BARS

1/4 cup almonds, toasted and chopped
1 cup rolled oats
1/3 cup whole-wheat pastry flour
1/4 cup unsalted sunflower seeds
1/4 cup dried currants
1/2 teaspoon ground cinnamon
2 tablespoons granulated cane sugar or maple sugar
1/4 teaspoon salt
1/4 cup almond butter
1/2 cup maple syrup
1 teaspoon vanilla extract
1/4 cup apple juice

Preheat the oven to 350°F. Oil an 8 by 8-inch baking pan.

Place the almonds, oats, flour, sunflower seeds, currants, cinnamon, sugar, and salt in a medium bowl and stir to combine.

Whisk the almond butter, maple syrup, vanilla, and apple juice together in another bowl. Pour the wet ingredients into the dry, stirring until the dry ingredients are thoroughly moistened.

Press the mixture evenly into the prepared pan and bake for 25 minutes. Remove the pan from the oven and cut into 8 bars. Return the pan to the oven and bake until golden brown, 10 to 15 minutes. Cool in the pan for about 10 minutes. Then remove the bars with a spatula, and cool them on a rack for at least 30 minutes.

NOTE: *For crisper bars, bake these in an 8 by 11-inch pan.*

Caramel Popcorn with Peanuts

Three kinds of sweet syrup make this caramel popcorn irresistible. Make sure to bake the popcorn on a baking sheet that has a rim so the sugar syrup doesn't spill into the oven when you stir it.

MAKES 5 CUPS

1/2 cup rice syrup
1/4 cup barley malt syrup
1/4 cup maple syrup
8 cups popped corn (from 1/3 cup kernels)
1/2 teaspoon salt
3/4 cup raw peanuts

Preheat the oven to 375°F.

Whisk the rice syrup, barley malt syrup, and maple syrup together in a small bowl.

Toss the popcorn with the salt and peanuts in a large bowl. Pour the syrup mixture over the popcorn and stir to coat evenly. Spread the popcorn out on a parchment-covered rimmed baking sheet, and bake for 15 minutes, stirring the popcorn thoroughly every 5 minutes. The popcorn should be well coated and golden brown. The sugars will be bubbly and hot.

Remove the baking sheet from the oven and let the popcorn sit for 10 minutes, until it is slightly cooled but still sticky. Then tear it into clumps and place them in a bowl. Refrigerate until crisp, 10 to 15 minutes. Store the popcorn in a jar or plastic bag at room temperature for up to 2 weeks.

FOR THE PERFECT POT OF POPCORN: Forget about cottony air-popped popcorn. Coconut oil is the tastiest and healthiest oil for popping popcorn. (This was the oil they used at movie houses before switching to hydrogenated soybean and canola oil.) Use a heavy-bottomed saucepan. Add the deodorized coconut oil (spread a thin layer on the bottom of the pot) and corn kernels. Do not add more kernels than can fit in a single layer at the bottom of the pot. Move the kernels around so that every kernel is coated with oil. Cover the pot, set it over medium heat, and wait until you hear the first kernels pop. Shake the pot a bit as the kernels pop. Within minutes the pot will be filled to the brim, and you'll have few if any unpopped kernels.

Chocolate Lovers' Brownies

These are the brownies to make when you don't just want chocolate, you *need* it. Oats are more absorbent than wheat flour, so they make for a lighter brownie. You can buy oat flour at a natural foods store or make your own by grinding rolled oats in a spice grinder or blender. Be sure not to overbake the brownies; the inside should still be moist when you stick a toothpick in the middle.

These brownies freeze beautifully.

MAKES 16 BROWNIES

4 ounces bittersweet chocolate, chopped
1/2 cup melted coconut oil *or* **1/2 cup (1 stick) unsalted butter**
3 large eggs
2 teaspoons vanilla extract
1 cup maple sugar, Sucanat, or unrefined cane sugar
1/4 cup maple syrup
1/2 teaspoon salt
1 1/4 cups oat flour
1 cup walnuts, chopped, optional

Heat the oven to 350°F. Line an 8 by 8-inch baking pan with parchment paper or aluminum foil, letting the paper overlap the pan to create handles. (See illustration.) Oil the two sides of the pan where the parchment is not touching.

Combine the chocolate and the oil in a small saucepan, and heat over low heat to melt the chocolate. When the oil is hot, remove the pan from the heat and whisk until the chocolate and oil are thoroughly combined.

Whisk the eggs and vanilla together in a large bowl. Whisk the chocolate mixture into the eggs and combine thoroughly. Add the maple sugar, maple syrup, salt, flour, and walnuts, and mix together with a rubber spatula or a wooden spoon.

Pour the batter into the prepared baking pan and press it evenly into place with an offset or large rubber spatula. Bake until a cake tester comes out a little wet when inserted in the middle but comes out clean when inserted on the sides, 30 to 33 minutes. Make sure not to overbake the brownies. Remove the brownies from the oven and let them cool for at least 30 minutes in the pan. Then run a knife along the edges where the parchment doesn't touch, and lift the brownies out of the pan. Cut into 16 pieces. Store at room temperature, covered, for up to 3 days.

Pecan Lace Tuiles

This is another example of kitchen magic: tiny amounts of flour and sweetener are transformed into a crunchy, lacy confection. Success depends on using a silicone pad or parchment paper to line your baking sheet. Store the cookies, covered, for a week at room temperature, or freeze them in freezer bags for up to a month.

MAKES 32 COOKIES

1/2 cup pecans, toasted

5 tablespoons whole-wheat pastry flour

2 tablespoons arrowroot powder

Large pinch of salt

2 tablespoons melted coconut oil or canola oil

1/4 cup rice syrup

1/3 cup maple syrup

1 teaspoon vanilla extract

Preheat the oven to 350°F.

Place the pecans in a food processor and pulse until coarsely chopped. Transfer the nuts to a medium bowl and add the flour, arrowroot, and salt. Whisk to combine.

In another bowl, whisk the oil, rice syrup, maple syrup, and vanilla until thoroughly combined. Add the wet ingredients to the dry, mixing with a wooden spoon or rubber spatula just until the dry ingredients are thoroughly moistened. Let the batter sit for at least 15 minutes.

Line two cookie sheets with parchment paper or a silicone mat (Silpat). Use a teaspoon to drop the batter onto one of the cookie sheets. Since the cookies spread to 4 to 5 inches in diameter, you will need to space them very far apart—only about 5 cookies to a sheet. Bake the cookies until they are evenly golden, 10 to 12 minutes.

Prepare your second sheet while the first one is in the oven. As soon as one sheet is done, place the second one in the oven to bake.

Let the cookies cool just long enough so that you can peel them off the parchment with a spatula, about 1 minute. Fold the cookies over a rolling pin and let them harden into that curved shape, about 3 minutes. Transfer the tuiles to a plate.

Repeat until all the batter is used.

NOTES: *If you have a convection oven, you can bake more than one sheet at a time. Otherwise, it's best to just bake one in the center of the oven so that the heat does not bounce from one baking sheet to the next. With one sheet in the oven at a time, it will take about 1 hour to bake all the cookies.*

Within a minute or so of coming out of the oven, the cookies are ready to be slipped off the baking sheet and slid over a shape to form a graceful bend. If you didn't bake the cookies long enough and they don't firm up, simply return them to the oven and continue baking as needed. Likewise, if they become too firm before you have a chance to shape them, return them to the oven for half a minute or so to soften them.

I like to form these over a rolling pin, but you can certainly improvise. I've baked tuiles in places where all I've had are condiment bottles to use as forms, and they still came out great.

Chocolate Chip Cookies

These delicious cookies are completely whole-grain and light on the belly. They freeze very well—you can eat them directly out of the freezer.

MAKES 30 COOKIES

1/2 cup (1 stick) softened unsalted butter *or*
    7 tablespoons coconut oil, at room temperature or semisolid
3/4 cup maple sugar, Sucanat, or evaporated cane sugar
1 egg
1 teaspoon vanilla extract
1 1/2 cups whole-wheat pastry flour or whole-grain spelt flour
1/2 teaspoon baking soda
Pinch of salt
1 cup semisweet chocolate chips

Preheat the oven to 350°F. Line two baking sheets with parchment paper or Silpats.

Using a stand mixer fitted with the paddle, or a hand-held mixer, cream the butter and sugar together on medium speed until fluffy, about 5 minutes. Beat in the egg and vanilla until smooth, and mix for another minute or so.

In a separate bowl, sift the flour, baking soda, and salt together. Mix the flour mixture into the batter, one third at a time, until completely moistened. Fold in the chocolate chips.

Tear off walnut-size chunks of the dough and place them 2 inches apart on the prepared baking sheets. Flatten the cookies with a quick whack, using the bottom of a jar or the palm of your hand. Bake, rotating the cookie sheet once, until the bottoms of the cookies are golden brown, 14 to 16 minutes. Transfer the cookies to a wire rack and allow them to cool. Store at room temperature, covered, for up to a week.

Peanut Butter Cookies

Made with peanut butter and chickpea flour, these cookies pack a tasty high-protein punch. They're great quick-energy snacks. Make sure to cream the oil or butter and sugar really well to give the cookies a beautiful look and texture. To measure 7 tablespoons coconut oil, start with 1/2 cup and remove 1 tablespoon.

MAKES 35 TO 40 COOKIES

1/2 cup (1 stick) softened unsalted butter *or* 7 tablespoons
    semisolid coconut oil
3/4 cup maple sugar or evaporated cane sugar
1/4 cup maple syrup
1 cup chunky peanut butter
1 egg
1 teaspoon vanilla extract
1 cup chickpea flour
1/2 teaspoon salt
1/4 teaspoon baking soda
1/4 teaspoon ground cardamom

Preheat the oven to 350°F. Line 2 baking sheets with parchment paper or silicone mats.

Using a stand mixer fitted with the paddle, or a hand-held mixer, cream the butter, maple sugar, and maple syrup together on medium speed until fluffy, about 5 minutes. Add the peanut butter and whip for another minute or so. Beat in the egg and vanilla just until smooth.

In a medium bowl, whisk the flour, salt, baking soda, and cardamom together. Mix the dry ingredients into the wet in three batches, mixing just until the batter is completely moistened.

Drop the batter by teaspoons onto a baking sheet, spacing them about 2 inches apart. Flatten with a fork. Bake, rotating the baking sheet once, until the bottoms are golden, 12 to 14 minutes. Transfer the cookies to a wire rack to cool. Store at room temperature, covered, for up to 2 weeks. These cookies freeze well also.

Semolina Cookies

These crisp butter cookies are flavored with orange and lemon and dressed up with drizzled chocolate. It takes just minutes to make the dough in a food processor. For a light sweet bite to finish a Moroccan or Turkish meal, serve the cookies with orange segments sprinkled with pistachios. You can substitute cornmeal for the semolina.

MAKES ABOUT 60 COOKIES

1½ cups semolina flour
¾ cup (1½ sticks) chilled unsalted butter,
    chopped into tablespoon-size chunks
¾ cup natural sugar, preferably maple sugar
    or evaporated cane sugar
⅓ cup unbleached white flour or whole-wheat pastry flour
Grated zest of 1 orange
Grated zest of 1 lemon
1 teaspoon vanilla extract
Pinch of salt
2 large eggs
4 ounces bittersweet chocolate, finely chopped

Combine the semolina, butter, sugar, flour, zests, vanilla, and salt in a food processor, and pulse just until the mixture resembles coarse meal. Add the eggs and pulse just until the dough forms a ball. Transfer the dough to a bowl, cover, and refrigerate until the dough is slightly firm, 30 minutes to 1 hour.

Preheat the oven to 375°F. Line three baking sheets with parchment paper.

Drop slightly rounded teaspoons of the dough onto the prepared baking sheets, spacing them about 2 inches apart. Flatten the cookies slightly with the moistened palm of your hand. Bake the cookies, turning the baking sheet once, until they are golden around the edges and on the bottom, 15 minutes. Let the cookies cool on the sheets for 5 minutes, and then transfer them to wire racks to cool completely.

Melt the chocolate in a double boiler. Place the wire racks over a cookie sheet, or over wax paper, to catch any chocolate drips. Using a spoon, drizzle the chocolate over the cooled cookies. Store at room temperature, covered, for up to a week, or freeze for up to a month.

Sesame Biscotti

These cookies have a nutty flavor reminiscent of halvah. Although the batter may look a bit oily, the biscotti come out beautifully crisp and dry when they are baked. These are wonderful cookies to serve after any meal with Middle Eastern flavors, such as Mujadarrah and Middle Eastern Salad (page 210) or Red Lentil–Chickpea Burgers with Sauce Taratour (page 133).

MAKES ABOUT 24 COOKIES

1/4 cup extra-virgin olive oil
1/2 cup tahini, preferably roasted
1/2 cup maple syrup
Grated zest of 1 lemon
1 teaspoon vanilla extract
Pinch of salt
1 1/2 cups unbleached white flour
    or whole-wheat pastry flour
1/4 cup sesame seeds

Preheat the oven to 350°F. Line a baking sheet with parchment or a silicone mat (Silpat).

In a medium bowl, whisk the oil, tahini, maple syrup, lemon zest, vanilla, and salt until emulsified. Using a spoon or a rubber spatula, stir in the flour until the dough is moistened and well combined.

Spread the sesame seeds on a plate. Divide the dough in half, and roll one half in the sesame seeds. Place the dough on the prepared baking sheet, and form it into a chubby log about 7 inches long. Repeat with the other half of the dough, leaving about 3 inches between the logs. Bake until the top is beginning to brown but the cookie is still soft, 15 to 20 minutes. Remove the baking sheet from the oven and let it cool for about 10 minutes. At this point the logs can remain on the baking sheet up to overnight.

Place the logs on a cutting board. Using a serrated knife, cut the logs into 1/2-inch-thick diagonal slices. Lay the biscotti on their sides on the cookie sheet and bake until they are golden brown, 15 minutes. Transfer the biscotti to a wire rack to cool. Then store them in an airtight container at room temperature for up to 2 weeks.

Chai

A great cup of chai is ambrosia for the healthy hedonist. I recommend making a big pot and storing it in the refrigerator so that you can heat it up at a moment's notice (or ice it on a hot day). I find that chai is a pick-me-up, a cozy comfort drink, a mood-alterer, a head-clearer, and a soothing warmer. Beware the ready-made variety; at best, it's way too sweet, and the flavor of the liquid concentrate pales by comparison to homemade. At worst, powdered chai is full of unhealthy ingredients.

Cow's milk, soy milk, and coconut milk all work beautifully, so use whatever suits your taste. Adjust the type of tea according to the caffeine level you can tolerate. I favor loose tea, though a couple of tea bags will work just fine in a pinch.

MAKES 2¾ CUPS; SERVES 2 OR 3

1 teaspoon (about 18) green cardamom pods

10 whole cloves

10 black peppercorns

1 cinnamon stick

3 stars of star anise

One 1½-inch piece fresh ginger, unpeeled, coarsely grated (about 6 tablespoons)

4 cups water, preferably filtered or bottled

1 cup full-fat soy milk, cow's milk, or unsweetened coconut milk

1 heaping tablespoon honey, preferably raw

1 tablespoon green, black, or rooibos tea leaves

Freshly grated nutmeg to taste

Place a heavy-bottomed skillet over medium heat, and dry-toast the cardamom, cloves, peppercorns, cinnamon, and star anise for about 2 minutes, until lightly browned and fragrant. Transfer the spices to a mortar and pestle and lightly crush them, or place them on a cutting board and crush them with a rolling pin.

Place the crushed spices in a medium saucepan and add the ginger and water. Bring the water to a boil, lower the heat, and simmer until reduced to 2 cups, about 10 minutes. Add the milk and the honey, and heat just until the liquid is about to boil, about 1 minute. Remove the pan from the heat and add the tea. Let the tea steep, 3 minutes for the green and rooibos and 5 minutes for the black. Strain, divide the chai among cups or mugs, and serve hot, sprinkled with fresh nutmeg.

Menus

FEASTS

TURKISH

Shredded Romaine Salad with Dill and Scallions • Turkish Tomato Salad with Fresh Herbs • Turkish Stuffed Trout in Parchment *or* Chickpeas with *Charmoula* Vinaigrette • Zucchini Latkes • Dolma Pilaf • Baklava

INDIAN

Mysore Rassam • Green Leaf, Date, and Cashew Salad with Tamarind Dressing • Coconut Green Beans with Mustard Seeds • Cucumber, Peanut, and Yogurt Raita • Cardamom and Coconut Basmati Rice • Tamarind Chickpeas *or* Sautéed Chicken with Mango and Red Onion Chutney • Ginger Coconut Ice Cream

SOUTHEAST ASIAN

Watercress and Grapefruit Salad with Thai Peanut Dressing • Salmon Medallions with Lime-Mustard Teriyaki *or* Baked Thai Tempeh Triangles • Yellow Pepper–Coconut Milk Sauce • Spinach-Basil Sauce • Grilled Pineapple-Mango Salsa • Thai Jasmine Rice with Chinese Black Beans • Crispy Rice Sticks • Coconut Green Beans with Mustard Seeds • Triple Gingerbread with Coconut Whipped Cream

VEGETARIAN THANKSGIVING

Spinach Salad with Lemon-Rosemary Vinaigrette and Smoky Shiitakes • Thanksgiving Stuffing Timbales • Cranberry-Chestnut Relish • Mashed Sweet Potatoes and Turnips with Caramelized Shallots • Sautéed Broccoli Rabe with Garlic and Red Pepper Flakes • Pomegranate-Pear Cornmeal Tart *or* "Pumpkin" Pie *or* Cranberry Apple Crumb Pie

SUPPERS, LUNCHES, AND BRUNCHES

Indian-Spiced Cauliflower, Chickpeas, Potatoes, and Kale • Cardamom and Coconut
Basmati Rice • Cucumber, Peanut, and Yogurt Raita

Tempeh Reubens with Caramelized Onions • Asian Slaw with Peanuts •
Celery Root and Red Bliss Smash

Red Lentil–Chickpea Burgers with Sauce Taratour • Shredded Romaine Salad
with Dill and Scallions • Sesame Biscotti

Cauliflower, Green Bean, and Mushroom *Kuku* • Shredded Romaine Salad with Dill and
Scallions • *Mujadarrah* • Orange Walnut Crêpes with Citrus Compote Supreme

Roasted Red Pepper Soup with Tofu Basil Cream • Watercress and Hearts of Palm Salad
with Plantain Chips • Salt Cod and Potato Cakes

Spinach Pie *Kuku* • Potato Salad with Caramelized Onions • Mediterranean Braise •
Strawberry Soup

Vegetable Quesadillas with Basil Pesto • Romaine Salad with Creamy Avocado Dressing •
Black Bean Burgers with Bell Pepper–Avocado Sauce • Roasted Peaches with Caramel Sauce

Bean and Cheese *Pupusas* with Tomatillo Salsa • Salvadoran Slaw

SPRING CLEANSING MEAL

Greens in Garlic Broth • Moong Dhal • Cardamom and Coconut Basmati Rice

DINNERS

Wilted Spinach Salad with Orange-Curry Dressing • Butterflied Barbecue Spice–Rubbed
Chicken • Delicata, Cauliflower, and Pearl Onion Roast • Cranberry-Lime Chutney •
Chocolate Lovers' Brownies

Spinach Salad with Lemon-Rosemary Vinaigrette and Smoky Shiitakes •
Porcini Mushroom Ragout with Chicken or Tempeh • Cranberry-Chestnut Relish •
Mashed Sweet Potatoes and Turnips with Caramelized Shallots •
Light-as-a-Feather Chocolate Mousse

Roast Chicken with Maple Glaze • Braised Cabbage with Cranberries • Garlicky Braised
Kale with Balsamic Vinegar and Capers • Lacquered Carrots with Coriander • Wild Rice
with Porcini Mushrooms, Pecans, and Dried Cranberries • Indian Pudding Cake

Watercress and Hearts of Palm Salad with Plantain Chips • Seared Sesame-Crusted Tuna
• Glazed Brussels Sprouts • Cajun Roasted Sweet Potatoes • Pecan Lace Tuiles

Kabocha Squash Soup with Gingery Adzuki Beans • Broiled Miso Black Cod • Forbidden
Black Rice • Green Leaf, Cucumber, and Wakame Salad with Carrot-Ginger Dressing •
Lemon Pudding

Braised Tempeh with Curried Coconut Sauce • Green Leaf, Date, and Cashew
Salad with Tamarind Dressing • Cardamom and Coconut Basmati Rice •
Triple Gingerbread

Chickpeas with *Charmoula* Vinaigrette *or* Fish in *Charmoula* • Quinoa-Grits Polenta with
Roasted Red Pepper Sauce • Roasted asparagus • Chocolate Lovers' Brownies

Porcini-Miso Broth with Stir-fried Vegetables and Soba Noodles • Baked Tofu *or* Teriyaki
Tofu • Green Leaf, Cucumber, and Wakame Salad with Carrot-Ginger Dressing *or* Asian
Slaw with Peanuts • Sesame Biscotti

Gazpacho Salad with Tomato Vinaigrette • Spicy Baked Beans • Swiss Chard with
Corn and Balsamic Vinegar • Pecan-Crusted Trout with Lemon-Sage Butter •
Peach-Raspberry Brown Betty

Indonesian Corn Chowder • Frisée, Endive, and Celery Salad with Anchovy Vinaigrette •
Butterflied Barbecue Spice–Rubbed Chicken with Barbecue Sauce • Beet, Tomato, and
Watermelon Salad • A Trio of Fruit Sorbets

Smoky Black Bean Soup with Tortillas, Avocado, and Lime Cream • Fish Tacos with
Designer Guacamole and Cabbage Slaw • Browned Butter Berry Galette

Baby Greens with Reduced Balsamic and Hazelnut Oil Vinaigrette •
Seven-Vegetable Moroccan Stew • Baklava

Resources

Asia Market Corporation
71½ Mulberry Street
New York, NY 10002
(212) 962-2028

Large selection of Southeast Asian foods, including galangal and lime leaves.

The Baker's Catalogue (King Arthur Flour)
P.O. Box 876
Norwich, VT 05055-0876
(800) 827-6836
www.kingarthurflour.com

Baker's supplies, flour, wonderful online resource.

Barry Farm Foods
20086 Mudsock Road
Wapakoneta, OH 45895
(419) 228-4640
www.barryfarm.com
e-mail: info@barryfarm.com

Good source for agar powder.

Bridge Kitchenware
711 Third Avenue
New York, NY 10017
Phone: (212) 688-4220
Fax: (212) 758-5387
www.bridgekitchenware.com

Excellent selection of kitchen tools. Extensive online catalog.

Coombs Family Farms
P.O. Box 117
Brattleboro, VT 05302
(888) 266-6271
www.coombsfamilyfarms.com

My favorite source for high-quality maple sugar, from 1-pound to 40-pound packages, and maple syrup. They have their own sugarhouse. Maple powder is the finest grind.

Dean and Deluca
560 Broadway
New York, NY 10012
(800) 221-7714
www.dean-deluca.com

Spices, dried beans, rice, masa harina, walnut oil.

Diamond Organics
Highway 1
Moss Landing, CA 95039
(888) ORGANIC (674-2642)
Fax (888) 888-6777
www.diamondorganics.com
e-mail: info@diamondorganics.com

Farm-fresh organic food, including vegetables and meat, with guaranteed overnight deliveries.

Fillo Factory
P.O. Box 155
Dumont, NJ 07628
(800) 653-4556 (800 OK FILLO)
www.fillofactory.com

Best commercial phyllo available. Available in stores around the country. Check their Web site to see which stores near you carry them. They ship directly also.

Goldmine Natural Food Company
7805 Arjons Drive
San Diego, CA 92126-4368
(800) 475-FOOD (3663)
www.goldminenaturalfood.com

Amazing selection of the highest-quality organic grains, including brown and golden teff, dried chestnuts, organic dried fruit, hard-to-find products, beans, sea vegetables, varieties of high-quality sea salt, and condiments. They ship within 24 hours. Orders take just a couple of days in the U.S., about 1 week internationally.

The Grain & Salt Society
4 Celtic Drive
Arden, NC 28704
(800) 867-7258
Fax: (828) 299-1640
www.celtic-seasalt.com

Great resource for Celtic Sea Salt.

J. B. Prince Company, Inc.
36 East 31st Street
New York, NY 10016
(212) 683-3553
Fax: (212) 683-4488
www.jbprince.com

Large selection of baking supplies. Mail order.

K. Kalustyan
123 Lexington Avenue
New York, NY 10016
(212) 685-3451
www.Kalustyan.com

Top on my list of places to visit in New York. Huge selection of spices, dhals, condiments from all over the world. Best place to get exotic ingredients, including fermented black beans, chiles, spices, beans and grains of every type, berbere *powder, farro. Mail-order available.*

Kitchen
218 Eighth Avenue
New York, NY 10011
(212) 243-4433 or (888) 468-4433

Southwestern ingredients. This is an excellent source for almost every kind of dried chile and chile powder, masa harina, black and white jasmine rice, large selection of beans. Mail-order catalog.

New York Cake and Baking Distributor
56 West 22nd Street
New York, NY 10010
(212) 675-CAKE, (800) 942-2539

Large selection of baking supplies. Mail order.

Omega Nutrition
6515 Aldrich Road
Bellingham, WA 98226
(800) 661-3529
www.omeganutrition.com
e-mail: Info@omeganutrition.com
Order online: www.omegahealthstore.com

Superior organic oils, including my favorite all-purpose coconut oil. They ship quickly.

Penzey's Spices
20 retail stores
(262) 785-7676, (800) 741-7787
Fax: (262) 785-7678
www.penzeys.com

Excellent quality and selection; 250 spices and spice blends, including dried chiles and vanilla beans. Mail-order spice catalog.

Poseidon Bakery
629 Ninth Avenue
New York, NY 10036
(212) 757-6173

A wonderful place to visit in New York. The best quality hand-made fresh phyllo. No mail order.

Radiant Life Wellness Company
(888) 593-8333
www.radiantlifecatalog.com

Wonderful products, information, and resources that promote optimal health and sustainable living.

Sur La Table
P.O. Box 34707
Seattle, WA 98124-1707
About 50 stores nationally with cooking classes in half of them.
(800) 243-0852
www.surlatable.com

Wonderful selection of kitchen supplies. Mail order, gift registry.

Udom Corp.
Thai and Indonesia Grocery
81A Bayard Street
New York, NY 10013
(212) 349-7662

Great place for Thai spices, galangal, kuri leaves, Thai chiles.

Weston A. Price Foundation
4200 Wisconsin Avenue, NW
Washington, DC 20016
(202) 333-HEAL
www.WestonAPrice.org
www.pricepottenger.org

Foundation based on the research of nutrition pioneer Dr. Weston Price. This organization is a clearinghouse of information on healthful lifestyles, ecology, sound nutrition, alternative medicine, humane farming, and organic gardening. Informative Web site with lots of links, including realmilk.com, which lists folks to contact about purchasing raw milk directly from the farmer.

Wilderness Family Naturals
P.O. Box 538
Finland, MN 55603
Orders toll-free (866) 936-6457
Questions (800) 945-3801
www.wildernessfamilynaturals.com

Delicious virgin coconut oil and coconut cream as well as other high-quality oils and products.

Glossary of Terms and Ingredients

Acidulated water. Water with lemon squeezed into it. Used to prevent vegetables such as artichokes and celery root from discoloring.

Adzuki beans. Small reddish brown beans with a white stripe along one edge, popular in Japan and China. Their low fat content makes them easily digestible.

Agar-agar. Vegetarian form of gelatin, made from a red seaweed that is processed into flakes, bars, or powder. The bars are also known as kanten bars. See discussion on page 296.

Ancho chile. Dried poblano, the most commonly used chile in Mexico. The sweetest of the dried chiles, it has a mild fruit flavor. The name means "wide" in Spanish. The chile is a dark mahogany color and measures 4 to 5 inches long and 3 inches across.

Arame. Slightly sweet and delicately flavored sea vegetable that grows in the seas around Japan. Comes in thin strands. Available in Asian markets and natural foods stores.

Arrowroot powder. Root starch used as a thickener, much like cornstarch. See discussion on page 316.

Asafetida. Also known as *hing*. Made from a resin. It's quite smelly, so close the jar immediately after using. When it is cooked in oil or ghee, however, it emits a pleasant oniony aroma. For this reason, it is often used in place of onions and garlic. An ingredient in many dhals, it is considered a valuable digestive aid. Available in Indian markets.

Barley. Small, stubby-kerneled grain with a lot of natural starch. Sold pearled or hulled.

Barley malt. Mild sweetener with a strong, distinctive flavor and a consistency and color like molasses. Made from sprouted barley. Add hops and yeast, and you've got beer.

Barley miso. A dark miso with a rich, salty, full flavor. Mellow barley is a much milder variety.

Basmati rice. Long-grain rice with a nutty aroma and fluffy texture. The most prized rice in India.

Belgian endive. Shaped like a short, fat cigar, a pale yellow crisp, bitter salad green. A member of the chicory family.

Berbere. Classic spice mix from Ethiopia. Also available as a dried mix at well-stocked spice stores.

Blanch. Cook briefly in boiling salted water. It facilitates the removal of skins, such as for almonds, pearl onions, tomatoes, and peaches; eliminates harsh or bitter flavors, such as for broccoli rabe; or partially cooks a food before it is cooked by another method, such as roasting.

Blood orange. More intensely flavored than juice oranges, with orange to crimson-colored skin and blood-red juice. Mostly available from January through March.

Bok choy. Large leafy green leaves and a large white, tender stalk. It cooks quickly. You can use leaves and stems in a stir-fry.

Braising. Cooking food first in fat and then simmering it in liquid until tender.

Broccoli rabe. Commonly eaten in Italy, a green with a pronounced bitter flavor (a blanch before cooking gets rid of some of the bitterness). Its leaves are similar to those of a turnip, with little broccoli-like florets interspersed among the greens. All parts are edible.

Brown rice vinegar. Traditionally brewed vinegar imported from Japan, made from rice, koji, and spring water. It has a smooth and mellow flavor with low acidity.

Bruise. To release the flavorful oils in herbs, spices, or citrus peels by laying the flat side of a knife over the item and giving it a firm smack, the way you would for peeling a clove of garlic.

Buttercup squash. Squat, round, usually dark green winter squash with dense, sweet orange flesh. Japanese kabocha, Honey Delight, and Black Forest are all in the buttercup category.

Capers. Pungent, intensely flavored flower buds of a Mediterranean shrub. They have a singular flavor that pairs well with fish, olives, and anchovies. They are sold either pickled or packed in salt.

Cassia leaf. The type of bay leaf used in Indian cooking is a leaf from the cassia tree. Like bay laurel, it is an evergreen member of the laurel family. Sometimes called Indian bay leaf, it is milder than a bay laurel leaf, with a sweet taste and mellow spicy aroma.

Celery root (celeriac). Primarily available in the autumn and winter, looks like a gnarly brown turnip. To use, peel away the thick skin and the mass of little roots with a wide

Y-shaped vegetable peeler or a knife. The firm white flesh has an intense celery flavor. If you're not going to cook the celery root immediately, hold it in acidulated water.

Chard (Swiss chard, red chard). Comes in green, red, and a mixed variety; all are interchangeable in recipes. Even though the thick stems are edible, it's preferable to remove them for most dishes. Chard is readily available year-round. Look for ribs that show no discoloration and for crisp, curly leaves.

Chiffonade. Finely shredded leaves, most often leaves that have been stacked, rolled, and then sliced. Frequently used for basil and spinach.

Chile de árbol. Tiny, dried, "tree-like" chiles. Closely related to cayenne, with a searing, acidic heat. Bright red, about 2 to 3 inches long and ½ inch wide.

Chinese black beans. Black soybeans that have been fermented. They give a distinctive flavor to Chinese black bean sauces. Sold in Asian markets and gourmet stores, they keep indefinitely. A quick couple of rinses removes the excess salt.

Chipotle chile. Smoked red jalapeños with a hot, smoky, sweet flavor.

Chipotle chiles in adobo sauce. Chipotle chiles (smoked jalapeños) packed in small cans in a tomato-based sauce. Convenient to use (you can store any extra in a jar in the refrigerator for many months). They are readily available in gourmet markets and natural foods stores.

Cremini mushrooms. Similar to button mushrooms in look and flavor but rounder and larger, with tan or brown caps.

Deglaze. To add liquid to a hot pan that has just had food cooked in it. The liquid facilitates scraping up any brown bits stuck to the bottom of the pan and enables reclaiming the juices that have cooked down.

Delicata squash. Small, elegant-looking oblong winter squash with characteristic green stripes. Its edible skin is easy to peel.

Dried chestnuts. Available in gourmet stores, Italian groceries, and natural foods stores, especially through autumn. They are sold either loose, from a bin, or in packages. They come already peeled and are convenient to use. Soak the dry chestnuts as though they were beans (either overnight or with the quick-soak method). This will reduce the cooking time considerably and make it easier to remove any skin left on. Remove any bits that float to the top of the soaking water. Any skin left in the grooves of the chestnuts will disappear when the dish is puréed. Fresh peeled chestnuts are also available bottled or vacuum-sealed.

Emulsify. To blend two or more liquids that would otherwise remain separate into a homogenous liquid, generally by whisking.

Farro. Spelt-like whole berry that is common in Italy. Available in Italian and gourmet markets.

Frisée. Known as curly endive for its light green, ruffled spindly leaves. It has an assertive, slightly bitter flavor. Most often used as a salad green. A member of the chicory family. Remove the heavier white stems before using.

Garam masala. A blend of Indian spices, usually including some sweet ones.

Ghee. Ghee is made from simmering butter to remove the water and milk solids. It has a long shelf life and is able to withstand high cooking temperatures. See discussion on page 6.

Hass avocado. Best-tasting avocado. Small and dark green, with pebbly, rough skin and buttery, dense flesh.

Hatcho miso. High-protein dark miso made from soybeans.

Hearts of palm. A delicacy taken from the core of the trunk of some species of palm trees. It is a crisp, white, watery vegetable, akin to a water chestnut but chewy, with its own distinctive taste. It is central to Cuban cooking and to regions in the world where palm trees grow. Hearts of palm (even organic) are readily available in cans.

Hijiki. One of the most mineral-rich sea vegetables. Comes in black spaghetti-like strands and has a briny sea taste. Needs to be soaked for at least 20 minutes and cooked for at least 20 more.

Indian red chiles. Similar to cayenne peppers, these are the chiles in Indian chile powder.

Jalapeño chile. Plump, shiny, bullet-shaped fresh pepper, about 2 inches long. The most widely eaten hot chile in the United States.

Jasmine rice. Long-grain, high-quality, slightly sticky white rice used in Thai cooking. Has a distinct fragrance when cooked.

Jicama. Large round tuber with hard, brown skin. The exterior masks a sweet vegetable with watery, crunchy flesh that is best eaten raw.

Kabocha squash. Squat, green winter squash with dense, flavorful orange flesh and dark green edible skin. Also called hokkaido pumpkin.

Kalamata olives. Large, purplish black olives from Greece. Great all-purpose olive, meaty and rich.

Kale. One of the hardiest greens, able to withstand frost and snow. Russian Kale, the most available variety, has dark green, crisp, tightly curled leaves. There are other varieties on the market such as Tuscan kale, which has narrow leaves and a sweet, mild flavor; curly kale, which is dark green with very curly leaves; and ornamental kale, which has ruffly violet-edged leaves and is used mostly as a decorative plant. The stem on all varieties should be removed before cooking. Young kale can be lightly cooked; the more mature it is, the longer cooking time it requires.

Koji. Fermenting catalyst for amasake, mirin, sake, soy sauce, and miso, among other products.

Kombu. Kelp that comes in flat, stiff ribbons and gives body to grains, stews, and soups. A natural flavor enhancer since it is high in glutamic acid, a natural form of monosodium glutamate. A small piece of kombu added to a bean cooking pot improves the beans' flavor and digestibility.

Kudzu. The powdered root of the kudzu plant, used as a thickener. Kudzu has the added quality of being a medicinal ingredient, specifically used in the East to alkalize acidic conditions such as colds, nausea, and indigestion. Soothing for the belly. See discussion on page 296.

Latke. Yiddish word for the pan-fried potato cakes most often associated with Hanukkah.

Lemongrass. Herb that looks like coarse, heavy grass. Used for its sour-sweet citrus flavor, associated with Southeast Asian cooking.

Liquid smoke. Made by placing high-grade smoking woods, such as mesquite or hickory, into sealed retorts where the intense heat makes the woods smolder, releasing gases seen in ordinary smoke. The gases are chilled to liquefy them, then filtered to remove impurities, then aged in oak barrels. Adds a smoky flavor to foods and keeps for years on the pantry shelf.

Maple sugar. Crystallized maple syrup.

Masa harina. Fresh corn masa that has been dried and powdered. The texture is much finer than that of cornmeal. Maseca is the best brand currently available. Stored in a dry place, masa harina will keep for a year.

Mirin. A sweet wine naturally brewed and fermented from sweet brown rice, koji, and water. The alcohol in mirin evaporates in the cooking, leaving behind a mild sweetness. For the best quality, purchase mirin in natural foods stores.

Miso. Fermented soybean paste, made by mixing cooked soybeans with koji, salt, and water, and fermenting the mixture for 2 months to 3 years. Used to make soup and as an addition to many different dishes. High in protein and loaded with enzymes that help digestion. The huge variety of misos range from mild and light to full-bodied and dark.

Moong dhal. Split and hulled mung beans, available in any Indian grocery. An easily digestible bean, it is used frequently in dhals.

Napa cabbage. Mild cabbage shaped like a football with crinkly leaves and broad white ribs. Cooked or raw, all parts are edible. Also called Chinese cabbage.

New Mexican chile. Scarlet, elongated, tapered chile measuring 5 to 7 inches long and 1½ to 2 inches across. It has an uncomplicated red chile flavor. Sold in the form of crushed flakes and ground powder. Also known as chile colorado.

Niçoise olive. Tiny, brownish black French olive with a large pit in proportion to its size.

Nori. Cultivated sea vegetable that is harvested, washed, chopped, and spread over bamboo mats to dry into paper-thin sheets. Most familiar as the sheets that wrap sushi.

Pasilla chiles. Dark raisin-brown dried chile measuring 5 to 6 inches long and 1½ inches across. It ranges from medium to medium hot. The name means "little raisin"; also known as chile negro.

Pickled ginger. Traditional sushi condiment, pickled ginger is marinated in seasoned vinegar to enhance a fresh, pungent taste. It turns light pink after a week of pickling. It enhances other flavors and cleanses the palate.

Pickled jalapeño peppers. Cans of pickled jalapeños, with a few carrots thrown in, are wonderful for giving a briny heat to dishes. They are widely available in the ethnic foods section of supermarkets and in gourmet markets. Once you open the can, store any leftover jalapeños in a covered container. These will last for months in the refrigerator.

Polenta. Thick, savory cornmeal porridge. Staple of Northern Italy, eaten soft or allowed to cool and firm so it can be cut into shapes before boiling or frying. Also referred to as a coarse cornmeal grind.

Pomegranate syrup. Also known as pomegranate molasses or concentrated pomegranate juice. Thick, deliciously sweet-tart syrup that is made from reducing pomegranate juice. It is used frequently in Turkish and Iranian cooking. It has so much flavor and viscosity that it needs only a small amount of oil to balance the flavor. You can find it in gourmet markets and Middle Eastern groceries.

Porcini. Intensely flavored Italian mushrooms, most often dried, which need soaking to soften and remove the sand. The soaking broth adds intense mushroom flavor to soups, sauces, and stocks.

Port. Sweet fortified wine. More alcoholic and sweeter than table wine, it keeps well even after the bottle is opened.

Portobello mushrooms. Versatile large-capped mushroom with a dense texture and full flavor.

Purée. To blend raw or cooked foods until smooth, using a blender, food processor, food mill, or hand masher.

Raita. Cooling Indian dish of yogurt with mint and cucumbers, served alongside hotter dishes to soothe the palate.

Rapadura. Similar to Sucanat. Sweetener made from dried granulated cane juice.

Refresh. To arrest the cooking process by immersing the food (usually a vegetable) in cold water or ice water to stop the cooking.

Rice syrup. Mild sweetener with a subtle butterscotch flavor, made from brown rice. Good for savory food as well as desserts, and for those who want the lightest possible sweetening.

Rice vermicelli (rice sticks). Thin rice noodles made from rice and water. Reconstituted in hot water, they are suitable for soups or use as pasta. When in contact with hot oil, they puff and become crisp. Rice noodles also come in wide widths, such as fettuccine-style, which are suitable for sauces. These need to be cooked for a couple of minutes. Rice pastas are readily available at natural foods stores, gourmet markets, Asian markets, and many supermarkets.

Rose water. Distilled rose petals in water, an important flavoring in Middle Eastern food. Buy it in gourmet groceries, natural foods stores, and Middle Eastern groceries.

Saffron. Dried, thread-like stigmas of the saffron crocus. A small amount flavors a whole dish and colors it a brilliant gold.

Sake. Rice wine of 15 percent alcohol content. Widely used in cooking.

Salt cod. Also known as baccalà, used in dishes from Brazil, Trinidad, France, and Spain. Often found in the refrigerator section in fish markets. You must soak it in cold water overnight, changing the water a couple of times to remove the saltiness. I bring it to a boil and discard the first boiling liquid before I cook it. It has a strong, distinctive flavor.

Sauté. To cook food quickly in a small amount of fat. Sauté pans are shallow skillets with either sloping or straight sides and a long handle.

Sea salt. Sea salt is either evaporated by the sun and wind or dried, additive-free, at low temperatures. The highest in trace minerals are those evaporated by the sun and wind and packaged to retain their moisture.

Seitan. High-protein chewy "wheat meat" made of wheat gluten. It's available in plastic tubs in the refrigerator section of natural foods stores.

Semolina. Flour made from durum wheat, a high-protein wheat suitable for pasta. Imparts a lovely texture to baked goods.

Serrano chile. Smaller and hotter than jalapeños. The hottest commonly available fresh chile.

Sherry. Fortified wine originally from Spain, also produced in California. More alcoholic and sweeter than table wine, it keeps well even after the bottle is opened.

Shiitake. Japan's most popular mushroom, sold fresh or dried. Widely sautéed or used as a basis for stocks. The hard stems are inedible but excellent for stock.

Shoyu. Traditionally aged soy sauce. The only ingredients in it should be soy, wheat, water, and salt. It has a bright, fresh taste. Readily available in natural foods markets, gourmet markets, Asian markets, and many supermarkets.

Simmer. To cook in bubbling liquid over low heat.

Soba. Buckwheat noodles with a robust, earthy flavor. They take only 4 minutes or so to cook, and should be rinsed with cold water after draining to prevent them from sticking together.

Soybean. High-protein bean from which all soy products (including soy milk, tofu, tempeh, shoyu, and miso) are made. Also eaten fresh in the form of edamame.

Soy milk. Liquid extracted from soybeans that have been soaked, ground, boiled, and pressed dry. Some types have flavorings and sweeteners added. Richness varies from brand to brand.

Spelt flour. Flour from spelt, an unhybridized form of wheat. Its high water solubility helps the body absorb its nutrients easily; also, it is a great source of fiber. Many people sensitive to wheat tolerate spelt well.

Stock. Flavorful liquid made by simmering vegetables and aromatics in water until the flavor is extracted. Used for soups, stews, sauces, and other dishes.

Tahini. Sesame seed paste originally from the Middle East. The tastiest tahinis are made from toasted sesame seeds. Available in gourmet markets and Middle Eastern stores.

Tamarind. Fibrous pod of a tropical plant native to India. Used as a souring agent in Indian and East Asian cooking. Comes pressed into cakes or as a liquid concentrate and can be found in Asian and Indian groceries. Refrigerated, it keeps indefinitely. Use it as a refreshing, tart pick-me-up in sauces and soups.

Tempeh. High-protein soybean cake, made by splitting, cooking, and fermenting and injecting the soybeans with a tempeh culture called a rhizopus mold. The fermentation binds the soybeans into a compact white cake and makes it, along with miso and shoyu, one of the most digestible forms of soy.

Thai bird chiles. Hot, tiny, red or green chiles used extensively in Southeast Asian cooking.

Thai fish sauce. Made from fermented anchovies, water, and salt, fish sauce is a salty dark liquid that gives Southeast Asian cooking its unmistakable flavor. A little goes a long way. It is also known as *nuoc mam* and *nam pla*. Avoid sauces that have additives such as corn syrup. Widely available in markets and specialty stores, this is the Southeast Asian "secret ingredient."

Thai green curry paste. Made from a combination of Thai chiles, *galangal* (Thai ginger), and other spices, it's available in natural foods stores, gourmet markets, and many well-stocked supermarkets. One brand to look for is Thai Kitchen. They also make a red curry paste.

Toasted sesame oil. Made from toasted sesame seeds, it has a rich flavor and dark color. It burns when heated directly and is best used as a seasoning agent.

Tofu. Made from soy milk coagulated with nigari or calcium sulfate and then pressed into blocks, tofu does not have much personality on its own. It absorbs the juices and flavors of ingredients it's cooked with, and marinated and manipulated in inventive ways, it affords countless varieties of satisfying tastes and textures.

Tomatillos. Small, plum-size, tart-tasting green fruit similar in appearance (but in fact unrelated) to the tomato. Leaflike husks must be removed before cooking or eating.

Umeboshi. Seasoning agent that imparts a sour-salty flavor. The fruit, resembling an apricot more than a plum, is fermented in salt with a shiso leaf, which gives it the fuchsia color. The whole plums or paste keep indefinitely at room temperature. The vinegar, which actually is not a vinegar at all—it's the liquid from pickling the plums—is delicious in salad dressings.

Umeboshi paste. Purée of pickled japanese plums. Pickled for a year with red shiso leaves, it is a bright fuchsia color and has a sour, salty flavor. Available in natural foods stores.

Umeboshi vinegar. Pink brine of the umeboshi plums. Used in place of vinegar and salt to boost flavor in soups, sauces, and dressings. Technically not a vinegar because it is pickled, not fermented. Available in natural foods stores.

Wakame. Familiar as the sea vegetable that floats in miso soup, it has a hard, spiny stem that needs to be removed. Wakame has a mild, pleasant taste, is loaded with minerals, and needs only a 10-minute soak to reconstitute it. Available in natural foods stores and Asian markets.

Wasabi. Japanese horseradish. It comes as a light green powder in Asian markets and natural foods stores. Fiery-hot flavor.

Wheat gluten. Elastic protein formed when hard wheat flour is moistened and agitated. Gives bread its characteristic elasticity. When the starch is washed away and only the gluten is left, it can be simmered in broth to make seitan.

Wild rice. Technically a grass, not a grain, this rice has a nutty flavor and a chewy texture. You must clean wild rice thoroughly before cooking.

Wonton wrappers. Wonton wrappers, also known as dumpling skins, are readily available in the refrigerator section in Asian grocery stores, and in some natural foods stores and supermarkets. They come in 4-inch rounds or squares, in 1-pound packages that contain 45 to 60 wrappers. Wonton wrappers can be refrigerated for about a week and frozen for a couple of months.

Yuca. Also known as cassava or manioc. A slender, elongated root that ranges from 4 inches to 2 feet in length. Characterized by a barklike skin and white flesh, it has a bland flavor and buttery texture. This is the root that tapioca is made from.

Zest. The brightly flavored colored rind—minus any white pith—of citrus fruits. A strip, or a spoonful of grated zest, infuses a dish with intense citrus flavor.

METRIC EQUIVALENCIES

LIQUID EQUIVALENCIES

CUSTOMARY	METRIC
¼ teaspoon	1.25 milliliters
½ teaspoon	2.5 milliliters
1 teaspoon	5 milliliters
1 tablespoon	15 milliliters
1 fluid ounce	30 milliliters
¼ cup	60 milliliters
⅓ cup	80 milliliters
½ cup	120 milliliters
1 cup	240 milliliters
1 pint (2 cups)	480 milliliters
1 quart (4 cups)	960 milliliters (.96 liter)
1 gallon (4 quarts)	3.84 liters

DRY MEASURE EQUIVALENCIES

CUSTOMARY	METRIC
1 ounce (by weight)	28 grams
¼ pound (4 ounces)	114 grams
1 pound (16 ounces)	454 grams
2.2 pounds	1 kilogram (1,000 grams)

OVEN-TEMPERATURE EQUIVALENCIES

DESCRIPTION	°FAHRENHEIT	°CELSIUS
Cool	200	90
Very slow	250	120
Slow	300–325	150–160
Moderately slow	325–350	160–180
Moderate	350–375	180–190
Moderately hot	375–400	190–200
Hot	400–450	200–230
Very hot	450–500	230–260

Index